The authors—

STEPHEN P. BRADLEY is Associate Professor at the Graduate School of Business Administration, Harvard University. Formerly with the Center for Exploratory Studies, IBM Corporation, he is co-author of a forthcoming book, *Applied Mathematical Programming*, as well as the author of several articles.

DWIGHT B. CRANE is Associate Professor at the Graduate School of Business Administration, Harvard University. Formerly Director of Operations Research for the Mellon Bank, he is Departmental Editor for Finance, *Management Science*, as well as author of several articles.

MANAGEMENT OF
BANK PORTFOLIOS

MANAGEMENT OF
BANK PORTFOLIOS

STEPHEN P. BRADLEY
DWIGHT B. CRANE

Graduate School of Business Administration
Harvard University

58363

A WILEY-INTERSCIENCE PUBLICATION
JOHN WILEY & SONS, New York • London • Sydney • Toronto

Library of Congress Cataloging in Publication Data:

Bradley, Stephen P 1941–
　　Management of bank portfolios.

　　"A Wiley-Interscience publication."
　　Bibliography: p.
　　Includes index.
　　1. Bank investments.　I. Crane, Dwight B.,
1937–　joint author.　II. Title.
HG1616.15B73　　332.6′7　　75-23030
ISBN 0-471-09522-2

Printed in the United States of America

10 9 8 7 6 5 4 3 2 1

To our parents

GEORGE and MARY BRADLEY
LESLIE and ABIGAIL CRANE

PREFACE

The environment in which bank portfolios are managed has changed dramatically in the past few years. Interest rates have become more volatile, short-term liabilities have become more available, and opportunities for expansion of bank assets into new and hopefully profitable fields have grown. In this new environment banks have been freed to some extent from old constraints on portfolio management, such as the need to use securities as the predominant source of liquidity, and some new constraints have been imposed, such as the shortage of taxable income at many banks.

These changes have raised some questions about the kind of portfolio strategies appropriate to the new environment. For example, what maturity structures are likely to provide the best performance? How is the maturity structure and return from a portfolio affected by the risk the bank is willing to tolerate? If purchased liabilities are used to meet liquidity needs, what are the implications for portfolio strategy? How are the desirable maturity structures of U.S. Treasury and tax-exempt portfolios affected when the total return and risk of the two portfolios are considered jointly?

This book reports the results of an extensive research study designed to help answer these and other important portfolio management questions. One of the two major purposes of the study was to provide guidelines that would help commercial banks and other financial institutions select a portfolio strategy. The second major purpose was to develop new decision-making aids that would assist institutions in the ongoing management of their portfolios. To accomplish these objectives we have developed new planning procedures to help assess future economic environments and new computer models to generate and evaluate alternative portfolio strategies.

One of the major problems in portfolio management, as in most aspects of asset and liability management, is the need to make decisions in the face of uncertainty about future economic conditions. In this book we propose a conceptual framework for planning in this uncertain environment. The approach, called scenario planning, involves an assessment of future portfolio environments that might occur and an evaluation of alternative portfolio actions that might be taken facing these environments. Assessing future conditions can be a significant task, but we have developed statistical procedures that will assist in the process. The conceptual framework and the statistical procedures are discussed in Chapters 2 and 3.

Once the potential future portfolio environments are described, the next step is to evaluate alternative sets of actions that might be taken. Computer models can greatly assist in this process. The most commonly used approaches are simulation models and linear programming models, which are discussed in Chapters 4 and 5. These models are helpful in exploring the implications of alternative actions and in evaluating bank policies that influence the portfolio structure.

A difficulty with the commonly used models is that they do not explicitly consider uncertainty about the future economic environment. We begin to address this problem in Chapter 6, which describes a Monte Carlo simulation model. This model was used to study the performance characteristics of alternative portfolio strategies, so that we are able to present some conclusions about the relative returns and riskiness of laddered and barbell maturity structures.

A major development of our research is a new optimization model capable of explicitly accounting for uncertainty about future events when it selects a portfolio strategy. Optimization models incorporating uncertainty have existed for some time, but these models have not been very practical because some important elements of the portfolio problem have had to be ignored in order for the model to be computationally feasible. The model and solution procedure reported in this book have overcome this difficulty. Chapter 7 provides a description of this model, while complete details about the model and solution procedure are provided in Appendix B.

The optimization model is used in Chapters 8 and 9 to study a number of portfolio management issues. Some of the issues addressed are the implications of using purchased funds to meet liquidity needs, joint versus separate management of U.S. Government and municipal portfolios, and the cost and implications of limitations on realized and unrealized losses. We then illustrate how such a model might be used in Chapter 10, where we describe the results obtained when the model was used to "manage" a hypothetical portfolio of municipal securities.

Finally Chapter 11 provides an overall summary of the findings of the book. It brings together the general conclusions reached about portfolio management strategies and discusses the potential role of each of the modeling approaches in assisting the continuing tactical decisions that have to be made.

The book was written to be useful to individuals in banks and other financial institutions. The intended audience is threefold, individuals responsible for asset and liability management planning, portfolio managers, and management scientists. The planners would be most interested in the scenario planning framework developed in Chapters 2 and 3 and in the discussion of alternative modeling approaches provided in Chapters 4 through 7. Portfolio managers would be interested in this material plus the findings from our study of portfolio strategies and other management issues. These conclusions are developed in detail in Chapters 6, 8, and 9, but Chapter 11 provides a convenient summary that can be read independently. Each of the chapters is written in nontechnical language and intended to be readable to portfolio managers willing to learn a minimum amount of new terminology. Technical discussions have been placed in appendices to be available to management scientists and other interested readers.

The book also provides useful reference material for educational courses. Its discussion of the portfolio management problem and evaluation of alternative strategies will be of interest for courses in financial institutions. In addition, the development and application of models described in the book will be useful in applied managment science courses.

Financial support for our research was provided by and through the Division of Research of the Harvard Business School. At an early stage of our work research support was received from the Cambridge Project to assist in the mathematical development of the modeling procedure. At a later stage a group of financial institutions contributed to the research. These institutions included Bank of America, Bankers Trust Company, Chase Manhattan Bank, Chemical Bank, First Bank System, First National Bank of Chicago, Harris Trust and Savings Bank, Manufacturers Hanover Trust, Metropolitan Life, National Shawmut Bank of Boston, and Toronto-Dominion Bank.

A number of individuals and banks have contributed ideas and data to our research project. Each of the banks participating in the project sent representatives to a workshop that provided a helpful forum for an exchange of ideas, and many of these banks also provided additional information. Bankers Trust Company was particularly helpful in providing an opportunity to try out our optimization model and scenario planning framework in a real environment. We also wish to acknowledge the help of another bank, which generously provided internal data on its assets and liabilities, but it must remain unnamed to protect the confidentiality of the data. We talked about our work with many at Harvard, primarily in

sessions of the Decisions under Uncertainty Seminar and the Foundations
Seminar on Financial Institutions. We are grateful to participants at these
seminars for their useful contributions.

STEPHEN P. BRADLEY
DWIGHT B. CRANE

Boston, Massachusetts
June 1975

CONTENTS

MANAGEMENT OF
BANK PORTFOLIOS

1

ISSUES IN THE MANAGEMENT
OF FIXED INCOME SECURITIES

This book concerns strategic and tactical planning for the management of fixed-income security portfolios. Of particular interest are situations in which the portfolio is actively managed over time and the choice of maturity structure and security type are important considerations. Commercial banks, savings and loan associations, and other banklike institutions are the major examples of institutions for which these issues are important, so we have chosen to concentrate on commercial banks for our planning framework and our examples. However, the concepts discussed in the book are relevant for management of fixed-income securities in other institutions where portfolio actions and performance are affected by the pattern of future interest rates and other elements of the portfolio environment. The number of such institutions is growing as more firms try to improve performance by managing the portfolio more actively and taking action in anticipation of future events.

Not all financial institutions are concerned with this portfolio management problem. Some life insurance companies, for example, tend to buy long-term bonds for their investment portfolio and hold them to maturity. Since their liabilities are long term in nature, they want the income stability provided by the long maturity securities. These securities have some risk since their market value fluctuates significantly when the general level of interest rates shifts, but this is less important to the institutions than the stability of income obtained. Even when these institutions do manage their portfolios more actively to improve performance, they tend to trade in and out of bonds of approximately equal maturity and risk of default. Thus the maturity and risk structure of the portfolio are not changed in anticipation of changes in the environment.

Commercial banks and other banklike institutions cannot avoid the maturity question so easily. They have more concern about fluctuations in the market value of their portfolio because the maturity structure of their liabilities is relatively short. As the economic environment shifts, there is some chance that part of the security portfolio will have to be liquidated to finance a runoff of liabilities or an increase in assets. This has become less of a problem in recent years because of a greater reliance on purchased liabilities for liquidity, but few banks can completely discount the potential need to reduce holdings during tight periods. Even when there is no perceived need to sell securities, banks are still concerned about potential declines in the market value of the portfolio. The resulting unrealized losses affect the bank's need for capital and limit its flexibility in a period of high interest rates.

Because of these concerns banks have a significant share of their portfolios in short-term securities, which have relatively little fluctuation in the market value. This limits the risk of capital loss, but it poses a new risk of fluctuations in income. Short maturities provide a relatively rapid turnover of securities so the interest income from the portfolio varies with changes in the level of interest rates. Banks thus face the continuing management problem of maintaining a balance between short- and longer-term securities so that a satisfactory return is obtained from the portfolio and an appropriate mixture of income and market value risk is achieved.

OBJECTIVES IN PORTFOLIO MANAGEMENT

Management of U.S. Treasury and state and local government security portfolios has always been a difficult task in commercial banks because of the conflicting objectives and the future uncertainties that face the portfolio manager. One objective is to increase bank earnings by improving revenues from the portfolio. Security holdings as a share of total assets have declined in recent years, but they still accounted for more than 22% of all commercial bank assets at the end of 1973. Improvement in earnings on this share of assets can have a significant impact on total bank performance.

This income objective conflicts to some extent with a second role performed by security holdings. These assets are a potential source of liquidity to help absorb changes in loan demand and to offset fluctuations in other sources of funds. During past periods of rising loan demand, security holdings have been reduced to provide funds to meet the demand. Increases in bank liabilities, such as demand deposits and savings deposits, may help to finance the loan growth, but this source is typically small. A more important source of assistance in recent years has been the use of "purchased funds," such as negotiable certificates of deposit and Eurodollar borrowings. These funds have been used for both secular growth in loan volume and for liquidity needs over an economic cycle, rising and falling as dictated by changes in loan volume. However, reliance on purchased funds has not completely insulated the portfolio from liquidity needs. Some relatively large banks significantly reduced their holdings of U.S. Treasury and municipal securities during recent tight money periods.

A second conflict occurs between the objective of improving long-run earnings on the investment portfolio and the desire of the bank to stabilize total earnings in the short run. In a period when interest rates are low and loan demand is weak, bank earnings are typically low and bank management looks to its investment portfolio for earnings improvement. The yield on long-term bonds in this environment is usually substantially above that on shorter-term securities, so there is pressure to lengthen the maturity structure of the portfolio. The conflict results because this is precisely when the portfolio manager wants to invest in short-term securities. To the extent interest rates move in a cyclical pattern, the period of low rates will be followed by one of rising rates. Thus the long-run earnings on the portfolio might be enhanced by waiting until rates have risen before buying the long-term bonds, even though interim earnings would be lower.

A similar problem occurs when rates are at their peak. The portfolio manager wants to buy long-term bonds, but loan demand is usually very strong at this time. There is a shortage of funds and consequent pressure to limit the size of the portfolio to help meet loan demand, rather than a surplus of funds that can be invested in new long-term securities. Frequently the only way to finance new bond purchases is to increase the amount of short-term borrowing at high rates. This high-cost money would then be invested in long-term bonds at a small or even negative profit margin in anticipation of longer-run profits as rates fall.

The conflicts between income and risk of capital loss and between short- and long-term earnings could be resolved relatively easily if future demand for funds and future interest rates were known with certainty. If loan demand were known, the portfolio manager could plan to have the proper amount of funds on hand at the right time and then invest the remainder without regard to liquidity needs. Similarly, the costs and benefits of alternative investment strategies at various phases of the interest-rate cycle could be accurately assessed and a proper choice made from among the conflicting needs.

Unfortunately, this forecasting utopia has not been reached. An improved understanding of the economy and its impact on banks permits a more complete knowledge of the forces shaping loan demand. It is possible, for example, to foresee a set of trends occurring that should lead to stronger loan demand. It is much more difficult to predict exactly when the loan increase will occur, how long it will last, and what the amount of the increase will be. In addition, it is difficult to predict how much of this increase can be financed with purchased funds. Thus the portfolio manager must contend with a considerable amount of uncertainty about the timing and amount of funds that might be required of the portfolio.

He also faces uncertain interest rates in the future. Rates that seem relatively high are not necessarily the peak rates that will occur. As with loan demand, it is difficult if not impossible to forecast how long a period of rising or falling rates will last and how high or low rates will go during the period. It may be more difficult to forecast rates than loan volume because the forces determining the level of interest rates are less well understood than those affecting loan demand. In addition, bank policy has some influence over loan volume, whereas it has no control over rates determined by supply and demand conditions in the money and capital markets.

TRADITIONAL APPROACHES TO PORTFOLIO MANAGEMENT

Over the years various means have been proposed and used to deal with the conflicts among objectives and the uncertainty of future funds requirements and interest rates. One approach for dealing with the conflict between liquidity and income is to separate the security holdings into "liquidity" and "investment" portions. Securities in the liquid pool would be primarily short-term, high-grade securities, which the bank could sell readily with relatively little cost or capital loss. The size of the investment pool would be relatively constant and could be invested with income as an important, but not the sole, consideration.

Woodworth [1967] is an advocate of this approach for managing cyclical liquidity. He suggests that the size of the liquidity portion be determined by a careful assessment of the size of a loan increase that might occur and the extent to which a decline in securities would be used to finance this loan expansion. The assessment would be based primarily upon the historical experience of the bank and comparable banks, but it would be adjusted for changes in bank policy. A bank planning to rely on borrowed funds to help finance cyclical loan increases would have to estimate its willingness to count on this source during a future expansionary period. Given an estimate of need for liquidity from security holdings, Woodworth recommended that this amount be invested in equal amounts of 2-, 3-, and 4-year U.S. Government securities or their equivalent.

Other approaches to the management of securities do not formally separate securities into liquidity and investment portions. Instead, an attempt is made to meet the objectives of income and limited capital loss by selecting a maturity strategy for a single pool of funds. In the management of either a single pool or the investment portion of a split portfolio, the two major types of strategies that have been used can be classified as "laddered" and "barbell" strategies.

The laddered approach to portfolio management is the more traditional and more commonly used.* In the pure form of this approach, holdings of securities are distributed evenly throughout the range of maturities the bank considers appropriate for its portfolio. A bank, for example, might hold a spread of tax-exempt securities so that equal amounts would mature in each of the next fifteen years. The maturity of these bonds would provide a continuing inflow of cash that could be used to meet other needs for funds or be reinvested. If the funds were reinvested, they would be used to buy the longest-maturity bond and maintain the laddered structure over time.

This approach has a number of advantages for some banks. Among the most important is that it is easy to manage. Cash proceeds from maturities are either used to meet a pressing need for funds or reinvested in the longest maturity, so that there is little or no trading activity in the portfolio. It is also argued that this approach produces a relatively high average rate of interest on the portfolio. In most environments, yields tend to increase with longer maturities, so that funds reinvested in the longest maturity are put to work at the highest yield available at the time.

A second advantage of the laddered approach is that it can be followed without trying to forecast rates. Little attempt is made to take advantage of interest rate swings, as would be the case were a bank to try to lengthen the portfolio in anticipation of a decline in rates. Thus there appears to be no need to try to assess the future direction of movement in interest rates. Some banks do try to modify the pure laddered approach to adjust partially for interest rate swings. For example, a portfolio manager might not immediately reinvest maturity proceeds in a new long-term bond if he thought interest rates would rise in the next few months. If the rate forecasts are accurate, this variant of the laddered approach provides a limited ability to take advantage of interest rate swings, but the spread-out maturity structure precludes a major shift of the portfolio in anticipation of interest rate changes.

The barbell approach involves a much different maturity structure and philosophy. In its pure form the securities in the portfolio are concentrated at the short and long end of the maturity range with no intermediate maturities held. As a practical matter the portfolio is unlikely to have the securities concentrated completely at the extremes since it would require a very

---

* Robinson [1962] provides a typical discussion of the laddered portfolio approach, which he calls a "spaced maturity" policy.

frequent turnover of the long-maturity bonds to keep them long as time passes.

Hempel [1972] provides an example of a barbell portfolio strategy. In his illustration 30% of the portfolio is placed in short-term securities and the remaining 70% in long-term bonds. The short securities are spread through maturities out to 5 years, with the majority in the 1- to 2-year range. This maturity distribution is maintained as time passes by investing proceeds from maturities in equal amounts of 1-, 2-, and 5-year bonds. The long-term bonds are spread evenly over the 20- to 30-year maturity range. As the 20-year bond becomes a 19-year bond with the passage of time, it is sold and the par amount of the bond is invested in a new 30-year maturity.

The rationale for the barbell approach is based on the concept that money invested in a mixture of short and long bonds provides a better combination of return and risk than would the same amount invested in an intermediate-term bond. For example, a 10-year bond would provide some expected return over a given planning horizon, but it would contain some risk, perhaps measured by its capital loss potential or the variability of its total return. The concept is that there is a mixture of short- and long-term bonds providing the same expected return over the horizon with less risk, or that a larger return could be obtained at the same level of risk.

The argument given to support this concept recognizes that portfolio decisions are made in an uncertain world. At the time of each decision, there is some chance that interest rates will rise over the planning horizon and some chance that rates will fall. If rates in fact do rise, the short-term securities will provide the least capital loss. On the other hand, if rates fall, the long bonds will provide the largest capital gain. In addition, the long bonds will produce the highest income if the yield curve had its normal upward slope at the time of the investment decision. In most instances the intermediate maturities do not provide the interest income and capital gain potential of the long maturities, nor do they provide the protection against capital loss of the short-term security. Thus a combination of the extreme maturities may be the most efficient way of obtaining return at a givel level of risk.

We will consider the evidence for and against these arguments carefully in a later chapter. At this point it is sufficient to note that there is some research evidence for desirability of barbell portfolios. The work of Wolf [1969] and Watson [1972] provides two examples. In addition to such published research, there are at least a few banks that utilize the barbell approach in the management of their security portfolios.*

---

* The virtues of barbell portfolios have also been discussed a little in traditional banking texts. An example is provided by Lyon [1960], although he refers to this as a "flexible maturity" policy.

Whatever its merits, management of a barbell portfolio is much more difficult than use of the laddered approach. A greater need for active portfolio management arises, in part because there must be some trading activity to maintain the barbell structure. As time passes, the long-term bonds become shorter and the portfolio loses its barbell structure unless some bonds are periodically sold and the proceeds invested at the long end of the maturity spectrum. It would be possible to use an arbitrary trading rule, such as the selling of bonds when their maturity shortens to nineteen years, as in the Hempel example. However, such arbitrary rules are not likely to work well in practice because of the important impact these sales of relatively long bonds can have on the earnings and tax position of the bank. The choice of when to sell some bonds and go long again is likely to be a difficult decision, which must take into account the bank's assessment of future credit market conditions as well as its current financial position.

A second problem to be resolved is the allocation of funds to the short and long end of the maturity distribution. A larger share of funds allocated to longer maturities will tend to increase returns, but the bank will be exposed to greater fluctuations in the market value of the portfolio. This risk of capital loss can be reduced by putting a larger share in short maturities, but this will both reduce average income and increase the volatility of interest income over time. The choice is further complicated if the portfolio manager wishes to try to adjust the relative amounts of short- and long-term securities in response to changing interest rate levels. The potential benefits of lengthening the portfolio when rates seem to be at their peak are substantial, but the risks are commensurate with the possible gains.

STRATEGIC AND TACTICAL PROBLEMS

The various approaches recommended for the management of bank security portfolios provide some useful ideas, but some difficult choices remain for the portfolio manager. At one level some strategic choices must be made. For example, how much risk is the bank willing to tolerate in the security portfolios? To what extent will the portfolios be relied upon to provide liquidity? What should be the distribution of maturities in the portfolio? Once these strategic issues are resolved, there remain the tactical problems encountered in implementing the portfolio strategy on a continuing basis.

A basic strategic choice is the selection of the maturity distribution of the portfolio since this determines the riskiness and other performance characteristics of the portfolio policy. This choice can be partly resolved by selecting one of the two approaches that have been recommended, the laddered or the barbell maturity structure. There are virtues in both of these alternatives, but they have different risk and return characteristics, which need to be understood when selecting a portfolio strategy. Besides, there is the problem of selecting appropriate maturity guidelines whether a laddered, barbell, or some other approach is adopted. If a laddered portfolio is selected, for example, what should the longest maturity be? In a barbell portfolio what share of the portfolio should typically be placed in long maturities?

These choices depend upon a number of considerations, an important one being the bank's tolerance for risk. Because future economic conditions are not known, there is risk stemming from uncertain portfolio income and from potential capital losses. If a bank is willing to incur more of either risk in its portfolio strategy, this normally means it can obtain higher returns on average. Although it is less obvious, the length of the bank's planning horizon also has an important impact on desirable maturity structures. If a bank has a long investment horizon, for example, long-term bonds are not very risky. They will provide stable income over the planning period and will have little risk of capital loss at the horizon since they will then be much shorter maturity bonds.

Major changes in the environment in which portfolios are managed may also have a significant influence on the nature of desirable portfolio strategies. One such change is that interest rates have become more volatile. Year-to-year fluctuations in rates from the mid-1960s to the mid-1970s were much greater than in previous years. If interest rates continue to be volatile, this may affect the relative performance of laddered and barbell portfolios. Which maturity structure provides the best balance between return and risk in a volatile interest-rate environment?

Another change in the portfolio environment is the greater availability and use of purchased liabilities. Their use to finance both secular growth and cyclical changes in loan demand has led to portfolios that are smaller relative to the rest of the bank's assets and more stable in size. This lessened use of portfolios for liquidity has been reinforced in banks that have substantial public deposits requiring securities to be pledged as collateral. Does this trend mean that a larger share of the portfolio should be placed in longer maturities? Does it change the relative attractiveness of barbell and laddered portfolios?

One of the results of a reduced need for liquidity in security portfolios is that banks have tended to place a larger share of their portfolio funds in tax-exempt securities. This has increased the aftertax return from the combined portfolios, but it also has contributed to another problem in many banks, a shortage of taxable income. The United States tax liability at these banks has declined because of their expansion into leasing, which generates large tax deductions, and the growth of foreign activities, which produce tax credits. An important consequence of this shortage of taxable income is that it limits the losses a bank wants to realize realizable from portfolio trading. There is some incentive to realize losses because of the tax deduction it creates, but only if there is sufficient taxable income to absorb the deduction. Thus one result of a taxable-income shortage is a lessened ability to undertake bond trading programs. How do this limitation and the other changes in the portfolio environment affect the strategic choices facing the portfolio manager?

Even after answering these questions, the portfolio manager is faced with the tactical problems of managing the portfolio. Some of these problems can be resolved by adopting a laddered portfolio strategy. This approach can be implemented with a limited amount of active management, but there is still some room for ongoing management initiative. For example, the portfolio manager has the option of automatically reinvesting cash from maturing securities in the longest maturity allowed, or he can wait for a while by reinvesting the cash temporarily in a short-maturity asset. This choice may not be easy if long-term rates are expected to rise or if the yield curve is inverted so that higher income can be obtained, at least temporarily, by purchasing some short-term securities.

If a barbell portfolio strategy or other flexible maturity policy is adopted, there are a number of continuing decisions to be made. The long end of a barbell portfolio becomes shorter as time passes unless some trading is undertaken to maintain the structure. The timing and amount of the trading should take into account expectations about future rates and the overall tax position of the bank. Similarly, continuing consideration needs to be given to the maturities of new securities being purchased. There may be times when the shape of the current yield curve and the bank's expectations about future rates may indicate that intermediate maturities are attractive purchases or that the distribution of short-term maturities should be changed.

The potential use of portfolios for liquidity purposes poses an additional set of tactical decisions that must be made. If funds are needed to finance loan growth or deposit runoff, should some securities be sold now or should the bank continue to rely on an expansion of liabilities? If securities are to be liquidated, which ones? The short-run costs of each of these alternatives are easy to see, but an evaluation of the longer-run implications requires some assessment of future uncertainties. The sale of short-term securities, for example, would probably be easier in the short run than liquidation of longer maturities. They are more marketable, and they probably can be sold with less capital loss and perhaps with less reduction in interest income. On the other hand, if the need for funds and interest rates continues to rise, it might be better to get rid of some long-term securities now before the cost of selling them becomes greater. Similar considerations plague the choice between increased use of purchased funds and reduction of security holdings. An intelligent choice requires some assessment of the future availability and cost of both sources of funds.

WHAT IS NEEDED?

The questions and decision-making problems posed suggest that portfolio managers could be assisted by two kinds of help. One is an evaluation of alternative portfolio strategies, including a study of how these policies are affected by changes in the portfolio management environment. The second is the development of improved techniques to assist in tactical planning and decision making.

An evaluation of alternative strategies might help a portfolio manager develop a new portfolio policy more appropriate to the current environment, or it might provide desirable confirmation of a policy currently in use. Thus one of the two major purposes of this book is to help banks answer a number of policy questions. These include the following:

1.   What basic portfolio structure is likely to provide the best balance between return and risk?

2.   How should the level of risk a bank is willing to tolerate affect the maturity structure of its portfolios?

3.   If a portfolio is not to be used for liquidity purposes so that its size is relatively constant, how does this affect the choice of a maturity structure?

4.   How does the availability of purchased funds affect portfolio strategy?

5.   How are the maturity structures of U.S. Treasury and tax-exempt securities affected when the total return and risk of the two portfolios are considered jointly?

6.   What is an appropriate planning horizon for a bank to use in selecting a set of portfolio actions?

Answers to these questions might be of significant help to banks and their portfolio managers, but they are not all that is needed. Even if the portfolio manager is completely happy with a set of policy recommendations, the tactical problems of managing the portfolio remain. These significant decisions must be made on a continuing basis within the context of the bank's strategy, its present position, and expected future economic conditions. Assistance in solving these problems requires different kinds of research than the work that explores alternative strategies.

Solving the continuing tactical problems could be greatly helped by improvements in two key areas:

1. Methods for simplifying the description of future environments, including interest rates and funds available for investment.

2. Methods for studying the implications of these future conditions for current portfolio action.

Forecasting is an essential element of describing the future environment, but there is more to it than the traditional definition of forecasting. Most banks go through the exercise of forecasting their loans and deposits and projecting interest rates on a regular basis. Such projections are helpful inputs to management of the security portfolios. Even with this information, though, the manager cannot base his portfolio actions on the assumption that the forecast will be completely accurate. No matter how good the track record of the forecaster or how sophisticated the forecasting model, the actual results can deviate significantly from the projections. The decisions of the portfolio manager must take this forecasting uncertainty into account.

What is needed then are not just more accurate forecasts, although they would help, but rather better ways of describing the future and its uncertainty. How high might interest rates go? What demands might be placed on the portfolio if these rates occur? What is the likelihood of this occurrence? Answering such questions is a much more difficult task than preparing the normal bank forecast. Indeed, many traditional forecasters feel decidedly uncomfortable when asked to specify the uncertainty in their forecasts.

Whatever method banks have for describing the future environment, they also need some procedure for deciding the implications of this future for their current portfolio actions. Traditionally banks have relied heavily on implicit procedures for moving from projections to action. Such methods have been variously called "feel of the market," "management judgment," and "intuition." These factors should and always will play a critical role in deciding on a portfolio action. However, in the past few years more and more explicit analytical procedures have been proposed as useful for portfolio management decisions.

Most of these procedures are embodied in the form of computer models or programs that at least partially describe the nature of the portfolio problem. Given information about the future environment and current portfolio, some of these models make it easier for a user to study the future implications of one or more portfolio strategies he wishes to specify. Other kinds of models will actually compute a recommended set of portfolio actions for the manager to consider.

Although such models have been increasingly available, they have met with a mixed reception in the banking community for many reasons, including the difficulty bankers encounter in trying to understand and use complex models, the difficulty model builders encounter in trying to understand the essential characteristics of portfolio management, and the difficulty both sides encounter in trying to communicate with each other. Even with complete understanding, however, problems have remained in many cases because the models did not consider satisfactory descriptions of the future environment or did not adequately structure the portfolio management problem. If models are to be useful in helping managers move from forecasts to action, what seems to be needed are both a better understanding of how they can be used and improved models that more adequately describe the portfolio management problem.

Thus the second major purpose of the book is to provide some improved analytical techniques that have been developed to assist portfolio managers in tactical planning and decision-making. These techniques include better methods for structuring assessments about future economic conditions. In addition, they include new computer models useful in studying the implications of these future environments for current portfolio actions.

Over the past several years substantial progress has been made in the development of new modeling techniques, both in and out of commercial banks. In this book we draw upon this work to show how it can be usefully applied in banks. However, previous procedures have not been able to deal adequately with all the critical aspects of portfolio management, particularly the need to make decisions in the face of uncertainty. In our research we have attempted to solve some of these problems by the development of a new conceptual framework for studying portfolio problems and some computer models for implementing the framework.

The procedures developed to help describe future portfolio environments and the new models developed to analyze the implications of these future conditions were designed to be useful for planning and decision making within banks. These same procedures and models can also be used as experimental tools to study the portfolio policy questions posed above. For example, we used our planning procedures to describe realistic sequences of interest rates. Our models could then be used to evaluate the performance characteristics of alternative portfolio strategies. As a result, the developments reported in this book allowed us to accomplish our dual purpose of helping answer strategic portfolio questions and presenting new analytical procedures useful for tactical planning and decision making.

There is a third level of decision making, operational decisions, which we have not attempted to consider in our research. These decisions must be made within the context of tactical and strategic plans, but they go beyond the scope of the book. As an example, the procedures discussed in the book will help a bank evaluate what share of its portfolio should be in relatively long-term municipal securities, but they will not help select specific bonds to be bought or sold to achieve this share. The choice of a specific security is an operational decision that depends more upon detailed current market information and other factors than on the assessment of future economic conditions.

For similar reasons we have not been directly concerned with day-to-day money management or the bank's bond trading department. Our methods of analysis are more appropriate for securities held for a few months or longer than for those held for a very few days, as would be the case in managing a money desk or trading department. For example, a choice between federal funds and U.S. Treasury bills for an investment over a few days depends primarily upon current market rates and the bank's intramonthly pattern of funds flows. The time horizon is too short for changes in economic trends to have a significant impact.

OVERVIEW OF THE BOOK

Because the assessment of future trends is the first step in evaluating portfolio strategies, the next chapter describes some of the common approaches to structuring bank and interest rate forecasts. It also goes beyond this to develop an expanded approach to forecasting in which several economic scenarios are specified. Moving from these economic scenarios to specific estimates of funds flows and interest rates can be assisted by the statistical techniques discussed in Chapter 3. As illustrated in that chapter, these aids are very useful in specifying the range of conditions which might occur.

Chapter 4 discussed how relatively simple computer models can be used to study the implications of an investment strategy for one or more economic scenarios. This is a simulation approach used by several banks to help select an appropriate set of portfolio actions. Other banks have developed and used more complex kinds of computer models that automatically compute an investment strategy based on a given forecast of loans, deposits, and interest rates. An overview of these "optimization" models is presented and their usefulness is reviewed in Chapter 5.

In Chapter 6 we begin our discussion of more complex models that take into account the amount of uncertainty in our forecast of future conditions. The first kind of model discussed resembles those in Chapter 4 in that it computes the implications of investment strategies specified by the user. It is different from the earlier models, though, in that it indicates the distribution of outcomes that would result from possible future environments.

Chapter 7 deals with the subject of optimization models that also take into account the uncertainty of future events. Earlier models could not deal adequately with this problem, but our research led to the development of a new model structure that can be usefully applied to portfolio problems. An example of this structure, called the BONDS model, is described in the chapter and sample results are presented.

By using the BONDS model in an experimental mode, it is possible to study the desirability of various portfolio strategies, such as the laddered and barbell approaches discussed above. In the concluding chapters of the book we present the results of an extensive study of several portfolio management issues. Chapter 8 discusses the nature of desirable portfolios and shows how the maturity structure is affected by the shape of the current yield curve and the portfolio manager's assessment of future interest rates. Furthermore, results are reported showing how portfolio strategies depend on the bank's use of the portfolio for liquidity and the bank's willingness to accept capital losses, both realized and unrealized. Some of these issues are expanded on in Chapter 9, which discusses the availability of purchased funds, the management of tax-exempt portfolios, and the joint management of U.S. Treasury and tax-exempt portfolios.

One of the important issues with optimization models such as the BONDS model is how it would perform over time if regularly used to help manage a portfolio. To help answer this question, we used the BONDS model to manage a hypothetical portfolio of municipal securities during the 10-year period from 1964 to 1973. The results of this experiment and a comparison with alternative portfolio strategies are provided in Chapter 10.

The final chapter in the book summarizes the conclusions reached from our research on each of the portfolio policy questions posed. We also review the types of models discussed in the book and discuss how a bank might use each of them to assist in portfolio planning and decision making.

2

DESCRIBING THE FUTURE PORTFOLIO ENVIRONMENT

Although future interest rates and other elements of the portfolio environment can never be predicted with complete accuracy, an important part of portfolio management is concerned with the assessment and description of what might happen in the coming months and years. Some approaches to investment management, such as the laddered maturity structure, can be carried out with little or no forecasting on a regular basis. Even with this approach, though, some attention must be paid to future events when the basic strategy is being designed or reviewed. For example, decisions about the maturity structure of the ladder should depend on the liquidity needs of the bank, which in turn depend on future loan and deposit volatility as well as availability of purchased funds. Whatever the bank's basic portfolio strategy, almost any attempt to improve portfolio performance requires that some action be taken in anticipation of future events. The better these future events can be understood and described, the better able the bank will be to assess the potential rewards if the action is successful and the possible costs if an unfavorable environment occurs in the future.

This chapter is devoted to methods for assessing and describing future portfolio environments. It might have been titled "Forecasting Loans, Deposits and Interest Rates," but traditional bank forecasts are only a part of the process that would be helpful to better management of portfolios. The chapter first reviews the critical elements in the portfolio environment and summarizes common bank approaches to the forecasting of these items. Then a more complete framework for describing the future is discussed. It is an approach to forecasting that better describes the uncertainty inherent in the process and allows the bank to take this uncertainty into account in its planning for the portfolio.

CRITICAL ELEMENTS IN THE PORTFOLIO ENVIRONMENT

A number of factors in the environment faced by portfolio managers affect the selection of an investment strategy. One of the most significant in the view of many banks is the amount of funds that might be made available to or withdrawn from the portfolio. If loan and deposit trends are very volatile and if the bank has limited access to purchased liabilities, it may rely heavily on sale of securities in the event of adverse trends. Estimates of this liquidity need vary among banks, but its magnitude affects the composition of bank security holdings.

Interest rates are similarly important factors in the environment since they determine the returns that will be obtained from holding each security. They are a particulary significant consideration for banks attempting to take advantage of anticipated swings in interest rates to improve portfolio performance.

In addition to the critical factors of liquidity needs and interest rates, there are other elements in the portfolio environment having an important influence in some banks. For example, the need to pledge securities against deposits of various governmental authorities can limit flexibility in management of the portfolio. Trading flexibility is also limited in some banks because they have a relatively small amount of taxable income available to utilize tax deductions resulting from losses realized on bond trades.

Liquidity Needs

A large part of the liquidity needs of most banks is determined by factors not directly under their control. This was particularly true before the advent of the negotiable certificate of deposit market in the early 1960s. Both before and after the introduction of CDs, however, the major need for liquidity has stemmed from increases in loan demand over an economic cycle. Banks do have some ability to stimulate loan demand in slack periods through promotional activities and to restrict loan volume somewhat during the tight periods. It is fair to say, though, that loan demand is determined largely by economic factors such as corporate spending that influence borrowers' needs for funds. Banks do not lightly say no to the legitimate credit needs of a corporate customer in tight money periods, since they would then face the possibility of losing the customer's business in future years.

In the past, the major sources of funds to banks have been demand deposits and nonnegotiable time deposits. Banks do have some influence over the volume of these sources, but, as with loan volume, deposit balances are largely determined by economic forces not under direct control by the bank. Federal Reserve monetary policy and the economic activity in a bank's market have much more impact on the cyclical changes in its deposit balances than do the bank's own activities.

Cyclical changes in loans and deposits continue to place substantial liquidity burdens on banks, but the growing use of CDs and other instruments have added an important element of control to the size of security portfolios. Beginning with the tight money period of 1966, banks have relied more and more on purchased liabilities to finance loan increases. Negotiable CDs were the predominant purchased liability in the mid-1960s, but the Federal Reserve limited access to the CD market in 1966 by maintaining relatively low interest rate ceilings on these instruments under its "Regulation Q." This encouraged a number of banks to more actively use the Eurodollar market as a source of funds, particulary in 1969–1970, when interest rate ceilings again limited access to CDs. Banks also relied heavily on the federal funds market and obtained funds through sales of commercial paper by bank affiliates to help finance their loan demand.

Although many banks now count on purchased funds extensively as both a continuing part of their liabilities and a source of liquidity, Federal Reserve policy has added some uncertainty to the availability and price of these funds. Regulation Q was used as an active policy instrument in both 1966 and 1969–1970, and reserve requirements were imposed on both Eurodollars and sales of commercial paper by bank affiliates. More recently, however, the monetary authorities have moved to provide freer access to CDs and other time deposits. The first step was taken in 1970 when the Federal Reserve moved to lessen pressure on the money markets following the Penn Central bankruptcy by removing the interest rate ceiling on large CDs with maturities under 90 days. In May 1973 ceilings were removed on all other maturities as well, and in July 1973 the way was paved for smaller banks to have greater access to interest-sensitive money. Rate ceilings were removed for time deposits of less than $100,000 for maturities of greater than 4 years. In October 1973 rate ceilings on these savings certificates were reimposed, but at the relatively high rate of 7.25%.

These actions by the Federal Reserve have made it somewhat easier to count on liabilities as a source of liquidity, expensive though they might be in tight periods. In spite of these changes, it is still unlikely that banks will be willing or able to rely completely on purchased funds and insulate the security portfolios entirely from liquidity considerations. It is too risky and perhaps too expensive to count on a single source of funds. In 1969 even the large banks, which had the most access to Eurodollars and other sources of purchased money, relied to some extent on sales of securities. Andrew Brimmer [1971], member of the Board of Governors of the Federal Reserve System at the time, reported some data for a group of twenty "multinational banks." In 1969 these large banks experienced an 18.1% decline in holdings of U.S. Treasury securities and a 16.0% decline in other securities. Thus security portfolios were hardly immune from the demands of this tight money period. Comparable data are not yet available for 1974, but a number of relatively large banks experienced some difficulty in selling CDs during this more recent tight period.

To summarize, the basic forces that create the need for liquidity in security portfolios are by and large beyond the bank's control. Cyclical changes in loans, demand deposits, and savings deposits move more in response to underlying economic forces than to efforts of the bank. However, bank policy does have an important influence on the extent to which liquidity needs are met from expansion of liabilities rather than contraction of security holdings.

Interest Rates

The general level of interest rates is obviously an important part of the portfolio environment. Expectations about the future direction of interest rates have a critical influence on decisions to lengthen or shorten the maturity structure of a bond portfolio. In spite of this importance, information about the general level of interest rates is not sufficient. It is also important to consider the shape of current and future yield curves in making a maturity decision.

One approach to taking advantage of swings in interest rates, for example, is to acquire longer-term securities when interest rates are considered to be at or near their peaks. In this manner relatively high income is locked in and the market value of the securities builds up if rates fall as expected. Unfortunately, as one bank becomes convinced that rates are at a peak, other banks and other investors also tend to become similarly convinced. This belief is then reflected in relatively flat, or even downward sloping, yield curves, which have frequently occurred for U.S. Treasury and Agency securities. In early August 1974, 3-month treasury bills had a yield to maturity of 9.22% as compared with the 8.35% yield available on 20-year Government bonds at the same time.

This market phenomenon makes the decision to lengthen maturities much more difficult. The investor must give up some interest income in the short run in return for the possibility of higher average interest over a longer horizon with a longer-term bond. Making the choice to lengthen maturities thus requires some assessment of how the whole yield curve will move as well as what the general level of rates will do. Will the short term rates fall enough within the bank's planning horizon so that it will be better off with the long-term bond than with a rollover of shorter term investments?

In addition to the general level of rates and the shapes of yield curves, further detail is important in some situations. Relative yields across various types of securities, for example, U.S. Treasuries and Agencies and state and local government bonds, are of use to some banks. This is particularly true in situations where banks try to take advantage of the spread between U.S. Treasuries and Agencies by trading between these two categories of securities. On the other hand, the allocation of funds between U.S. Treasuries and tax-exempt securities is determined in most instances by factors such as pledging requirements and the bank's taxable income position rather than by the relative yields on these security categories.

At the finest level of detail, yields and other characteristics of individual securities are important in the day-to-day trading decisions of portfolio managers. However, since the primary focus of this book is concerned with tactical planning and executing broader portfolio strategy, these detailed interest rates play a relatively minor role.

In overall planning for the bank and the portfolio, interest rates on various sources of funds and yields on assets other than securities are a part of the portfolio environment. Costs of funds, such as negotiable CDs, are particularly significant since expectations about these costs affect the bank's willingness to rely on purchased funds for liquidity needs rather than the security portfolio. Moreover, the availability of these funds makes it possible to consider using them to expand the size of the portfolio. Rates of return on loans and other assets not considered a part of the security portfolio do have a role in bank planning and forecasting, but they are normally a less important part of the portfolio environment. In most situations the allocation of funds between loans and securities depends on other factors that weigh more heavily in the decision than the relative interest rates on loans and securities.

While banks do have some influence on the extent to which portfolios will be used to meet liquidity needs, they have little or no control over interest rates relevant to the portfolio environment. The general level of interest rates is determined basically by the demand and supply of funds in the money and capital markets, while the shapes of yield curves are also affected by expectations about future interest rates. Bank lending and investment policy in the aggregate has some influence on these interest rates, but individual banks in effect borrow and lend at prevailing rates. The rates on which decisions of individual banks seem to have the most impact are the CD rates and loan interest rates such as the prime. These rates are ostensibly set by bank policy; however, an individual bank would be hard pressed to loan a significant amount of funds at rates above those offered by competing banks or to sell large volumes of CDS at rates below those prevailing in the money market.

Thus assessments of future interest rates in the portfolio environment require some understanding of the economic forces determining movements in rates rather than knowledge of future bank policy.

TRADITIONAL FORECASTING PROCEDURES

The most common approach to forecasting within banks is associated with the annual budgeting and planning cycle of the bank. Many banks go through this process, in which loan, deposit, and expense forecasts are prepared by each branch and department. The total of these forecasts then forms the bank's plan for the coming year. In some banks the major purpose of this planning process is to prepare a budget and an earnings forecast rather than to make decisions about future activities or strategies. The nature of the process, though, requires that some thought be given to future activities and to how resources of the bank will be allocated.

The annual planning cycle in one large bank starts with an economic forecast for the coming year. This is prepared in the early fall and distributed to the various departments of the bank as background for their planning. These departments then individually prepare forecasts of their loan and deposit trends, taking into account their own plans, what they know about their customers' activities, and the implications of the economic forecast. These departmental forecasts are added together to obtain a forecast for the bank as a whole.

The senior management of the bank then reviews the individual plans and their implications for the bank. At this time consideration is given to the implications of these forecasts for the bank's need for funds and how the need might be financed. Also the total loan and deposit forecasts are compared with corresponding forecasts prepared by the economist based upon his projections of economic trends. Finally, management reviews the projected bank trends in the light of their objectives and plans for the bank. If the departmental projections seem to be out of line with the aggregate trends projected by the senior management or with the economic outlook, the plans may be recycled through the departments and branches for reconsideration.

This planning process results in a pro forma statement of condition and income statement for each quarter of the coming year, as well as for the year as a whole. Apart from the general planning and budgeting purposes these statements serve, they also provide a description of the future portfolio environment and incorporate some tentative plans for managing the portfolio within that environment. Most of the content of the financial statements represents forecasts of items over which the bank has no control, such as loan and deposit trends and interest rates. Other items, though, require that tentative planning decisions be evaluated and made. How will projected deficits of funds be financed or surpluses invested? How will maturities in the portfolio be reinvested? To what extent will the bank take losses in a trading program and how will this program affect the structure and returns from the portfolio?

It is a useful exercise for the portfolio manager to interact with the annual planning process and work out some tentative plans, but from his viewpoint this approach to forecasting has some inadequacies. For one thing, being a very cumbersome process, it is difficult to do more than once per year. Thus it is not done frequently enough to be of use on a continuing basis. In fact the process takes so long that the numbers are frequently out of date by the time the calendar year starts.

A major reason for these "bottom up" forecasts becoming out of date quickly is that individuals preparing the forecasts have limited ability to incorporate information about economic trends. Some banks have found that commercial loan officers, for example, have information about their customers' plans that provide some accuracy in near-term projections. They know expected takedown rates for outstanding loan commitments and repayment schedules on outstanding loans, and perhaps they have some knowledge about new borrowing requests. The difficulty is that there are some underlying economic forces at work that a loan officer cannot be expected to incorporate in a company-by-company forecast. Even if a loan officer is aware of an economic uptrend in the process, it is difficult to predict when spending plans and borrowing needs of individual companies will respond. The farther into the future the officer is forecasting, the more chance the economic trend will have to influence corporate plans and the more opportunity for errors in the projections. Thus longer-term forecasts require that more attention be given to the relationship between aggregate loans and deposits at the bank and the regional and national trends affecting them.

Several banks that place emphasis on their planning for borrowing and investing strategy have attempted to overcome these problems by forecasting on a more regular basis and by tying projections more closely to economic trends. (Some of these banks still use bank officer forecasts as an important factor in short-term loan and deposit projections.) To provide this continuing forecasting service, these banks have established staff groups to do the analysis on a regular basis. Such groups are frequently located in the bank's economic department, but it is also common to find the staff support coming from the management science group or from a separate planning staff. The role of these staffs is usually to develop projections of the bank's loans and deposits and interest rates, based upon expected economic trends. Economic forecasts required for these projections might be developed within the bank or obtained from commercial forecasting services.

These projections form the framework for regular planning and consideration of the investment activities. However, since the bank's policy does have some influence on its loan and deposit trends, it is also important to bring management's plans to bear in the process. In addition, some of the components of the plan require that assumptions be made about borrowing and investment policy, loan policy, and general bank management. Such committees then meet on a regular basis to arrive at combined judgments about future trends and their implications for the bank.

USE OF ECONOMIC SCENARIOS

The traditional bank planning procedure can be viewed as an attempt to relate the bank's planning effort to a scenario describing what the bank expects to happen in the future. In effect, banks using these or related procedures are doing "scenario planning." In the "bottom up" forecasting approach, the bank officers are asked to condition their projections upon the economic forecast provided to them. In the more formal forecasting effort by a special staff, projections of loans and deposits may be tied very tightly to forecasts of future economic trends. Whether the link between the bank and external factors is formal or informal, the bank's plans are developed in the context of its expectations about the future environment.

Scenario planning is an important concept for portfolio management. As discussed above, the critical elements in the portfolio environment are for the most part outside the control of the bank. Thus the bank needs some way of coming to an informed judgment about factors that will affect the portfolio. By linking the bank's projections to external economic factors, it is possible to obtain a better understanding of these trends and produce a set of forecasts consistent with each other and the expected economic environment.

The process of scenario planning starts with a definition of the relevant environmental factors for the bank. These factors depend upon characteristics of the bank such as size, geographic location, and the nature of its customer mix. The loans and deposits of a large bank doing a substantial volume of business with national corporations will be significantly affected by the trend of the national economy. Regional banks, which deal with a more narrowly defined market, will be more directly affected by local population and business trends. In some cases loans and deposits at a bank might be very insulated from national trends. Even in these instances, though, some interest rates relevant to management of the portfolio will be determined by national market conditions.

The next step in the planning process is the development of a scenario that represents the expected path of the relevant environment. If we take as an illustration a large bank with a broad customer mix, the bank would be concerned with overall trends of the economy. Thus the definition of the scenario would include projections of the major trends in the economy. The bank might be concerned with such representative factors as the rate of growth of the total economy, the rate of inflation, how the growth would be divided up among the major sectors, and the likely posture of monetary and fiscal policy.

Within this broad scenario there are some key economic variables particularly important to the bank. For example, commercial loans at the bank are probably related to the corporate need for external funds. It would therefore be important to focus on variables such as corporate plant and equipment spending and inventory accumulation on the one hand and corporate profits and depreciation on the other. These measures of corporate spending less the internally generated funds would provide an indication of the external funds needed by companies. Going one step further, the amount of this need that corporations will rely on the banks to provide depends to some extent on the cost of bank funds relative to other sources. As a result, interest rate assumptions are also needed to move from an economic scenario to a specific forecast of commercial loan volume.

After specifying a scenario and projecting the key economic variables within it, the bank must next translate these assessments into forecasts of loans, deposits, and interest rates that are needed for portfolio and other planning. This translation is done informally in the bottom-up forecasts prepared for the annual planning cycle. The more formal approach is to do a statistical study to estimate the relationships between the variables in the scenario and the bank's data. As will be discussed in Chapter 3, this approach can be used by an internal staff group to efficiently prepare detailed bank forecasts from the scenario.

The forecasts resulting from this part of the process provide a framework that can be used to explore alternative portfolio actions. What are the implications of lengthening the maturity structure of the portfolio, given the expected scenario? If loan growth is expected to exceed deposits, should the deficit be financed by increasing the amount of purchased funds or by shrinking the size of the portfolio? As these and other possibilities are explored, their implications for the size of the bank's portfolio and its earnings can be combined with the forecasts to obtain a complete financial picture for each alternative. Finally, the planning process is completed by selecting one of the alternatives as the recommended set of actions for the current planning period.

INCORPORATING UNCERTAINTY IN SCENARIOS

Several banks use this scenario planning process to help evaluate portfolio actions. If they regularly update and extend the forecasts, they seem to find it a useful way to monitor portfolio actions and evaluate short-term decisions. However, there is an underlying assumption in the described approach to scenario planning that limits its usefulness for some important aspects of portfolio management. The problem stems from the use of only one scenario to develop a plan. This environment is very unlikely to occur as projected. Normally the scenario used is the one considered "most likely" to occur, but there will almost always be some error in the projections.

It is important to recognize the uncertainty inherent in the scenario, particularly for portfolio planning. A portfolio manager must take into account the fact that future interest rates are uncertain. He would not invest all of the portfolio in long-term bonds even if the most likely forecast called for substantial interest-rate declines.

One method of solving this problem is to explore the implications of more than one scenario. A bank using this approach might describe one scenario representing the economic environment it thinks is most likely to occur over time. This scenario is then supplemented by one describing a path the economy might follow if its growth is more rapid than expected and another representing a weaker economy that might occur. For each scenario, "high," "most likely," and "low," the economic variables that are key to the bank's trends are projected. These variables are then used to develop specific bank forecasts for each projected environment. With this information it is now possible to explore more thoroughly a portfolio strategy by looking at its implications in each of three possible environments.

A few banks have adopted the practice of developing projections for more than one economic scenario for internal planning purposes. At least one bank has made available to the public some results of its scenario planning as it relates to earnings forecast. As described in an article, NCNB Corporation's most likely scenario for 1973 included a GNP growth rate of 11 to 12%, a restrictive monetary environment with the money supply growing at 5 to 6%, and an average prime rate of 7%.* The corporation's "high earnings" scenario assumed a more expansionary monetary policy and a larger spread between the prime rate and its cost of money. The "low earnings" path assumed a restrictive monetary policy and low margins on loans. This scenario presumably took into account the possibility that political pressures prevailing in 1973 would make it difficult for banks to raise the prime in response to rising money costs.

While the major purpose of the NCNB Corporation's scenario planning might have been to prepare earnings forecasts, similar analysis is useful for the development of a portfolio strategy for the bank's current planning horizon. This use of multiple scenarios recognizes that the future cannot be

---

* "Predicting Earnings with More Precision," *Business Week*, June 30, 1973, p. 52

perfectly forecasted, and it allows the bank to evaluate how much of the portfolio should be kept in short-term securities. Suppose the most likely scenario shows relatively stable interest rates and a moderate loan growth that can be financed through a deposit increase and a use of purchased funds well within the bank's policy limits. If the bank were sure that this most likely scenario would occur, it might decide that relatively little liquidity would be needed in security holdings and that it would be a good time to lengthen maturities to take advantage of higher rates on the longer bonds.

The high scenario, however, might indicate further increases in rates and a more rapid loan growth, which will require some reductions in security holdings if it occurs. For this scenario the portfolio manager might want to shorten up maturities to prepare for the potential reduction in security holdings and to have some funds available for investment in longer maturities after rates have risen. Finally, the addition of the low scenario to this picture indicates the continuing dilemma of the portfolio manager. In this environment rates and loan demand might fall from their present levels, in which case some of the portfolio should be invested in longer maturities before rates fall.

In this hypothetical case and in the real world, there is no way for a portfolio manager to prepare simultaneously for all of the possible future environments. The manager therefore has to pick a hedging strategy that will provide an acceptable return in each of the various scenarios and not pose too much risk in any of them. By evaluating portfolio actions in each of the three scenarios, it is possible to obtain a helpful picture of the returns and risks these alternative strategies pose and select an appropriate hedging strategy. Some difficult choices must finally be made, but the thorough evaluation of possible strategies in the potential environments aids an informed judgment by providing information about performance characteristics of each of the alternative policies.

CONTINGENCY PLANNING WITH SCENARIOS

Moving from single-scenario planning to the exploration of multiple scenarios adds a level of complexity to planning that several banks have found helpful. One further level of complexity can be added that allows banks to do contingency planning. It is a useful step to take, but one new to banks and requiring more forecasting and analysis. In spite of these difficulties, a few large banks have begun to incorporate this additional level of analysis. New developments in the use of computer models, which are reported in this book, have made contingency planning significantly easier.

In single-scenario planning there is, in effect, an underlying assumption that this is the only path the portfolio environment might take. Moving to three scenarios recognizes that there is more than one future path the environment might take. This is a more realistic and useful description of what might happen, but the approach still contains an implicit assumption that should be recognized. The three-scenario approach assumes that once the environment begins to move along one of the paths, it will continue to follow that scenario for the rest of the planning horizon. In reality the economy might begin to move along the high path, for example, but then return to a more normal growth rate or start to decline. To recognize this possibility in scenario planning, we have to add additional branches to the three paths of the environment originally envisioned. This suggests the use of a "tree of scenarios" because of the large number of possible branches.

The structure of these scenarios does indeed resemble a tree as branches are added. Looking ahead for the coming period, the economic scenario might move along a high, most likely, or low branch. At the end of this period, it need not continue to move along the same branch. If it started along the high branch, it might slacken its pace and diverge from this scenario at the end of the first quarter or other time period. Or the economy might start out on the most likely scenario and then grow more rapidly. A number of combinations are of course possible.

Although these scenarios are more complicated, it is useful to recognize that the environment is unlikely to move steadily along any single scenario. The high scenario might show a continuing growth in loan volume and difficulty in purchasing funds that lead to a steady drain of funds from the portfolio. There is some small probability that this chain of events will occur, and this possibility should be taken into account. However, it would be very costly to adopt a portfolio policy of providing enough liquidity to protect the bank against this unlikely long-term trend. The more detailed set of scenarios indicates more likely alternatives as to future directions of the economy, and the bank is then better able to choose which level of liquidity protection it wishes to provide.

An even more important reason for developing a tree of scenarios is to allow a more complete consideration of what actions might be taken as the future unfolds, that is, contingency planning. When only three scenarios are used, the bank evaluates a policy alternative by assuming it is used throughout the length of the planning horizon. In reality the bank has the option of revising its tactics as it gets new information. This can be reflected in a tree of scenarios since the bank can develop a plan that is contingent upon which branch occurs. Although a bank is not going to make a firm decision now on what to do in the future, it is still helpful to think through what might happen in the future and what actions might be taken in response to those events. Such contingency planning can lead to a more informed decision on the actions taken now.

Obviously contingency planning with a tree of scenarios imposes much greater demands on banks than do single- or three-scenario plans. The number of future environments to consider is potentially very large and the number of portfolio alternatives to explore is even larger. However, there are some techniques available that make the problem more manageable. In the next chapter we discuss some statistical techniques helpful in providing the projections needed for contingency planning with a tree of scenarios. Later chapters describe some computer models that utilize this concept and are very useful in the evaluation of portfolio alternatives.

3

TECHNIQUES FOR ASSESSING FUTURE ENVIRONMENTS

Scenario planning requires a procedure for developing a set of bank projections consistent with future environments the bank might encounter. When the planning is done infrequently or when projections are prepared for only one future environment, there is opportunity for a substantial amount of human effort, as in the traditional annual planning cycle. When the planning is done more frequently and a collection of scenarios are being explored, it becomes important to have more formal procedures to produce projections. The purpose is not only to have a more convenient and faster way of preparing forecasts, but also to have more assurance that each set of projections is consistent with the scenario being analyzed.

The process of developing projections described in the previous chapter started with the identification of scenarios the bank considers worthy of investigation. Each of these scenarios is defined in terms of a few key variables that are particularly relevant to the bank. These variables are then used to develop a set of loan, deposit, and interest-rate projections for each scenario.

The purpose of this chapter is to describe some statistical techniques useful in identifying the key variables and in preparing projections from these variables. Projections of loans and deposits will be discussed first, followed by procedures for generating future interest rates. It should be noted that the techniques discussed require some procedure for identifying possible paths of the key variables to be used in developing the detailed forecasts. The most likely path, for example, would probably be obtained from a standard forecast of the economy. Other scenarios might tend to be variants of this trend. Some procedures for developing these scenarios are discussed, but for the most part it is assumed that the bank has access to economic forecasts either prepared internally or obtained from external sources. This chapter is concerned with how to get the most out of these forecasts rather than how to produce them.

FORECASTING LOANS AND DEPOSITS

Commercial Loans

The process of developing projections based on economic scenarios can be illustrated by reviewing a procedure some economists use to forecast commercial loan volume. In this approach the economist first tries to forecast the variables determining total corporate need for external funds. This need depends on spending of corporations less the amount of funds they generate internally. Thus the variables that have to be forecast are measures of spending, such as corporate plant and equipment expenditures and inventory accumulation, and measures of internal funds, such as profits and depreciation.

The difference between corporate spending and internal funds provides a measure of need for external funds in total, but it is necessary to take the process another step in order to forecast the share of this need banks will be asked to fulfill. This allocation of the demand for funds depends on the present and expected future cost of bank credit versus other sources, such as the commercial paper market and the bond market. Some economists attempt to take these factors into account by forecasting relevant future interest rates and trying to assess their impact on where the demand for funds will be placed.

The final step in this process is to estimate the share of corporate demand for bank loans that will be experienced by an individual bank. For some large banks, their share of the total commercial loan volume may be quite stable; for others the market share may vary in response to some special factors. These factors might include a tendency to lead or lag the credit cycle, concentrations in some industries behaving differently than the rest of the economy, or bank policy decisions that have caused loan trends to vary. If these or other factors account for variations in loan volume, they are a part of the scenario that needs to be defined in order to forecast loans.

This process of moving from an economic forecast to a commercial loan forecast is something bank economists have traditionally tended to do either formally or informally. The difficulty with the process is the need to quantify the relationship between the explanatory variables and loan volume. If plant and equipment spending is expected to increase, how much of this increase will be translated into growth in loan volume? In the past, economists have relied on their experience or judgment to estimate these relationships. Such judgments will always be an important part of the process, but there is a growing use of statistical models to assist in the estimation problem.

Banks are normally reluctant to discuss forecasting models in use, but a published study by Budzeika [1971] provides an example of a statistical model for loans. He developed a forecasting model for business loans at the large New York City banks reporting weekly data to the Federal Reserve. Although Budzeika used aggregate data for the reporting banks, his approach is typical of what an individual bank might do. He found that business loan demand at New York banks could be explained well by a statistical equation including the following variables: capital spending by business, inventory accumulation by manufacturing and trade firms, changes in corporate accounts receivable, business saving of nonfinancial firms, and the rate of interest charged by New York banks on business loans. As would be expected, loan volume tended to increase with increases in spending for plant and equipment, inventories, and accounts receivable. Volume tended to decrease with increases in business saving and the interest rate on loans. Of all these variables, capital spending played the predominant role. Budzeika estimated that roughly half of the business loans at large New York City banks were traceable to capital spending.

Thomson [1973] also reports a business-loan forecasting equation. Although the particular form of his equation differs from Budzeika's, he also found that business loan volume could be estimated well by an equation including corporate investment in inventory, plant and equipment spending, internal cash flow, and the level of interest rates as economic variables.

The primary value of statistical equations such as Budzeika's and Thomson's is that they make it easy to go from a scenario to a forecast needed by the bank. In these statistical models the explanatory variables such as plant and equipment spending, inventory accumulation, and business saving are the variables that form a scenario. Thus, specifying a sequence of future values for each of the relevant variables defines a scenario. These values are then put into an equation to compute the implications of the scenario for the bank's commercial loans.

If the future values specified represent the bank's most likely forecast of corporate spending and the other variables, the equation will produce a most likely loan forecast. If the bank wants to evaluate the implications of a more rapidly growing economy, this scenario can be defined by assigning future values more appropriate to this environment. The equation can then be used to compute the commercial loan volume implied by this scenario. Thus the equation provides a convenient means of computing loan forecasts consistent with any scenario.

Demand Deposits

For each forecast of commercial loans there is a need to have appropriate projections of other loans and deposits. These forecasts should be based on the same scenario as used for commercial loans so that the complete set of forecasts will be internally consistent. To accomplish this objective it may be necessary to expand the definition of the scenario by adding new variables that help explain the behavior of the loan and deposit series being forecast.

Forecasts of demand deposits provide a case in point. At one large bank a forecasting study by Crane and Crotty [1967] indicated that demand deposits had an underlying growth trend resulting from the general growth of the bank as it added branches and customers. This underlying trend was a significant component of deposit projections, but it obviously would not help the bank predict when demand deposits would deviate from their trend. Further analysis pointed out that deviations were caused largely by deposits of corporate customers. Thus there was a need to incorporate one or more variables to explain this behavior.

The variables selected were commercial loans at the bank and a corporate bond rate. There was a feedback between the bank's commercial loans and its trend of corporate balances. Growth in loans led to a more rapid expansion of demand deposits. Working against this trend was the fact that higher interest rates provided added incentives for corporate treasurers to place short-term funds in interest-bearing assets rather than demand deposits. This phenomenon was incorporated in the model by adding the interest rate variable to the equation. The result was a demand deposit forecasting equation that used as explanatory variables a time trend to reflect normal growth, and commercial loans and an interest rate to reflect cyclical behavior.

This equation would allow demand deposits to be forecast with only a minor addition to the scenario used to project commercial loans. The interest rate variable needed could probably be the same interest rate used in the loan forecasting equation, and the loan variable needed is the one being projected. The only addition to the scenario required is a measure of time, such as a number for each quarter of data, which is used to incorporate the growth rate of deposits.

Other Loans and Deposits

The examples of commercial loans and demand deposits illustrate how the trends in these items might be explained by a scenario defined by relatively few economic variables. However, not all loans and deposits will be significantly affected by economic trends. Some categories of assets and liabilities tend to grow more or less steadily and are unaffected by the cyclical changes in the surrounding economic environment. Future values of these items can then be adequately projected by incorporating a measure of time in the scenario definition.

Other categories of loans and deposits depend heavily on bank policy. Installment loan volume, for example, can depend significantly on how actively the bank bids for dealer paper. A more important example is the level of CDs and other similar kinds of purchased funds. In normal times banks have considerable discretion over their use of these funds, so that a judgment has to be made about bank policy for each scenario. This can be a difficult judgment for most banks to make, given the possibility of limited access to these funds in tight money periods. While there is no easy way for a bank to decide how much reliance to place on purchased funds, the analytical procedures discussed later in the book provide a means for evaluating alternative policies.

In rapidly growing institutions, the bank's policy toward growth can have a dominant influence in most or all major categories of loans and deposits. These banks might be growing rapidly through acquisitions or expansion of branches, so that rates of deposit and loan growth might depend heavily on these expansionary policies. When this is true, future expansion plans are a critical part of each scenario studied.

It can be seen that there is no one set of factors appropriate for all banks. However, for a particular bank there is probably a relatively small set of variables that will help explain the trends in its loans and deposits. These factors will reflect some mixture of economic cycles, bank policy decisions, and the passage of time.

FORECASTING NET NEED FOR FUNDS

For some planning purposes it is helpful to prepare a forecast of each loan and deposit category, as discussed above. In thinking through the bank's credit posture, for example, it is important to know what categories of loans will account for the demand for funds placed on the bank. Projections of bank earnings will also depend on detailed forecasts of sources and uses of funds. For the purpose of portfolio planning, however, the specific categories of loans and deposits are less important. More important is the net amount of funds that will be available for the portfolio and how much this net amount might vary over the bank's planning horizon.

This suggests the use of some aggregate measure, which might be called the "net need for funds." A way of defining this measure is to divide the bank's assets and liabilities into two categories, one representing items not directly under the bank's control and the other containing assets and liabilities subject to the bank's discretion. Items in the first category would probably include loans and all other assets that are not part of the security portfolios, as well as liabilities such as demand and savings deposits. The dollar difference between these "noncontrollable" assets and liabilities represents the net need for funds to be financed by the discretionary sources. If this net need for funds increases, it must be financed by either reductions in the security holdings or increases in sources of funds such as CDs or federal funds.

The net need for funds is a critical item to be specified for each scenario. Estimates of this need will help determine, for example, the amount of liquidity that should be built into the portfolio. One approach to forecasting net need is to prepare a projection of each asset and liability included in the definition of net need. Then the projected liabilities are subtracted from assets to estimate the aggregate amount of net need. An alternative procedure is to project the net need directly. In this method a historical data series is prepared to indicate how the net need has behaved over past years. These data are then used to develop a forecasting equation allowing net need to be computed directly from a scenario.

If the net need for funds is the primary item to be forecast, there are some advantages to the aggregate approach in which it is computed directly from the scenario. It is computationally easier since only one item must be projected for each scenario. This is particularly important when collections of scenarios are to be evaluated. A second advantage is that it may be possible to define a scenario with a smaller number of variables. Some variables that might be needed to forecast individual asset and liability categories may play an insignificant role when the net need in aggregate is being projected. A final advantage is that projections of an aggregate figure tend to be more accurate than the sum of individual projections.

In spite of these advantages, some banks may find that complete aggregation does not work well. One or more components of net need may behave so differently from the other asset and liability items that their behavior cannot be adequately explained by the same set of key variables. In this situation it is probably better to identify such items and project them separately for each scenario. Then net need excluding these items is forecast and added to the separate forecasts to arrive at a total net need projection.

A procedure for projecting net need can be illustrated with data from a large national bank. Although the data have been disguised to protect the confidentiality of the bank, the solid line in Figure 3.1 illustrates the pattern of net need over the period 1966 through 1972. The net neet for funds shown in the chart reflects primarily the trend of loans minus demand deposits. Savings deposits were excluded since their pattern was determined by a different set of forces from those that seemed to explain the remaining amount of net need. A change of bank policy in the mid-1960s and disintermediation, which occurred in the late 1960s and early 1970s, significantly affected the trend of

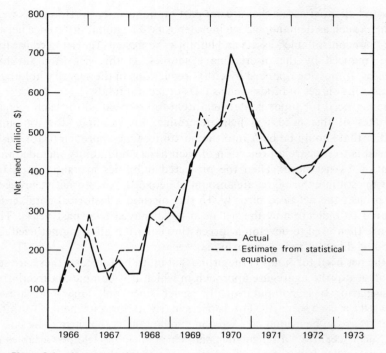

Figure 3.1.   Net need for funds.

these deposits. Thus it seemed better to exclude them from the net need measure and project them separately for each scenario.

The remaining need for funds displayed a generally rising trend as loan volume grew more rapidly than demand deposits and the bank began to rely more heavily on purchased funds. Substantial cyclical swings are also present in the pattern, reflecting fluctuations in the demand for bank funds that occurred during the 1966–1972 period. Both of these phenomena need to be explained by the variables used to define the scenarios.

An analysis of the data suggests that three variables explain a large share of the variation in net need for funds. These include a time trend, a measure of corporate need for external funds, and an interest rate. The time trend was measured simply by assigning a number to each quarter of data. Corporate need for external funds was estimated by using a variable to reflect the amount of corporate spending less internally generated cash. Thus the measure included plant and equipment spending plus inventory accumulation, less undistributed corporate profits and depreciation. The interest rate variable used was the 90-day treasury bill rate. Although corporate borrowing plans are not directly affected by this particular interest rate, it is a good surrogate for relevant rates, such as the prime rate, and it serves as a useful base for projecting other interest rates, as discussed below.

Regression analysis was used to estimate the relationship between these explanatory variables and the bank's need for funds. The following equation resulted:

$$NN_t = -370.7 + 17.3\ CERF_t + 52.1\ BILLS_t + 27.2t \qquad (R^2 = .886)$$

where NN_t = net need for funds in quarter t
  $CEFR_t$ = corporate external funds requirement in quarter t
  $BILLS_t$ = 90-day treasury bill rate in quarter t
    t = number of the quarter

This equation fits the historical data well, explaining 88.6% of the variance of net need for funds. A visual perspective of the fit is provided in Figure 3.1 by the dashed line, which indicates the net need computed from the regression equation.

Although the equation was developed from historical data, its purpose is to help project net need, given some scenario about the future. The scenario is defined by a set of values for the explanatory variables, corporate external funds requirements, the 90-day bill rate, and time. Thus, given an estimate of future values for these variables, the equation provides an estimate of the corresponding value of net need.

To illustrate how the equation could be used to develop a forecast, the statistical relationship was reestimated using data for 1966 through 1971 only. It was then used to project the net need for each quarter of 1972. The projection was made as of the end of 1971, but the actual 1972 values of the explanatory variables were used to define the scenario. As shown in Table 3.1, the projection correctly predicted an uptrend in net need, although the actual increase was less than predicted.

This points out that the amount of net need computed from a scenario is only an estimate subject to error, even if the future scenario is known with

Table 3.1 Predicted Net Need for Funds

	1972			
	I	II	III	IV
Actual	618	625	666	699
Predicted	588	623	705	820

certainty. The amount of error or uncertainty in the forecast can be computed, though, and it is an important piece of information to have. It can be expressed as a distribution of possible values of net need. For example, a range can be computed such that there is an 80% chance that the actual net need will fall within it, if the specified scenario occurs. This range is shown in Table 3.2 along with the actual value of net need. The 10% line was computed so that there was a 10% chance that net need would be lower than the amount indicated. Similarly, there was a 10% chance that the value would be higher than the upper limit, or an 80% chance of net need being between the two limits. As shown in the table, the actual value did fall within the limits in 1972.

The width of the forecast range is a measure of the predictive accuracy of the equation. It depends primarily on how well the equation fits the historical data, but accuracy is also influenced by the values of the explanatory variables used to compute the forecast. The forecast is most accurate when the future values specified for these variables are close to their historical values. As the future values move away from their past average, the forecast range becomes wider, that is, the forecast becomes more uncertain. For example, the forecast is more uncertain when the treasury bill rate is specified at unusually high or low levels.

The error in this forecasting equation is not the only source of uncertainty in predicting the net need for funds. An important additional source is that future values of the explanatory variables are not known with certainty. If these variables move along a path other than that of the forecast scenario, estimates of net need will be wrong even if the forecasting equations have perfect accuracy. A less important source of additional uncertainty is that savings deposits are excluded from the definition of net need. These deposits must also be forecast for each scenario to obtain total net need for funds, and there will undoubtedly be some potential error in this forecast.

One of the purposes of scenario planning is to recognize that there is sig-

Table 3.2   Forecast Range for Net Need for Funds

	1972			
	I	II	III	IV
Upper forecast limit (90%)	725	760	842	951
Actual	618	625	666	699
Lower forecast limit (10%)	450	486	569	689

nificant uncertainty about future needs for funds and to describe it in terms useful to portfolio management. Uncertainty in the explanatory variables is taken into account by specifying a collection of scenarios representing the possible paths future values of these variables might take. For each of these scenarios the projection of net need can be computed and the forecast error estimated. If the forecast error for a single scenario is small relative to the variation in net need across all of the scenarios, the identification of each scenario may provide a sufficiently complete description of the total uncertainty. However, if the forecasting errors are large, it may be necessary to prepare a high, most likely, and low projection of net need for each scenario. There is, of course, a practical limitation to the number of different paths of funds requirements that can be explored. Thus it will be necessary to arrive at some compromise between the number of scenarios described and the number of projections prepared from each scenario.

STATISTICAL AIDS FOR ASSESSMENT OF INTEREST RATES

Interest rates play a dual role in the scenario-planning process. As discussed above, at least one interest rate is needed as a key variable in the scenario definition in order to forecast the net need for funds. In addition to this rate, though, a multitude of rates need to be specified for each scenario being analyzed. These interest rates include yields for the various maturities of U.S. Government and tax-exempt securities and the cost of liabilities such as CDs. Each of these rates is needed to evaluate portfolio strategies for a particular scenario.

Just as the net need for funds is forecast to be consistent with each scenario definition, these interest rates should also be specified for the same scenarios. One or a few interest rates will be a part of each scenario definition, but the remaining rates will be derived from these key variables. Because of the large number of rates that must be forecast for each scenario, it is almost imperative that statistical aids be developed to help specify the set of interest rates required. Fortunately, the money and capital markets are intertwined so that there is a high degree of correlation among yields on the various kinds and maturities of securities. This correlation makes it possible to estimate statistical relationships and specify equations of significant help in generating a complete set of interest rates consistent with the rate or rates included in the definition of a scenario.

In this section we shall first discuss methods for tying projections of a few important short-term rates to scenario definitions. Then approaches for longer-term rates will be described. Finally, a technique for estimating yields on the remaining maturities of major security classes will be presented.

Short-Term Rates

A number of short-term rates are relevant to the bank's management of assets and liabilities. Figure 3.2 shows the pattern of a few of the important rates including the 3-month treasury bill rate, the prime rate, the secondary market rate on 3-month CDs, and the yield on 1-year "good grade" municipals as reported by Salomon Brothers [1974]. These rates have tended to move together, as can be seen for the 1965–1972 period in Figure 3.2. Thus, if one of them is specified in a scenario, the others can be esimated from a statistical equation with a relatively high degree of accuracy.

The treasury bill rate is a likely candidate for selection as the rate to be included in the definition of the scenario. It is a rate that moves freely in response to the demand and supply of funds in the money market. In addition, the market for bills is well established, with a larger number of buyers and sellers and a large outstanding volume of securities.

An analysis of the data suggests that changes in the short-term rates of interest are closely correlated with changes in the 3-month bill rate. One equation that captures this phenomenon uses as explanatory variables changes in the bill rate and the previous value of the rate to be explained. This can be illustrated by the equation used to explain the level of the CD rate.

$$CD_t = 1.00\, CD_{t-1} + .88\, (BILLS_t - BILLS_{t-1})$$
$$(R^2 = .928, \text{ standard error} = 36 \text{ basis points})$$

where
$$CD_t = \text{the 3-month CD rate in quarter } t$$
$$CD_{t-1} = \text{the 3-month CD rate in the previous quarter, } t - 1$$
$$BILLS_t - BILLS_{t-1} = \text{the change in the 3-month bill rate from quarter } t - 1 \text{ to quarter } t$$

The coefficients in this equation suggest that the CD rate will be about the same level as in the previous quarter if there is no change in the bill rate. However, if the bill rate changes, the 3-month CD rate tends to move about 88% as much in the same direction. Over the period 1965–1972 this equation explained 92.8% of the variance in the 3-month CD rate, and its standard error of estimate was 36 basis points. (The standard error is a measure of the dispersion between the actual interest rates and rates estimated from the statistical equation. About 95% of the actual CD rates will be within twice the standard error, 72 basis points, of the computed rate.)

Similar results can be obtained for the other short-term rates in Figure 3.2. These are shown in Table 3.3 together with the coefficients of the equations.

These results suggest that the 3-month bill rate can be a very important variable when included in the definition of a scenario. However, although it can explain the level of other short-term rates well, there are other factors

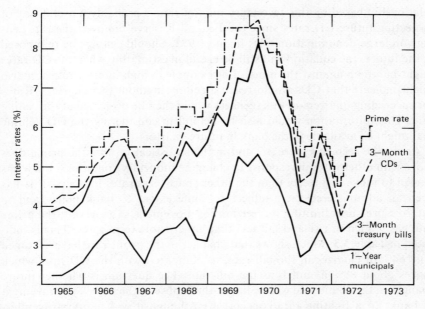

Figure 3.2.   Short-term interest rates. (Source: Salomon Brothers [1974].)

that must be considered in projecting some of these rates, particularly the CD rate and the prime. Negotiable CD rates paid by banks in the past have been subjected to ceilings through Federal Reserve use of their "Regulation Q." In order to obtain a historical data series, we used the rate on CDs sold in the secondary market. Since it is free to move in response to the demand and supply of funds, it provides a measure of what the primary 3-month CD rate might have been had banks been allowed to pay the going rate. A statistical

Table 3.3   Sample Short-term Interest Rate Equations

| | Coefficients | | | |
Interest Rate	Lagged Value of Rate	Change in Bill Rate	Percent Variance Explained	Standard Error of Estimate
3-Month CDs	1.00	.88	92.8	36 bp
Prime rate	1.00	.64	92.1	33
1-Year municipals	1.00	.53	86.4	31

relationship based on this secondary market rate is probably a useful way of projecting future CD rates since the Federal Reserve removed the rate ceilings on large denomination CDs in July 1973. Should ceilings be reimposed in the future, the equation will still be useful in estimating when the CD rates might bump up against the limits. For example, a high interest rate scenario might indicate that CDs would reach a ceiling in about two quarters. Rates for succeeding quarters in this scenario would then be projected at the ceiling rate. This information would also be helpful in considering the CD volume that might be available to the bank in future quarters.

As can be seen in Figure 3.2 and in the statistical results, the prime does move with other rates in response to changing monetary conditions, but it has tended to move less freely than the other short-term rates in the past. It has been an administered rate, subject to some extent to bank policy and to external pressures limiting its freedom of movement. As a result, the prime rate has tended to rise and fall less than other short-term rates. This is indicated in Table 3.3, which shows that changes in the prime rate have averaged only 64% of changes in the bill rate, as compared with the CD rate, which moves about 88% as much as the bill rate. The question is whether future changes in the prime rate will be larger than those in the past. The movement of banks to a floating rate concept, even though it was temporarily interrupted in early 1973 because of government pressure to keep rates down, may mean that future changes in the prime will correspond more closely to other money market rates. If so, this adjustment will have to be made in the statistical results.

Longer-Term Interest Rates

Procedures for projecting longer-term rates on the basis of a given scenario can be illustrated with a sample of rates such as the 10-year treasury rate, the 20-year "good-grade" municipal rate, and the rate on new issues of AA utilities with deferred call options. The Government and municipal rates are obviously important in the management of bank portfolios. The utility bond rate was included because it might be useful to help explain loan volume and net need for funds at some banks. Each of these rates is shown in Figure 3.3 along with the treasury bill rate.

One approach to projecting long rates is to select one of them as the explanatory variable, just as the bill rate was selected earlier to help explain changes in other short-term rates. As shown in Figure 3.3, the long-term rates do tend to move closely together over the monetary cycles. Thus, given a value for one of them, say the 10-year Government rate, estimates of the others can be obtained.

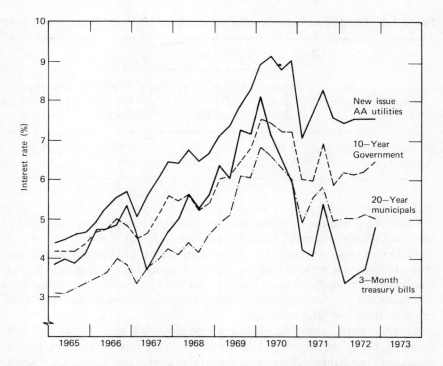

Figure 3.3.   Intermediate and long-term interest rates. (Source: Salomon Brothers [1974].)

The statistical results shown in Table 3.4 confirm this. As in the previous table for short-term rates, the equation for each long-term interest rate contains the previous value of the rate and the change in the 10-year Government rate. For example, an estimate of the 20-year municipal rate is given by the past value of the rate plus 78% of the change in the 10-year Government rate. These equations work well, explaining 94.1% of the variance in the 20-year municipal rate and 94.5% for the AA utility rate.

Since the bill rate and the 10-year Government rate can be used to explain the short and long-term rates, respectively, a possible approach to planning would be to use both of these rates as explanatory variables in the scenario definitions. Future paths of both of these rates would be identified for each scenario, and they would then be used to project the remaining short and long-term rates. While this approach is a useful one, a problem remains. How can a 3-month and a 10-year Government rate be selected so as to be consistent with each other within a particular scenario?

Table 3.4   Long-term Rate Equations Based on 10-Year Government Rate

| | Coefficients | | | |
| | Lagged Value of Rate | Change in 10-Year Government Rate | Percent Variance Explained | Standard Error of Estimate |
Interest Rate				
20-Year municipal	1.00	.78	94.1	26 bp
AA utility	1.00	.95	94.5	33

There are economic forecasting techniques that permit these two rates to be specified independently, but still based upon the same economic environment so that they are consistent. These approaches, discussed in a later section, are based on the idea that the factors determining the long rate are significantly different from those determining the short-term rate. Thus these different economic factors must be taken into account when specifying future values of short and long-term rates.

An alternative approach, which may be easier for some banks to implement, is based on the idea that movements in long-term rates can be explained reasonably well by short-term rates alone. The theoretical foundation for this approach lies in the term structure of interest rate theory, which attempts to explain the relationship between short and long rates. There is no universally accepted explanation of this relationship, but there is a widely held belief that the markets for short and long securities are interrelated. It is argued that a sufficient number of investors are free to select maturities so that returns in the long-term market cannot be determined independently of the short-term rates. If short rates are expected to rise, then an investor will not buy long securities unless the yield is sufficiently high to cover the average of the increasing returns that are expected to be available in the short-term market. This phenomenon is a major cause of the steeply sloped yield curves that occur when investors expect rates to rise. A similar market phenomenon can cause the yield curve to become inverted. When investors expect short-term rates to fall they are willing to buy lower yielding long-term bonds since they expect the return over their holding period to equal or exceed that of a series of short-term investments with falling interest rates.

If market expectations about the trend of future short-term rates are based on past rates, and if expectations about future short rates are a major factor in determining the shape of the yield curve, then there is reason to expect some statistical relationship between short- and long-term rates. Most students of the structure of interest rates do believe that expectations are based in part on past rates and that these expectations are a significant factor in the shape of the yield curve. The only controversy concerns factors other than market expectations that might also influence the shape of the yield curve.

Some believe, for example, that there is a liquidity premium in the structure of interest rates. Because of the added risk in long-term securities, it is argued that investors will not invest in them unless the return exceeds the return expected from a rollover of short-term securities. Thus the yield to maturity of a long-term bond will be larger than it would be if rate expectations were the only factors involved. Modigliani and Sutch [1966] have proposed a variant of the liquidity premium theory. They argued that many investors have a preference for a particular maturity range for their assets, based in part on the maturity structure of their liabilities. Some investors might have a preference for long-maturity securities if their liabilities also have a long average maturity. Whatever their natural preference, it is argued that investors will have to receive some premium to be enticed to purchase maturities outside this desired range.

For the purpose of projecting interest rates we do not need to choose from among the conflicting theories. If there are liquidity or other premiums in the interest rate structure, they will not be detrimental to forecasting equations so long as the size of any premium is relatively stable over time. This appears to be the case inasmuch as a substantial amount of empirical evidence suggests that a large share of the movement in long-term rates can be explained by short-term rates.

The structure of the equation previously used in Tables 3.3 and 3.4 is also useful to express the relationship between short- and long-term rates. (The rationale for this equation and its relationship to other empirical work is discussed in Appendix A.) Table 3.5 shows the results obtained when the 3-

Table 3.5   Long-term Rate Equations Based on 3-Month Bill Rate

| | Coefficients | | | |
Interest Rate	Lagged Value of Rate	Change in Bill Rate	Percent Variance Explained	Standard Error of Estimate
10-Year Government	1.01	.43	90.0	31 bp
20-Year municipal	1.01	.39	90.9	32
AA utility	1.01	.44	90.0	42

month treasury bill rate is used to explain the long-term rates. The 10-year Government rate, for example, can be explained by its past value plus 43% of the change in the bill rate. As would be expected, the change in the 10-year rate is substantially less than the change in the short rate. This equation explains 90.0% of the variance in the 10-year rate and has a standard error of 31 basis points.

The standard errors of estimate in Table 3.5 are slightly larger than those in Table 3.4, reflecting the fact that there is a closer relationship among the long-term rates than between the short- and long-term rates. The 10-year Government rate can explain the 20-year municipal rate with a standard error of 26 basis points. This standard error rises to 32 basis points when the change in the bill rate is used as the explanatory variable. This does not necessarily mean that the 10-year rate is the better approach to specifying the long-term municipal rate for a scenario.

There are basically two approaches to projecting long-term rates for a given scenario. One is to include a long-term rate in the definition of the scenario and then use it to project the other long rates using equations such as those in Table 3.4. The second approach is to include only a short-term rate such as the 3-month bill rate in the scenario definition. This rate is used to project each of the long-term rates using equations similar to those of Table 3.5. If this approach is taken, it is more accurate to go directly from the bill rate to the municipal rate, for example, than to project the 10-year Government rate and then use it to project the municipal rate.

The choice between including one or two rates in the scenario definition depends in part on the availability and accuracy of procedures for specifying both the short- and long-term rates so that they are consistent with each other within a scenario. There are procedures available for this purpose. Pierson [1970], for example, has developed a statistical model in which long and short Government rates are estimated using a number of explanatory variables. These included the earning assets of banks, GNP, the Federal Reserve discount rate, and the volume of outstanding treasury debt of long, intermediate, and short maturities. These equations explained a large percent of the variance in each of the interest rates. However, she also found that an equation based on the term structure of interest rates alone worked as well as the other approach. In this equation movements in the long-term Government rate were explained well by using current and lagged values of the bill rate.

This result suggests that a procedure in which all rates are tied to a single rate, such as the bill rate, will work reasonably well. Of course, if the bank believes there is some chance that the structural relationship between long and short rates might change, this phenomenon can be embodied in one or more of the scenarios being explored regardless of the approach used in other scenarios.

Intermediate Rates

For portfolio management purposes it is frequently necessary to specify complete yield curves for both treasury and municipal bonds, not just the short- and long-term maturities of these securities. Taking Governments as an example, this could be accomplished by estimating a statistical equation for each maturity that related its yield to the 3-month bill rate. This would be a cumbersome process, but it is possible to shortcut this procedure by using a mathematical formula to fit a yield curve through yields for a few maturities. In this approach only a few yields are estimated from the scenario and the others are filled in using the formula.

A formula that seems to work well is based on an equation identified by a statistician, K. Pearson. The form of the equation is

$$R_m = am^b e^{cm}$$

where R_m is the yield to maturity of an m-period bond, and a, b, and c are parameters selected so that the equation fits the yield curve.*

To use this equation to describe a yield curve, three interest rates on the curve need to be specified. These three points are then used to determine values of the parameters in the equation. As an example, consider the Government yield curve of January 1, 1974 reported by Salomon Brothers [1974]. The 3-month rate was 7.59%, the 3-year rate was 6.72%, and the 20-year rate was 7.30%. Given these three rates, values for a, b, and c can be computed, yielding the following equation:

$$R_m = 6.944(m^{-.062})(e^{.012m})$$

This equation specifies a curve passing through each of the three points, and it can be used to compute rates for any other maturity of interest. The resulting curve is shown as the dashed line in Figure 3.4 for the January 1974 date. The solid line represents a plot of the actual Salomon Brothers' yields.

Equations of this form can be used to describe a variety of yield curve shapes. Some examples of typical shapes are shown in Figure 3.4 along with the inverted yield curve of January 1974. Each of the dashed curves was computed by fitting the curve equation through the 3-month, 3-year, and 20-year yields to maturity.

* This equation was suggested to the authors by Kenneth Gray. It is a simplification of the Pearson "Type III" frequency which is a generalization of the chi-square distribution. For a discussion of these curves see Cramer [1946].

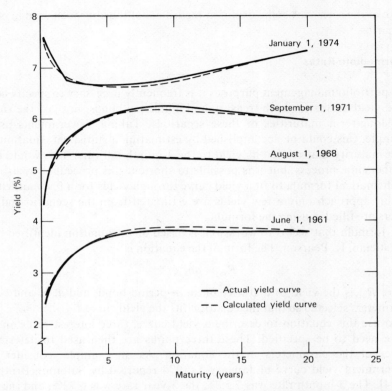

Figure 3.4.   Selected government yield curves. (Source in part: Salomon Brothers [1974].)

STRUCTURING INTEREST RATE SCENARIOS

While the curve equation can be used to fit past data reasonably well, its major purpose is to make it easier for a portfolio planner to specify future yield curves consistent with the scenarios being explored. It can be used in conjunction with statistical procedures discussed earlier to develop sets of yield curves for each scenario with relative ease. One possible sequence of steps for Government securities would be as follows:

1.   Define the scenarios to be explored. Values for the 3-month rate would be included as a part of each scenario's definition. (Rates for other securities could also be included in the definition if desired.)

2.   Specify values for two other interest rates, such as the 3-year and 10-

year rates, for each 3-month rate. This could be done using statistical equations such as those in Table 3.5.

3.   Use the yield curve equation to fill in rates for other maturities on each curve.

To illustrate this process, assume that the portfolio planner wishes to consider three possible interest rate scenarios over the next time period. He defines these three scenarios by a 100-basis-point increase in the bill rate, no change, and a 100-basis-point decrease, respectively. The hypothetical starting Government yield curve is shown in Figure 3.5 as the "current yield curve." In this curve the 3-month bill rate is 5.4%, the 3-year Government rate is 5.95%, and the 10-year rate is 6.35%.

Given the planner's scenario definitions, the bill rate might rise to 6.4%, remain the same, or fall to 4.4%. For each of these rates we can estimate a 3- and 10-year rate using statistical equations such as those in Table 3.5. The results shown in that table indicate that changes in the 10-year rate have averaged about 43% of the change in the 3-month rate. Similar statistical analysis was conducted for the 3-year Government rate, suggesting that changes in the 3-year rate can be estimated by using 74% of the 3-month rate change. These assumptions combined with the designated changes in the 3-month rate for each scenario can be used to obtain three points on each future yield, as shown in Table 3.6. For example, the 3-year rate, which occurs when

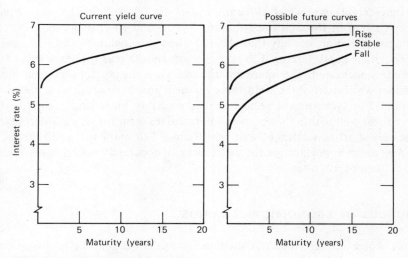

Figure 3.5.   Illustration of rate scenarios.

Table 3.6   Sample Interest Rate Scenarios

| Maturity | Current Yields (%) | Next Period's Rates (%) | | |
		Rise	Stable	Fall
3 months	5.40	6.40	5.40	4.40
3 years	5.95	6.69	5.95	5.21
10 years	6.35	6.78	6.35	5.92

interest rates rise, is equal to the old rate plus 74% of the 100-basis-point change in the bill rate, $5.95\% + 0.74\% = 6.69\%$.

The next step in the process is to estimate complete yield curves for each set of three points in this table using the yield curve equation discussed above. This results in the set of yield curves plotted in Figure 3.5. In the rising interest scenario the yield curve becomes flatter as the short-term rates rise more than intermediate- and long-term rates. Similarly if rates fall, the estimation process results in a more steeply sloped yield curve. These results are typical of those occurring in periods of rising and falling interest rates. In fact, the proposed estimating process will also provide the humped and inverted yield curves that occur when Government rates rise sufficiently.

It should be noted that the yield curves resulting from this process depend to some extent upon which three maturities are selected for the curve equation. A curve fit through the 3-month, 3-year, and 10-year points may, for example, rise more rapidly than desired when extrapolated out to 20 years. On the other hand, forcing it to pass through the 20-year rate may make the curve less accurate in the intermediate area. Thus the portfolio planner must consider which part of the yield curve for each group of securities is most important. For Government securities it is probably more important for the curve to fit well within the short- to intermediate-term range, considering the relatively short maturities held by most banks. For municipal yield curves, it may be more important for the yield curve to accurately reflect assessments about longer-term rates.

SOURCES OF ECONOMIC SCENARIOS

This chapter has described statistical techniques for estimating future interest rates and funds available to the portfolio based on economic scenarios defined by a few key economic variables. These techniques are particularly useful in generating the large number of projections required for planning under uncertainty. Their use, however, requires access to forecasts of the key economic variables.

One source of economic forecasts for many banks could be the regular forecasts prepared by the bank's own economics staff. These forecasts normally include projections of the variables needed for scenario planning. However, a difficulty is that many economists commonly prepare only one forecast, corresponding to the "most likely" scenario. They have traditionally been reluctant to specify more than one scenario. This pattern has begun to improve recently, so that many large banks now regularly prepare more than one scenario.

The trend to consideration of more than one scenario has been helped by the use of bank forecasting committees and the availability of commercial forecasting services. Forecasting committees made up of interested officers from several parts of a bank are now used by several large commercial banks. They serve a number of purposes, including the expression of more than one viewpoint in the committee meetings. These differing points of view encourage consideration of alternative assumptions and can lead to specification of more than one scenario to express these differences.

Commercial forecasting services are now available that regularly provide economic projections for different scenarios. For banks having little or no internal economic staff these forecasts can serve directly as the basis for the detailed projections needed for portfolio planning. In the larger banks the commercial forecasts still serve useful purposes in providing information helpful in the preparation of the bank's own forecasts and in encouraging consideration of the several scenarios that might occur.

As a result of the increasing sophistication of both the banks' economics staffs and the commercially available forecasting services in dealing with the future uncertainty, the kinds of analysis discussed in this chapter are feasible for a variety of banks, not just those with sophisticated analytical or management science staffs.

4

MODELS FOR SIMULATION
OF PORTFOLIO ACTIONS

Having described future portfolio environments that need to be considered, the bank next studies the implications of these scenarios for current portfolio action. Computer models can be very helpful in this process because of their ability to calculate the implications of a set of portfolio actions within the context of a specified portfolio environment. While it is possible to work out the implications of a portfolio strategy manually, computer models have made it feasible to both evaluate a much wider range of alternatives and do the evaluation in a more complete manner.

Simulation models have proven to be the most commonly used kind of model for this purpose, in large part because they are relatively easy to implement and use. A number of such models have been developed, some for proprietary use within individual banks and others available to banks generally on a commercial basis. The basic structure of most of these models is quite similar. The bank planner or portfolio manager supplies three types of information to the model: data describing the current financial position of the bank, including information about its portfolios; assumptions about future trends of loans, deposits, interest rates, and other relevant items; and a set of actions to be evaluated. The computer model then simulates what would happen if the assumed scenario occurred and the proposed decisions were implemented. The results of this simulation are then displayed, most commonly as pro forma balance sheets and income statements or other financial reports.

Although these simulation models are the most frequently used, they are not the only kind of model helpful in scenario planning. The distinguishing features of these basic models, called deterministic stimulation models, are that the decisions to be evaluated are supplied to the model by the user and that these decisions are studied within the context of one scenario at a time. There are alternative models, called optimization models, that will search through possible portfolio actions to select the best set of actions according to some well-defined criteria. In addition, there are "Monte Carlo" simulation models that are useful in exploring the implications of a user-specified portfolio strategy over a large number of possible scenarios. These more complex models are discussed in later chapters.

This chapter is devoted to deterministic simulation models. We shall first describe a representative simulation model to illustrate its structure and how it can be used. In the subsequent section we evaluate the role of these models and discuss some refinements that have been developed to make this type of model more useful in portfolio management. These refinements have been included in a financial planning model called BANKMOD, which was developed by the Bank Administration Institute for use by commercial banks. Finally, we summarize a study illustrating how a simulation model can be used to explore the implications of alternative portfolio strategies.

STANDARD SIMULATION MODELS

The simulation models most readily available through commercial vendors and large correspondent banks are useful primarily for aggregate planning purposes rather than detailed analysis of portfolio decisions. The categories of assets and liabilities included in the model are not very detailed, and the planning periods built into the model typically cover a whole year at a time. However, the relatively simple structure of these models makes them easy to use and allows them to serve as an introductory example of simulation models.

Simulation models are frequently structured around the three types of information that are to be supplied by the user:

- Current and historical data.
- Forecasts of future conditions.
- A set of actions or decisions to be evaluated.

The current information to be provided describes the starting position of the bank for the simulation. This position is typically described in terms of the bank's statement of condition as of a recent date or perhaps in terms of the average level of these assets and liabilities over a recent period. Data on current loan volume are commonly categorized into the major loan groups, such as commercial loans, consumer loans, and real estate loans. Deposit data are frequently grouped as demand deposits, savings deposits, certificates of deposit, and other time deposits. In the aggregate simulation models, data on current security holdings are usually grouped into broad balance sheet categories such as U.S. Treasury securities and state and local government securities.

In addition to this current balance sheet information, many models also make use of historical information to help in the projection of financial data. A model might, for example, require balance sheet data and some income and expense data for each of the past five years. Theae data are then used by the model to compute historical growth rates, which are reported to the user. This information is frequently helpful in making assumptions about the future growth rates of the bank's assets, liabilities, and other items.

In supplying projections to the model a distinction needs to be made between items not under the direct control of the bank and the asset and liability categories representing decisions made by the bank. Simulation models differ in the variables that are assumed to be decisions made by the user, but normally the major loan categories and deposits other than CDs are treated as projections rather than considered to be under the active control of the bank. Thus a scenario to be studied by the model would include some projection of the level or growth rate of each of these kinds of variables.

Interest rates are also a part of the scenario definition. A rate is needed for each earning asset and interest-bearing liability in each future time period. For example, an interest rate is needed to represent the average yield in each future year on the U.S. Government security portfolio. As discussed in earlier chapters, these interest rates need to be consistent with the patterns of loans and deposits included in the scenario.

A number of miscellaneous assumptions also need to be made to complete the list of projections. As examples, these items would include federal and state income tax rates, reserve requirements for each deposit category, and pledging requirements.

The "decisions" that the user needs to supply these models are limited. They are usually concerned with decision rules for investing any excess funds and for financing any deficit. One common approach is to have the user decide what level of CDs will be maintained in each year of the planning horizon and specify some volume of security holdings. These holdings might be stated as a percent of total assets or some other ratio that would be maintained.

Given the starting position, projections, and decisions, the simulation model then calculates what would happen and prints results, normally in terms of pro forma balance sheets and income statements. These or other reports typically highlight particular items of interest such as the surplus or deficit of funds, the bank's liquidity position, a measure of capital adequacy, and the earnings trend of the bank. As a result the planner obtains a good feeling for what would happen if the projected scenario occurred and the proposed decision rules were implemented.

In comparison with the more complex modeling techniques to be discussed later, the standard simulation models have the significant advantages of being readily available and easy to understand and use. In fact some users of these models may even feel they are so simple that they contribute little to the planning process. The user must supply a large quantity of data to the model, including the critical assumptions and projections. The computer model then does a small amount of straightforward calculating and prints out the results. There is some truth to this criticism, but the simulation model does provide some useful structure to the planning problem, and it makes possible the exploration of many more scenarios and bank decision alternatives than are feasible with hand computations.

For banks that have done relatively little formal planning, the process of looking at historical trends and thinking about likely future trends as required by the model can be a helpful exercise. In addition, the implications of these projections as computed by the simulation model may include some surprises that will initiate some action by the bank. The kinds of conclusions from the analysis could include information such as the following:

- Given the expected trends in loans, deposits, and interest rates, the bank's earnings will not grow as rapidly as hoped.
- Additional capital will be needed in the next year or two to support the bank's growth.
- Expected future loan growth cannot be funded unless the bank relies more heavily on purchased funds than desired.

These or other conclusions might suggest that the bank begin to take some action to head off the future problem. The simulation model can be used to help evaluate alternatives available to the bank by trying out new assumptions with the model. Sample questions that might be studied include the following:

- If the bank shifted its mix of taxable and tax-exempt securities, what would the impact be on the trend of bank earnings and its taxable income position?
- How much must the growth in expenses be curtailed to obtain a satisfactory earnings trend?
- If the bank added to its capital base, what would be the impact on its earnings per share and its ability to support loan growth?

Even if initial results of the simulation model do not point to potential future problems, it is helpful to look at the implications of alternative scenarios. As suggested in Chapter 2, this is a means of taking into account the fact that future conditions are uncertain. By altering assumptions about loan growth or interest rate trends, it is possible to see how sensitive the bank's earnings and other performance measures are to changes in the expected environment. This "sensitivity analysis" might suggest that the bank take some action to hedge against the possibility of unexpected changes in interest rates, for example, even if there are no problems expected in the most likely environments.

While useful in exploring these important questions, the simplicity and ease of use of standard simulation models do limit the kinds of analysis that can be undertaken. These limitations occur in two primary areas. First, the broad categories of assets and liabilities used in most of these models limit the amount of detailed analysis, particularly in the evaluation of portfolio strategy. Second, it is difficult to do contingency planning in which consideration is given to actions that might be taken as the future unfolds.

More detail about bank security holdings can be included in simulation models, and some models have moved in this direction. One such model, developed at Dartmouth,* divides U.S. Treasury and municipal securities into maturity groups. BANKMOD, a simulation model discussed more fully below, includes even more detail, such as quality groupings of municipal securities.

As detail is added, the simulation model becomes more complex and more information has to be supplied to it. In the Dartmouth model, for example, the user must supply data for each maturity category including the dollar amount and the average coupon rate in each group. In addition, interest rate projections must now be stated in terms of yields for each maturity rather than just one interest rate for each period. The benefits of this greater detail are that it allows a more accurate consideration of the bank's liquidity position as well as an evaluation of changes in the structure of the security portfolios. If the level of interest rates increases, what will happen to the market value of the portfolio? Should the maturity structure be changed in anticipation of a rate increase? What are the implications of such a change for current earnings and capital gains or losses? These are important questions for a portfolio manager to consider, but the simpler simulation models are of little help.

These models also have some weaknesses when they are being used to do the contingency planning outlined in Chapter 2. In the scenario planning ap-

* A summary of this model is provided by Bower and Simpson [1970].

proach described there, we suggested that at least three scenarios of future portfolio environments be specified to indicate the possible conditions that might occur. By considering portfolio strategies that might be appropriate in each of these scenarios, it is possible to see how these environments affect the structure of desirable portfolio actions. Unfortunately, no single portfolio action will be appropriate for all the scenarios, so the portfolio manager has the difficult task of selecting a strategy providing both a satisfactory return and a hedge in case rates rise or fall unexpectedly.

Simulation models are potentially useful in this step since they offer the possibility of testing strategies in several different environments. The portfolio manager might, for example, select a candidate strategy that performs well for the most likely scenario and try this strategy in other scenarios to see what would happen if a high or low interest rate environment occurred. By comparing these results with the performance obtained from strategies specifically appropriate for high- and low-rate environments, respectively, it is possible to see how much worse the candidate strategy would do if rates were higher and how much opportunity for gains would be foregone if rates fell. Modifications in this strategy could then be considered that might provide better performance if the most likely scenario did not occur. Again, this modified strategy could be tried in each of the environments to study its overall performance characteristics. This process of working back and forth between scenarios and portfolio actions could be continued until the portfolio manager developed what he considered to be an appropriate policy.

Use of a simulation model for this kind of planning suggests a number of desirable characteristics of these models. The model should be designed so it is relatively easy for the user to specify more than one scenario to be studied. When working out portfolio actions for each of these scenarios, it is also helpful to be able to work through the plan on a period-by-period basis rather than specify a strategy at the beginning of the simulation for the whole planning horizon. This allows the planner to take into account previous periods' decisions and their results when he is working on, say, the third quarter or the third year of the plan. Finally, it is helpful to be able to work back and forth easily between the scenarios and the portfolio strategies being evaluated. This requires some means of "saving" or storing both the scenario definitions and the portfolio decisions so that the user can tell the computer model to try out candidate portfolio strategies in alternative environments.

The standard simulation models do satisfy the first of these criteria. It is possible to specify more than one scenario and to work out a strategy appropriate for each. However, these models typically do not allow period-by-period decisions nor do they provide for easy interaction between scenarios and the sets of decisions being evaluated.

BANKMOD

Faced with these weaknesses in the simpler simulation models, a number of banks have developed their own internal models that have a level of detail and flexibility considered appropriate for the bank. One simulation model that is available to banks generally and that does meet the needs for more complete scenario planning is called BANKMOD.* This simulation model was developed by the Bank Administration Institute, which provides the model via a national computer time-sharing company for use by interested banks on a commercial basis. The types of decisions that can be evaluated by BANKMOD are detailed enough that the portfolio planner can explore trading strategies in the security portfolios and study alternative financing policies for the bank. In addition, the structure of the model makes it possible to store both scenarios and strategies so that courses of action can easily be studied under different assumptions about future environments.

The components of BANKMOD, although more complex, correspond to the three types of information a user must supply to the standard simulation models: current information about the bank, assumptions and forecasts about the future, and a set of decisions to be evaluated. This model requires some additional information, though, since it allows the user to specify some parts of the planning structure. For example, if the portfolio planner wants to work out a fairly detailed plan for the current year, he may specify a monthly plan for up to 12 months. If he wishes to plan for a longer horizon, the planner may decide to plan on a quarterly basis for up to 8 quarters. The user has the additional capability of specifying some optional asset and liability categories and selecting different levels of detail in the description of security holdings.

The decisions that can be evaluated in BANKMOD are much richer than those of the standard simulation models. In each planning period the user can select the level of short-term investments desired in a number of categories including federal funds sold, bankers acceptances, and others. He also determines the volume of securities held in treasury bills, U.S. Governments, agencies, prime municipals, and other municipals. The U.S. Governments, agencies, and municipals are further broken down into maturity groups so that the planner can specify purchases and sales of particular maturities. In addition, he can specify the coupon rate on the maturities to be purchased or sold.

While the standard simulation models typically have a very limited set of options for liability management, BANKMOD provides a number of liability

* An overview of the structure and use of BANKMOD is provided by Robinson [1973]. We are grateful for permission to draw upon his article, which was published in the *Journal of Bank Research* (Autumn 1973).

categories that can be managed by the planner. In the short-term area, the planner is allowed to set levels of federal funds purchased, borrowing from the Federal Reserve, large negotiable CDs, and commercial paper of the bank's holding company used to fund loans of the bank. The CDs and commercial paper are divided into maturity categories so the planner can select the maturities to be sold as well as the total amount outstanding. In the long-term area, the bank planner can specify sales of capital notes along with their maturity, and he can evaluate the sale or repurchase of shares of the bank's stock.

The information about the current status of the bank required by BANKMOD is of necessity more detailed than that for simpler models. Typical balance sheet data are required, but it is also necessary to provide information for each maturity of the assets and liabilities that have maturity groupings. For example, the volume outstanding and the coupon rate are needed for each maturity group of outstanding Governments and municipals. BANKMOD does provide some assistance in supplying data for municipal bonds. If the user desires, he can provide the computer with information on punched cards for each municipal security currently held, and the computer will do the grouping according to the specifications supplied.

The assumptions provided to BANKMOD are divided into two groups, "unnamed" and "named" assumptions. The unnamed assumptions are those not likely to be changed from one simulation to another. These might include factors such as tax rates and the book value of buildings and equipment. A set of named assumptions corresponds to a scenario definition that would include items such as projected loan growth and interest rate levels. Once specified, this scenario definition can be stored in a computer file and used later if the planner wants to try out a new set of decisions in this portfolio environment.

As would be expected, the scenario definitions in BANKMOD require much more data than those for simpler models. There are a number of asset and liability categories that have maturity groupings. These require interest rate assumptions for each maturity in each planning period. Fortunately the model provides some assistance so the user needs to supply the yields for only a few designated maturities. BANKMOD then computes the rest using techniques similar to those discussed in Chapter 3. In addition the user needs to supply these yield-to-maturity data for only four security categories, federal funds purchased, U.S. Governments, agencies and prime municipals. Other yields to maturity are calculated by the model using estimated yield spreads supplied by the user.

A planner has considerable flexibility in the types of decisions supplied to BANKMOD. It is possible to use it in much the same way as a standard simulation model. Portfolio and other decisions can be prespecified for each planning period before running the simulation model. Alternatively, the user can work through the plan one period at a time. With this procedure a set of decisions is made for the current period. The model is then told to simulate what would happen if these decisions were implemented. If the results are unsatisfactory, the planner can alter the decisions and ask for another simulation. When satisfactory results are obtained, the planner moves on to the next period and works on decisions for it. This capability of the model allows the user to work out a careful plan in which each period's decisions take into account earlier decisions and their impact.

In practice a planner will probably want to use both the prespecified feature and the ability to make period-by-period decisions. For example, he might want to work through the whole planning period quickly to get a general feeling for the implications of the scenario under study. For this purpose he would prespecify a rough set of decisions for each period and tell the model to simulate the impact of these decisions. This simulation might indicate, for example, that the environment is one in which actions will be needed to fund rising loan demand and to provide protection against rising rates. Knowing this or some other general background, the user might then work through the plan period by period. Some of the original decisions might be retained and others changed, but the model allows this flexibility.

BANKMOD provides some important assistance in working out a plan one period at a time by allowing the user to specify the reports desired at each step. After specifying a set of decisions for one period, the planner wants to see what would happen under this course of action, but he probably doesn't need complete financial statements. He has the option in BANKMOD of obtaining much less information. As an example, the planner has the option of requesting a "flash report," which provides information about current status and performance in terms of six primary measures, such as net operating income per share and a liquidity ratio. The value of each of these measures is shown on a before-and-after basis so the user can see what the impact of the current decision would be on bank performance. More detailed reports are also available after each period's decisions, up to and including complete balance sheets and earnings reports. Each of these reports is also available at the end of the planning horizon to provide a complete picture of the implications of the plan.

An important feature of BANKMOD is that both the scenario definitions and sets of decisions can be stored in a computer file. This makes it very easy for the planner to move back and forth between scenario definitions and sets of decisions. Assuming scenarios of interest have been defined and one or more sets of decisions have been specified, the planner can readily simulate what would happen if a set of decisions were implemented in the different future environments. This ability to mix scenarios and decisions provides an important assist to scenario planning.

RESULTS FROM A SIMULATION MODEL

Hempel and Kretschman [1973] used a deterministic simulation model to study several portfolio strategies in different economic environments.* Although they used a special purpose model dealing only with security portfolios, their study illustrates the kind of analysis that can be undertaken with a simulation model. Models such as BANKMOD are designed to help a portfolio manager select a specific set of portfolio actions based upon the bank's existing portfolio, the current interest rate environment, and economic environments that might occur in the future. The work by Hempel and Kretschman has implications for these decisions, but their model did not have this specific decision-making point of view. Instead they were concerned about the characteristics of portfolio maturity structures to be maintained over a period of time.

To study these characteristics via a simulation model, Hempel and Kretschman had to supply the three kinds of information discussed above: data on the starting position of the portfolio, economic scenarios, and decisions to be evaluated. In their work the decisions supplied to the simulation model were portfolio trading rules that would maintain the maturity structure being studied. The authors were particularly interested in the characteristics of laddered and barbell portfolios, so the maturity structures studied were all variations of these two basic maturity patterns. The scenarios supplied to the model were assumed paths of future interest rates. Thus by specifying several laddered and barbell maturity structures and simulating their performance in a variety of economic scenarios, Hempel and Kretschman were able to draw some conclusions about the characteristics of these two types of portfolio strategies.

They selected municipal securities for the sample portfolio used in the study. The composition of the portfolio was assumed to be 50% prime municipals and 50% good grade securities as defined by Salomon Brothers. This allowed them to use Salomon Brothers' historical data on municipal yield curves to obtain a past scenario of interest rate movements and a starting point for future scenarios.

In the laddered portfolios studied, it was assumed that the bond maturities would be evenly distributed from one year out to a longest maturity. For

* We are grateful for permission to draw upon the Hempel and Kretschman article published in the *Mississippi Valley Journal of Business and Economics* (Fall, 1973).

example, a 10-year ladder would have 10% of its funds allocated to each maturity from 1 to 10 years. This structure is maintained in the simulation model just as it is by banks using this maturity pattern. With the passing of each year in the simulation, the cash provided by the maturing 1-year bond is reinvested in a new bond of the longest maturity allowed at the prevailing interest rate. The authors considered a number of such ladders including portfolios laddered out to 2, 7, 15, and 20 years.

The barbell maturity structures had bonds concentrated in the short and long end of the maturity range. Short-term bonds were grouped in the maturities under 5 years, while the long bonds were spread from 20- to 30-year maturities. To maintain this structure in the simulation model, proceeds from maturing 1-year bonds were reinvested in equal amounts of new 1-, 2-, and 5-year securities. This reinvestment policy resulted in a concentration of most of the short-term bonds in 1- and 2-year maturities with smaller amounts in the 3- to 5-year range. Long-term bonds were spread in equal amounts from 20- to 30-year maturities. With the passage of time in the simulation model the 20-year bond was sold when it became a 19-year, and the proceeds were used to purchase a new 30-year bond. These decision rules were used for each barbell portfolio studied, but the share of the portfolio allocated to the short- and long-maturity categories was varied to correspond to the laddered portfolios of various lengths. The shortest barbell portfolios studied had 90% of the funds allocated to the 1- to 5-year maturity range and 10% in 20–30 years. Other distributions studied had allocations to short-term maturities of 70, 50, 30, and 10%, with the remainder in each case put in the long maturities.

Hempel and Kretschman were interested in how these strategies would have performed in the past, so one of the economic scenarios studied was the path of municipal interest rates in the period from 1950 through 1970. Some future scenarios were also investigated. In these scenarios actual municipal rates were used for the first half of 1971, but then rates were assumed to follow one of the following four paths:

- constant at mid-1971 levels.
- cyclically fluctuating rates, assuming 2-year up and down movements with about 50 basis points from peak to trough.
- steadily rising rates with the level of rates increasing about 250 basis points over the 10-year period studied.
- steadily falling rates with the level falling about 250 basis points.

It should be noted that one of the assumptions made for their scenarios was that the municipal yield curves moved in parallel. In other words, long-term rates moved up or down the same amount as did shorter rates. This has not been the pattern of rates of recent years, as discussed in Chapter 3, so the approach of Hempel and Kretschman may have overstated the potential capital gain or loss on the long municipals in their simulated portfolios.* For example, in the scenario with steadily rising rates the long-term rates would probably not rise as much and market value would not fall as much as assumed in the simulation.

As with other simulation models, they needed to specify a starting portfolio for the simulation. They assumed that the portfolios were initiated in 1950 by buying new securities at par. The portfolio laddered to 10 years, for example, was initiated in 1950 by purchasing equal amounts of new 1-year, 2-year, and so forth, securities. For simulations based on future scenarios they tried two different starting portfolios. In one they assumed that the securities held from the historical scenarios were the starting portfolios for the future simulation. The alternative assumption tested was that the starting portfolios in January 1970 were purchased new on that date. Since rates were relatively high in early 1970, this assumption increased the return on portfolios containing long maturity bonds.

The period from 1950 to 1970 was one of generally rising rates; so, as Hempel and Kretschman [1973] note, some of the simulation results were not surprising. Portfolios with shorter average maturities performed better in both the laddered and barbell strategies. It is interesting that the average annual yields (not including the effect of any unrealized gain or loss) were very close for all the portfolio strategies. The portfolio laddered to 10-year maturities provided the highest average yield over the period, 2.16%, but this was only 10 basis points above the yield of the two-year ladder, which provided the worst yield. The average annual yields of the barbell portfolios were all within the range of 2.10 to 2.12%. These yields on the barbell portfolios include any after tax gain or loss realized when bonds were sold to maintain the 20- to 30-year spread on the long end of the barbell.

Apparently the yields were so close across all strategies because two effects offset each other. On the one hand, long maturity bonds provided higher yields when purchased because the yield curves were upward sloping. This positive effect was offset by the more rapid turnover of shorter maturity portfolios, which provided more cash for reinvestment during the period of rising interest rates.

The major impact of lengthening the average maturity was, of course, in the market value of the portfolios. The authors computed the average market value and the lowest market value for each portfolio strategy during the historical period. For both the laddered and barbell portfolios, lengthening the

---

* In more recent work Hempel and Yawitz [1974] show why longer-term rates tend to be less volatile than short-term rates.

average maturity led to lower market values according to both measures because of the general uptrend of interest rates that occurred.

Which of the two basic strategies would have performed better during this 20-year period? The answer is probably a laddered portfolio. Because of the rising interest rates, the long maturity bonds in each barbell hurt the portfolio's performance. Thus the best barbell had 90% of its funds allocated to the short maturities. This strategy would have performed fairly well. It performed better than the portfolios laddered to maturities of 15 and 20 years, about the same as the 10-year ladder, and its performance was worse than the shorter ladders. To do this well, though, required a very short barbell. It is unlikely that a portfolio manager using barbell strategy would have put only 10% of its funds in long maturities.

The future scenarios specified by Hempel and Kretschman provide some insights into the performance characteristics of these two portfolio strategies under different environments, but no clearcut conclusions can be reached about whether ladders are better than barbells. One important conclusion that can be reached is that the starting portfolio makes a difference. Long maturity bonds held in the portfolios at the end of the 1950–1970 simulation tended to have low market values. Thus, simulations using these portfolios as the starting point were significantly affected by the presence of long-term bonds in both barbell and laddered portfolios. As a result the barbell portfolios did not perform as well as the laddered portfolios containing no long-term securities.

The simulations that started with new portfolios in January 1971 provide a comparison not tied to the secular uptrend in rates of the historical period. In these cases the barbell portfolios tended to provide higher annual yields (including realized gains and losses after tax). For example, the barbell portfolio with 70% in short-term securities provided higher average annual yields in each of the four scenarios than those achieved by the portfolio laddered to 7 years. The price paid to receive the higher yield was more variability in the market value of the portfolio. In the scenario with falling interest rates the barbell had a higher average market value than the ladder, and its average value was about equal to the ladder in the cyclical rate scenario. On the other hand the barbell had lower average market values in the constant- and rising-rate scenarios.

It is somewhat surprising that the two portfolio strategies would have different market values if interest rates were constant over time. This results from Hempel and Kretschman's scenario definition. In all four of the scenarios actual rates were used for the first half of 1971 and the scenario of future rates was assumed to begin with July 1971 rates. Thus the constant-rate scenario held interest rates constant at the July level even though the simulation was started in January. Long-term municipal rates rose about 75 basis points in this six-month interval, so that any long-term bonds in the initial portfolio were substantially "under water" at the level of the constant-rate scenario.

This assumption affects the numbers in their results, but it does not affect the general nature of portfolio behavior. Barbell portfolios by their nature include some long-term bonds, whereas the longest bond in many laddered portfolios might be 15 years or less. These long bonds can make a positive contribution to the interest income from a portfolio, but at the cost of more variability in the market value. Thus there is no easy way to say whether the ladder or barbell structure is better.

CONCLUSIONS

Hempel and Kretschman [1973] demonstrated how a simulation model could be used to try out portfolio strategies under different economic scenarios. Portfolio managers can do similar kinds of analysis to help with their portfolio decisions, although their analysis would be more specific to their own banks. For better or worse, the portfolio managers have an actual portfolio to work with rather than cash. The question is how this portfolio should be adjusted in light of the current environment and possible future conditions. Some of the scenarios a manager might evaluate could be general uptrends and downtrends in interest rates such as Hempel and Kretschman used, but he is also likely to explore specific scenarios that represent his judgment as to how the economy and interest rates might behave. A final difference in the way simulation models are used in planning is that the portfolio manager would be more actively involved in the portfolio decisions being studied. Hempel and Kretschman used mechanical trading rules for their study, making no attempt to try to take advantage of interest rate swings in either the laddered or barbell portfolios. One of the purposes of a simulation model would be to allow the manager to evaluate trades that allow the bank to prepare for expected changes in interest rates or other elements of the portfolio environment.

When selecting a course of action for a portfolio, one of the broader questions faced by a manager is whether to move the portfolio toward a laddered or barbell maturity structure. The simulation study summarized here raised some of the risk and return issues involved in this choice. We will return to the evaluation of portfolio performance characteristics in Chapter 6, when we begin to consider models dealing explicitly with the uncertainty of future portfolio environments.

5

LINEAR PROGRAMMING MODELS
FOR PORTFOLIO MANAGEMENT

The deterministic simulation models discussed in the preceding chapter provide a very flexible modeling technique. After supplying information about the current position of the bank and a forecast of the future economic environment the portfolio planner can specify any set of decisions that he wishes to evaluate. The model will simulate what would happen if the decisions were implemented and the assumed economic environment took place. When selecting a set of portfolio decisions to be evaluated the portfolio manager probably takes into account some bank guidelines for portfolio policy and some limitations on actions that might be imposed by the financial markets, but he does not need to make these considerations explicit. Similarly, he need not supply the model with information about his criteria for evaluating the results of the simulation. Although this makes deterministic simulation models flexible and relatively easy to use, these models can do nothing more than compute the implications of strategies against a particular planning scenario where both the strategy and the scenario are supplied by a portfolio planner or manager.

If the portfolio manager is willing to supply explicit information about limitations on portfolio actions and about the criteria for evaluating portfolio actions, linear programming models can be used. These "optimization" models essentially search through the possible portfolio actions that satisfy the limitations or constraints specified by the planner and select the strategy that provides the best performance according to a particular criterion also defined by the planner. Since the model generates its own portfolio strategy, it has the potential for suggesting a set of actions that may not have been considered by the portfolio manager. Further, even if the general structure of the strategy was one being actively considered, the model's refinement of that structure is extremely useful. Because it is selected by the model, the portfolio manager can have confidence that the strategy is the best available, given the assumed future environment and the constraints and objective specified.

Linear programming models are distinguished in a major way from deterministic simulation models in that they select their own portfolio strategy rather than evaluate one supplied by the portfolio manager. However, they share a similar characteristic in that neither explicitly considers the uncertainty about future environments. Both deterministic simulation and linear programming models evaluate a portfolio strategy assuming that a particular economic scenario will occur. There are two important ways in which these models have been generalized to include uncertainty. First, "Monte Carlo" simulation models take uncertainty into account by evaluating a portfolio strategy across a large number of possible economic scenarios. Second, optimization models can explicitly consider uncertainty when selecting a strategy by constraining portfolio actions on each of several scenarios and maximizing the expected value of the portfolio. The Monte Carlo simulation models are taken up in Chapter 6 and the discussion of optimization models that incorporate uncertainty is begun in Chapter 7.

In this chapter we develop the basic structure of linear programming models and discuss their usefulness for portfolio planning. Generally these models have been concerned with aggregate planning for the entire bank, including, but not devoted specifically to, the investment portfolio. Several banks have developed such linear programming models and a number have been reported in the literature. The forerunner of these models was one developed more than fifteen years ago by Chambers and Charnes [1961]. Cohen and Hammer [1967] built upon this work in their pioneering linear programming model developed at Bankers Trust Company. Other banks have followed with their own models, such as those reported by Chervany, Strom, and Boehlke [1970] for the Northwestern National Bank of Minneapolis, Komar [1971] for the Bank of New York, Robertson [1970] for the Industrial National Bank of Rhode Island, and Lifson and Blackmarr [1973] for an unnamed bank.

In the sections that follow we draw upon this published work, as well as our own experience with other banks, to discuss the role of linear programming models in portfolio management. The first section is devoted to an overview discussing how these models are structured, the decisions the models can make, and possible objectives for the models to optimize. Then the commonly employed types of constraints are categorized and presented. Finally the uses of these types of models as well as an evaluation of their strengths and weaknesses are discussed.

DYNAMIC BALANCE SHEET MANAGEMENT

The linear programming models designed for aggregate planning for the bank as a whole have been referred to as aids for dynamic balance sheet management. The essential nature of these models is that a sequence of balance sheets for the bank over time is generated in such a way as to "optimize" the performance of the bank according to some criterion while satisfying constraints on the bank's policies. These models have been called dynamic since they plan for a number of time periods into the future, but they are not dynamic in the sense of contingency planning as discussed in Chapter 2 in that uncertainty has not explicitly been taken into account. Linear programming models determine the sequence of balance sheets for the bank based on one particular scenario of the future economic environment. Contingency planning, on the other hand, takes into account that more than one scenario is possible and that the bank can alter its policy as future environments evolve.

Linear programming models generally consider a number of time periods extending far enough into the future to cover the usual planning horizon of the bank. In determining the sequence of balance sheets over this planning horizon, the decisions made by the model are the levels of the various asset, liability, and capital accounts that are under the control of the bank. For example, the model can select the amounts of various categories of investments, as well as bank borrowing, for balance sheets corresponding to each period in the planning horizon. The sequence of balance sheets generated for the bank is chosen so as to optimize some objective of the bank. For example, the bank might wish to maximize the present value of earnings and net capital gains over the planning horizon. The optimization takes place subject to a number of constraints on the bank's actions, including funds availability, demand for funds, pledging requirements, trading limitations, liquidity needs, and capital adequacy considerations among others.

Decision Variables

In order to be able to formulate a linear programming model for dynamic balance sheet management, it is first necessary to distinguish between controllable and uncontrollable items of the balance sheet. The controllable items are basically the decision variables of the model, and we want to determine their optimal levels. The uncontrollable assets and liabilities are items that need to be forecast as part of the economic scenario along with interest rates. It is important to point out that depending on the planning problem being addressed, some items may move from one category to the other. For example, in an aggregate planning model, commercial loans would probably be a forecast item. However, in a more detailed model the linear programming model could be used to decide how much of the demand for commercial loans should be met.

In Table 5.1 we have categorized the controllable accounts of the balance sheet. Although a variety of other categorizations might be used, this one provides a good basis for discussion.

Many of the categories listed in Table 5.1 potentially include a large number of maturity categories within them. Investments in securities, including Governments, agencies, prime municipals, and other municipals, all need to be classified according to their various maturities. Hence, a typical decision variable might refer to the level of holdings in a particular period of U.S. Government bonds of about two years' maturity. It is also true that maturity classifications may be needed for liabilities, such as large negotiable CDs. The degree of aggregation or refinement depends upon the particular planning problem being analyzed. Use of a linear programming model for a set of monthly planning periods, for example, would require detailed maturity categories within the shorter-term assets and liabilities.

We complete the items that make up the balance sheet in Table 5.2 by listing some uncontrollable items that need to be forecast. It should be kept in mind that banks may have some control over these items but that they are typically determined by events or decisions external to the model.

There are some assets and liabilities that are uncontrollable but, strictly speaking, do not need to be forecast either. For example, reserve requirements can be computed by the model based upon the deposits forecasted.

Table 5.1 Controllable Accounts

Assets	Liabilities and Capital
Money market	Money market
Federal funds sold	Federal funds purchased
Eurodollar investments	Federal Reserve borrowing
Bankers acceptances	Negotiable CDs
Securities	Eurodollar borrowing
U.S. Treasury bills	Commercial paper
U.S. Treasury notes and bonds	Long term
Agency securities	Sales of capital notes
Prime municipal bonds	Sales or repurchases of stock
Other municipal bonds	Capital
Other bonds	Reserve for loan losses
	Dividend payments

Table 5.2 Forecast Accounts

Assets	Liabilities and Capital
Cash and due from banks	Deposits
Loans	Demand
Commercial	Savings
Consumer	Other time
Real estate	Capital
Other	Common stock and surplus
	Undivided profits

Similarly, undivided profits in one period can be computed from their level in the previous period plus net income less any dividends paid. These balance sheet accounts involve both controllable and uncontrollable items but are computed from basic accounting identities rather than controlled or forecast directly.

One example of how these categories have been applied is given by Robertson [1970] in his discussion of the model employed at the Industrial National Bank of Rhode Island. He includes six categories of government bonds based on maturity, three of agency, six of tax-exempts, other bonds, stocks, and city-town loans, for a total of eighteeen investment categories. Also on the asset side, he discusses twelve categories of loans including various types of mortgages, automobile loans, commercial loans, and personal loans among others. On the liability side, he has seven categories of deposits including CDs, Eurodollars, borrowed funds, and undivided profits.

The assets, liabilities, and capital accounts listed in Tables 5.1 and 5.2 are often categorized further in a variety of ways depending on the planning problem being addressed. For example, loans that are linked to certain deposits through some kind of "loan-deposit feedback" mechanism need to be identified as such. Further, some investments may be used for repurchase agreements while others may be pledged against demand deposits of a particular type.

An example of such a further categorization has been suggested by Chervany, Strom, and Boehlke [1970] in their presentation of the model developed at the Northwestern National bank of Minneapolis. The basic categories in their model include fifty-five controllable accounts and forty-six forecast accounts. Cash is broken down into five items of which three are considered controllable, investments into thirty items of which twenty-eight are controllable and generally reflect maturity categories for various securities, loans into twenty items of which all but four are forecast, deposits into twenty-five items of which all but two are forecast, borrowed funds into four contollable items, and capital into seven items of which two are controllable. Since a principal use of this model is for liquidity planning, some of these items are further classified into marketable securities, volatile deposits (those likely to be withdrawn during a planning period), and vulnerable deposits (those large deposits which, if withdrawn, would cause liquidity pressure). This further categorization allows for specifying a group of constraints that reflect the bank's policy for maintaining certain types of liquid assets in relation to the two categories of deposits.

Objective Function

To permit the construction of a sequence of balance sheets for a bank that are "optimal" in some sense, it is necessary to decide on an objective function to be maximized or minimized. There are a number of different possible objective functions that could be reasonable depending upon the planning problem being analyzed. There are situations in which we might consider maximizing any of the following: net worth of the bank, total cash flow, discounted present value of cash flow, average earnings over some period, return on investment over some period, growth rate of earnings, and so on.

Although we can specify a large number of possible objective functions that might be of interest to the portfolio manager, there are essentially only two important ones to note for the general balance sheet management problem: (1) maximize the net worth of the bank at the end of the planning horizon and (2) maximize the present value of the stream of cash flows generated during the planning horizon plus some adjustment for increased net worth of the bank at the horizon.

The other more specialized objectives may be quite appropriate for some applications. For example, a bank concerned with its stock price may choose to maximize its growth rate of earnings over the next three to five years. However, in general these more specialized objective functions reflect secondary objectives of the bank. As such they may be quite important to the bank planner and therefore should be incorporated in any planning model. This can be easily accomplished by specifying minimum levels of performance for those objectives to be included and treating each as a constraint in the model.

There is an important distinction between the two primary objective functions suggested. The first objective, maximizing the net worth of the bank at the horizon, requires that all net interest income, net capital gains, and other cash generated be reinvested by the model during the planning horizon. The model then internally compounds the effect of any investment by reinvesting any cash it generates. If all future as well as present investment opportunities are explicitly incorporated in the model as decision variables, then there is no reason to withdraw any cash from the model except possibly for an exogenous schedule of payments such as dividends. Therefore the net worth of the bank will be maximized by reinvesting all cash generated, and the rate of return of these investments will be determined internally by the model.

In contrast with the first objective function, the second, maximizing the present value of the stream of cash flows plus increased net worth at the horizon, requires that an appropriate discount rate be selected to calculate the present value. Determining the appropriate discount rate can be a very difficult problem, and financial analysts do not in general agree as to how this should be done. Most agree that theoretically the bank's cost of capital should be used as the discount rate, but few agree on how the cost of capital should be determined. Some would argue, for example, Baumol and Quandt [1965], that the appropriate discount rate ought to be determined by solving the linear programming model that was developed to construct the optimal sequence of balance sheets using a discounted objective function. However, they ask how can this be accomplished if the discount rate must be known before the linear program can be solved? Others argue that the discount rate ought simply to reflect management's subjective time rate of preference for cash flows. Still others argue that the discount rate ought to be determined by appealing to some appropriate external market for funds. In any event, determining an appropriate discount rate is not a simple issue to resolve.

Because of the problem of selecting an appropriate discount rate, we believe that the first objective function has an important advantage. If all investment opportunities have been included in the model, it can be considered as a closed economy completely describing the bank's earnings opportunities; therefore, maximizing the undiscounted terminal value is the correct objective for the bank. This approach eliminates the necessity of determining the correct discount rate to use for computing present values. Moreover, it allows the "shadow prices" on the funds flow constraints to be reinterpreted as the true opportunity costs for additional funds in each period of the model. "Shadow prices" will be defined and interpreted later in this chapter in the section "Uses and Limitations of Linear Programming models." Bradley, Frank, and Frey [1975] have developed the relationship between discounted and undiscounted capital budgeting models and have shown that appropriate discount rates for each period can be determined by proper interpretation of the shadow prices of the undiscounted case. These discount rates can then be used as a device for screening investment opportunities that arise but have not been included in the model.

Although maximization of the present value of future cash flows poses the problem of selecting a discount rate, there are some reasons why this approach might be appropriate. First, all investment opportunities may not be explicitly incorporated in the model. In this case the discount rate specified for the model acts as a surrogate for these opportunities. For example, if the point of view of a bank holding company is taken, the company might be interested in maximizing the present value of the stream of dividends withdrawn from the bank. The discount rate used to determine the present value of this stream in general will be different from a rate that reflects the alternative investment opportunities of the bank. Note that in this example it is appropriate to reinvest interest income and other internal cash flows generated, because the only cash flows included in the present value computation are those actually withdrawn from the model as dividends.

Another reason for using the discounting approach is that it provides an ad hoc method for considering the uncertainty in future cash flows. By selecting a discount rate which is higher than the expected rate of return on the bank's investment opportunities, the model implicitly recognizes the risk of uncertain cash flows and weights the future flows less. Finally, a bank may wish to use discounting to emphasize current earnings if this is viewed as an important factor in influencing the market valuation of the bank's stock. In these two examples the discount rate essentially reflects management's time rate of preference for cash flows.

Although many planners might prefer the discounted objective function for the reasons given, besides the question of determining the appropriate discount rate there is a further difficulty with this approach that should be mentioned. As Cohen and Hammer [1967] point out, the choice of the discount rate will definitely affect the "optimal" solution selected by the linear programming model since higher discount rates will emphasize generating cash flows earlier. Therefore simply discounting at some "reasonable" rate will not suffice. A great deal of care has to be taken to determine a rate consistent with either the bank's marginal cost of capital or management's time rate of preference for cash flows. In either case this is difficult to do in an unambiguous way.

Cohen and Hamer [1967] and Chervany, Strom, and Boehlke [1970] generally prefer a discounted objective function, while Robertson [1970] employs an undiscounted one, as we suggest. Cohen and Hammer introduce a third objective, which would appear to be the same as our discounted objective except for having no adjustment for the increased net worth of the bank at the horizon. This latter alternative is undesirable since it implicitly values all holdings at the horizon as zero, and any model would tend to avoid investing in long-term assets that could not be sold before the end of the planning horizon. For most applications we feel that maximizing the net worth of the bank at the horizon is most appropriate precisely because it avoids the need of externally determining a discount rate and, further, gives insight into what the appropriate discount rates for each period should be.

Time-Period Structure of the Model

For the asset and liability management problem we basically wish to specify the balance sheet for each of a number of planning periods in the future. The number of planning periods to be considered and their length depend on the planning procedures of the bank and the use to which the model is to be put. Typically, asset and liability management models of this variety are used to analyze planning problems with horizons anywhere from 1 to 5 years into the future. The length of the periods would depend upon the horizon but tend to be anywhere from 1 month to 1 year. Since it is not necessary for the lengths of all periods in the model to be the same, a useful model might consist of six periods as follows: three 1-month periods, a 3-month period, a 6-month period, and a 1-year period. Such a period structure would cover a 2-year planning horizon, which is probably sufficiently far into the future to make the forecasting of loans, deposits, and interest rates not a simple matter. It would also cover the upcoming quarter in monthly detail, which would be sufficient to define the basic strategy. The longer future periods reflect the increasing uncertainty as we attempt to forecast further into the future. In some instances where strong seasonalities in loan and deposit levels as well as interest rates are anticipated, periods of equal length, such as four quarters or twelve 1-month periods, might prove quite useful. Also in the initial stages of the development of such a model it is often useful to model in equal time periods to insure that the model is behaving reasonably.

Since the linear programming model is structured in terms of time periods, a second structural question to be resolved is the definition of the balance sheet variables. Should the balance sheets computed by the model be end-of-period financial statements, or should they be based upon average balances for each period? Cohen and Hammer [1967] express the partitioning of a bank's balance sheet in terms of average balances during a planning period and assume that changes in a particular balance sheet category occur at a constant rate during the period. We also consider it reasonable to assume that changes occur at a constant rate during a planning period, but we prefer to express decision variables in terms of their suggested levels as of the end of each planning period. Consider, for example, the investment category of U.S. Government bonds with the maturities of about 2 years. Figure 5.1 depicts the holdings of the securities over a 1-year planning horizon by quarters. The decision variables of the linear programming model specify the level of holdings in each category at the beginning of the year and at the end of each quarter during the planning horizon. Within any quarter the actual levels of the decision variables are unspecified; however, in constructing the objective function for a model it may be convenient to assume that changes from one level to the next occur at a constant rate. Although other assumptions are

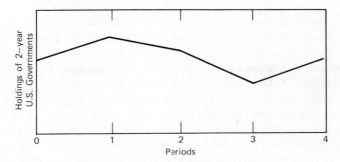

Figure 5.1. Specifying the levels of Holdings.

possible, they are not likely to add anything useful to the model. We feel that it is often more convenient for a bank to think of end-of-period balance sheet relationships and categories rather than averages since published statements are reported on this basis.

CONSTRAINING THE BANK'S ACTIONS

In the simulation models discussed in the previous chapter we specified the current position of the bank, the forecasts of future earnings and uncontrollable accounts, as well as the actions to be taken. In linear programming we do not specify the actions to be taken but rather let the "optimal" actions be generated by the model. However, we need to make explicit a number of policy and other constraints on bank actions that were only implicitly considered in the policies specified for simulation models. Without these constraints, the model may select strategies that are clearly not reasonable. In any particular situation the bank will have to determine for itself which constraints are applicable and which are not, but we discuss below a number of those commonly used. We can roughly categorize these constraints as follows: structural, forecast, market, legal, and policy.

Structural Constraints

There are two types of structural constraints that are the "glue" that holds the model together. The first set of constraints deal with funds availability within a planning period, while the second set deals with how the balance sheets are linked from one planning period to the next.

The structural constraint on *funds availability* is that the balance sheet must balance. For each period in the planning horizon we must have a constraint ensuring that total assets equals total liabilities plus capital. Of course a bank's sheet will balance at all times, but we need to make this normal accounting relationship explicit for the linear programming model.

The second set of structural constraints are those that link the planning periods together. As time passes, there is normal deposit run-off, maturing of securities, and amortization of loans. Therefore the levels of the asset and liability categories of one planning period have to be related to those of the following period. For example, a 2-year government bond might be a medium-term security for liquidity considerations; however, when that bond becomes a 1-year bond, it may be considered a short-term security for the same purpose. Therefore inventory *balance equations* must be constructed defining the levels of all asset and liability categories on hand at the start of a period in terms of the levels of these categories on hand at the start of the previous period.

Forecast Constraints

When defining an economic scenario for the linear programming model, a forecast must be specified for each uncontrollable variable. For example, a forecast is needed for each of the categories of deposits included in the model except for the decision variables such as negotiable CDs. These forecasts are incorporated in the model through *forecast constraints*. In effect, demand deposits and other uncontrollable variables are constrained to be equal to the values specified in the forecast for each time period.

In some cases constraints are set as upper and lower limits on variables rather than as a specific value. Commercial loan volume provides a common example. Some banks forecast the demand for commercial loans rather than the actual loan volume. This puts an upper limit on these kinds of loans but does not force the model to meet all of the potential demand. If this approach is taken, a lower limit is also normally used to make sure that the model meets a reasonable share of the forecast demand. The difficulty is that the current income from commercial loans is sometimes lower than that of alternative investments or that it is lower than the cost of funds used to finance the loans. Even though this occurs, the bank still wants to meet a reasonable amount of the loan demand because of the longer-term benefits of the customer relationship.

Some banks have tried to incorporate these future benefits in the model through the use of loan-deposit feedback relationships. The fact that certain types of loans generate present and future deposits has been taken into account in two different ways. First, the rate of return on loans that produce additional deposits has sometimes been adjusted upward to reflect the added earnings produced by the related deposits. This is theoretically incorrect since it assumes a specific use for these deposits that should be determined by the model. Second, constraints have been added to the model that relate these additional deposits to loans of a particular type. Theoretically this is a reasonable way to approach the problem. It then becomes unnecessary to attempt to impute an increased rate of return to such loans since the reinvestment of the additional deposits is done optimally by the model. However, it is generally rather difficult to estimate the relationship between future deposits and making particular types of loans, although Chervany, Strom, and Boehlke [1970] and Robertson [1970] claim to have done this empirically. Robertson further indicates that these loans should not be given "much more" credit for deposits than the average compensating balances maintained.

Market Constraints

There are a number of different types of *daily liabilities,* including, for example, federal funds, repurchase agreements, Federal Reserve borrowing, and Eurodollars, each of which can be used as a source of funds. However, there are limits on the use of these funds imposed by market conditions. As an example, models typically include some upper limit on the use of federal funds. This upper limit is set by bank policy, but it is based in large part on the bank's judgment about its ability to obtain this amount in the market. Repurchase agreements might be limited by an absolute amount during a planning period and are only possible to the extent that appropriate securities are available for sale. Borrowing from the Federal Reserve also requires securities for collateral and might be limited by other considerations.

Some types of *daily assets* and daily liabilities result from trading in the same market and hence impose some behavioral constraints. In order to maintain a position as a net borrower of federal funds it is necessary to some extent to sell federal funds. For example, large banks are typically net borrowers, but they operate on both sides of the market to service correspondents. Hence federal funds sold might be constrained to be above some percentage of federal funds borrowed.

Legal Constraints

Some constraints are essentially legal requirements, such as reserve requirements on deposits. Members of the Federal Reserve System, for example, must keep deposits on reserve at a Federal Reserve Bank based upon their demand deposits, time deposits, and some other liabilities such as Eurodollars and commercial paper of the bank's holding company used to fund loans in the bank. In September 1974 reserves against demand deposits (net of float) were on a graduated basis, rising from 8% of deposits under $2 million to 18% of demand deposits above $400 million. The requirements for time deposits were a 3% reserve requirement on savings deposits, 3% on other time deposits under $5 million, and 5% on other time deposits above $5 million. From time to time special reserve requirements have also been applied to discourage certain kinds of deposits. An example is the "marginal," or additional, 3% reserve requirement on negotiable CDs with original maturities of less than 4 months. This marginal reserve requirement has been applied to negotiable CDs without regard to maturity, but in September 1974 it was dropped for maturities of 4 months or longer to encourage banks to lengthen the maturity structure of their liabilities.

Some investments must be held simply for *pledging* purposes. There is a minimum of U.S. Government securities that will always be held to pledge for fiduciary powers and other restricted collateral deposits. Further, the bank must have pledgeable securities for public fund demand deposits, treasury tax and loan demand deposits, public fund certificates of deposit, and a percentage of the trust demand and time deposits. In general, the minimum amounts held of certain investments that can be used for pledging purposes must be specifically related to the appropriate deposit categories.

Policy Constraints

We have already mentioned some implicit policy constraints in our discussion of forecast and market constraints. Here we mention a group of constraints to emphasize that they are indeed policy constraints under the control of the bank.

There are a number of *traditional ratios* used to measure bank safety and liquidity. As long as these measures are commonly computed and referred to, a bank may wish to keep them within certain ranges in order to avoid possible adverse reactions from stockholders, depositors, and examiners. Examples of these types of constraints include the following: lower bound on the ratio of governments to assets, lower bound on the ratio of capital to risk assets, lower bound on the ratio of loans to deposits, upper bound on the ratio of CDs to total deposits, and so forth.

Because of legal requirements already mentioned and other reasons, a bank must maintain a minimum level of *cash and due from banks*. Cash items besides the Federal Reserve balance include cash on hand for operations, float considerations, and deposit balances at other banks as compensation for services received. The total level of cash and due from banks is a policy decision.

Since actual deposits fluctuate from day to day during a planning period, some minimum *liquidity buffer* is necessary in terms of cash and near-cash items. It is most common to have rather simple forms of liquidity constraints. One commonly used constraint has been outlined by the Comptroller of the Currency and requires that net liquid assets be at least equal to a percentage of net deposits.

At least one bank (Chervany, Strom, and Boehlke [1970]) has constraints on what they call short-, medium-, and long-term liquidity simultaneously. These constraints in general limit the sum of percentages of various investment categories to be greater than the sum of percentages of various loans, deposits, and capital stock. For example, their short-term liquidity constraint requires that U.S. Government securities less than 1 year, plus municipal bonds less than 1 year, plus federal funds sold, plus money market investments must be greater than 82.5% of volatile demand deposits, plus 94% of secured and unsecured certificates of deposits, plus all seasonal loans, plus 10% of capital stocks and surplus. The medium- and long-term liquidity constraints are similar but involve longer term maturities. These constraints protect the bank from different types of fluctuations in the economy, including daily variations, seasonal patterns, and major trends in the business cycle.

In general, there are a number of constraints on *borrowed funds,* some of which have been mentioned already. The important policy considerations are to place some limits on the total use of borrowed funds while maintaining a diversified portfolio. A typical constraint on the total use of borrowed funds would be to require that this amount be less than or equal to a percentage of the total capital funds of the bank. Alternatively, we might set an absolute dollar limit on the total amount. Limits on the use of individual types of funds, such as CDs, repurchase agreements, federal funds, Federal Reserve borrowings, and Eurodollars, are often imposed so as to insure a diversified portfolio of borrowings not too dependent on any one source. Without such constraints the model might tend to rely exclusively on CDs rather than Eurodollars since Eurodollars are generally more expensive than CDs.

Banks differ on exactly how to approach the problem of *capital adequacy.* However, regardless of the approach used, the amount of capital is clearly an important policy decision. In the constraints mentioned above, a number of restrictions on capital have already been suggested. We generally favor a simple approach to capital adequacy by including constraints on some ratios such as risk assets to capital, deposits to capital, and loans to capital. Others have included more complex forms.

Much of the debate concerning capital adequacy has centered on the capital adequacy formula suggested by the Board of Governors of the Federal Reserve System. The basis of this criterion is that it becomes more restrictive as the need for liquidity becomes greater. Capital requirements are considered in three groups: capital is levied directly against assets, additional capital requirements are imposed against possible fluctuations in deposits, and finally, capital requirements are levied against the bank's trust operations. Chambers and Charnes [1961] have shown that although this measure of capital adequacy is a nonlinear relationship, it can be modeled by linear programming.*

Cohen and Hammer [1967] as well as Chervany, Strom, and Boehlke [1970] make important use of this capital adequacy formula in their models. However, both take the position that, although the form of the constraint is quite appropriate, the percentages suggested by the Federal Reserve Board are too conservative since these were derived from figures based on a period of extreme depression. They suggest that the constraint be used but that the bank's management should establish the policy for the percentages used in the relationship. Robertson [1970], on the other hand, reports that the constraint was initially included but eventually was so relaxed that it might as well have not been there at all.

Finally, there are intertemporal constraints that link all the planning periods in a particular *tax year*. It is not uncommon to have a limit on the net realized losses from the investment portfolio during any tax year. Also there may be a constraint on the unrealized losses in the investment portfolio over the horizon to limit the amount that the portfolio can be depleted for current income. Constraints specifying lower bounds on taxable income are also quite common. Taxable income must cover operating expenses plus losses so that the bank ends the year in a net taxable position specified by the bank.

In this section we have given examples of different types of constraints that might be included in a linear programming model for dynamic balance sheet management. Obviously there are numerous other examples that could have been given. In any analysis the choice of objective function, categorization of assets and liabilities, and the particular constraints included depend on the particular planning problem being analyzed by the bank. In the next section we discuss some of the uses and limitations of such linear programming planning models.

USES AND LIMITATIONS OF LINEAR PROGRAMMING MODELS

The primary information provided by linear programming models is a recommended set of actions presented in the form of a sequence of balance sheets. These models are generally used in a case study approach, much as deterministic simulation models are, to study the implications of a particular

---

* For a mathematical explanation of how the Federal Reserve System criterion can be modeled by linear programming, see Chambers and Charnes [1961], or Cohen and Hammer [1966].

economic scenario. The portfolio planner specifies a starting position for the bank and defines an economic scenario. Then, assuming this scenario occurs, the linear programming model selects the set of actions that maximizes the bank's objective while satisfying the constraints imposed. The recommended decisions are in some ways more useful than the output of a simulation model since they indicate the best that can be done over this scenario, given the constraints and objective specified for the model.

Of course, models such as these do not make decisions but merely suggest reasonable courses of action based on the inputs supplied to them. An important advantage of these models is that they allow for the thorough analysis of a scenario under a variety of assumptions, whereas without such a model only a few strategies could be evaluated. Since linear programming models generate their own strategy consistent with the constraints specified, they have the potential for suggesting changes in strategies that were unnoticed by management. In fact one of the most powerful aspects of linear programming is that it accounts for all the secondary and tertiary effects of changing policy besides the primary effects that are more evident to management.

Linear programming also provides a very useful procedure, called parametric programming, for conveniently carrying out analyses that require the systematic variation of some of the attributes of the scenario. In these analyses the model is automatically solved for a sequence of specified values of some parameter describing the attributes of the scenario. With this procedure it would be easy to examine, for example, how the optimal sequence of balance sheets changes as the growth rate of demand for commercial loans is varied over some range. In another example Robertson [1970] used parametric programming to determine how much credit would have to be given to loans for generating deposits over and above compensating balances in order to effect the optimal solution. He concluded that the amount required was unrealistic and, therefore, that only crediting loans with the average compensating balances maintained over a reasonable period of time was appropriate.

In addition to the recommended actions, linear programming models provide other information not available from simulation models. Of this information most important are probably the "shadow prices" for each constraint, which are provided automatically when the model generates actions for a specified scenario. The shadow price associated with a constraint tells how much the objective function could be improved if that specific constraint were relaxed somewhat. This information provides insight into the following types of questions. What is the marginal value of obtaining additional capital? What is the maximum interest rate to pay on various types of borrowed funds during any period? What is the potential benefit associated with relaxing various policy constraints? The shadow prices are nonzero only for constraints that are binding, and this tends to focus attention on the constraints that in fact are dictating the solution of the model.

An example of how the shadow price information can provide helpful insights into the benefits and costs of alternative policies has been provided by Cohen and Hammer [1967]. They found that the shadow prices on the capital adequacy constraints were high, indicating that the incremental benefits from additional capital would far exceed the cost of capital notes. Some of the additional earnings would come from the spread between the cost of the notes and the earnings on assets acquired with the funds. The major impact, though, came from shifts in the investment portfolio to higher yielding assets, which were allowed if the capital base was expanded.

We can further illustrate the use of shadow prices by considering the bank's policy limit on the use of federal funds. The shadow price on this constraint would indicate how much the objective function would be increased if the bank were willing to use an additional amount of this source of funding. The shadow price is also an upper bound on the interest rate the bank can afford to pay for these additional funds. The rate of return on the additional funds is the difference between the shadow price and the interest rate paid.

This example brings up another type of useful information automatically made available when a linear program is solved. For each constraint in the model a range is given that indicates how much that right-hand-side can be varied without changing the shadow prices. In our example the range on the federal funds constraint indicates the amount of additional funds that could be borrowed while obtaining the return indicated by the shadow price. Beyond this range the shadow price on federal funds can never be more but may indeed be less. If it looks promising to borrow funds beyond the range, the linear program must be solved again to determine the rate of return on the additional funds beyond the range.

Another type of shadow price, called the "reduced costs," provides information about the cost of adopting actions not recommended by the model. This allows us to identify alternative optimal solutions, or solutions that are close to being optimal that may have other desirable properties. Suppose, for example, that the model decided to make the minimum amount of commercial loans allowed. The reduced costs associated with the commercial loan decision variables would indicate how much the objective function would be reduced if funds were diverted from other investments and put into these commercial loans.

One of the criticisms of linear programming models is that they assume the economic scenario specified will occur with certainty. This is an important problem that cannot be completely resolved by linear programming models; nevertheless, such models can be used to help explore some of the implications of uncertainty in the forecasts. As with the deterministic simulation models, it is helpful to specify more than one scenario, such as high interest rate, most likely, and low interest rate economic scenarios. By utilizing the model to obtain a suggested action in each of these scenarios, it is possible to see how a change in the environment affects desirable actions.

It is also possible to take this analysis one step further to see what can happen if the economic environment changes after some decisions have been implemented. For example, the starting position of the model can be altered to assume that the actions recommended for the coming period under the most likely scenario were actually implemented. Then the economic scenario for the rest of the planning horizon is changed to, say, the high rate scenario, and a new set of actions computed. These results will not be as good as if the high rate scenario actions had been implemented from the beginning, so a comparison of the two results indicates the cost of guessing wrong about the scenario. In addition, the actions that must be taken after the scenario shifts might indicate other problems caused by not planning for the higher interest rates.

By studying the implications of alternative scenarios for current actions, it is possible for the planner to arrive at a strategy providing a reasonable return in likely future environments but avoiding costly problems if adverse scenarios occur. Linear programming models are helpful in this process, but they will not automatically develop such a hedging strategy. Because these models assume that a specified scenario will occur with certainty, strategies that are good hedges must be forced upon the model through the use of constraints. Since these constraints are specified by the planner, many of the critical decisions are not made by the linear programming model even though it does generate its own strategy within these constraints. This is the most important criticism of linear programming models.

A related problem is that strategies recommended by these models tend to become predictable after a period of use, a consequence of the assumption of certainty and of the constraints imposed. If we assume that rates will fall with certainty and that there are limits on how much of the portfolio should be placed in long maturities, it is not too difficult to predict what the model will recommend after some experience with it has been obtained. This tends to limit the usefulness of linear programming models for routine portfolio decision making.

Although linear programming models are helpful in selecting portfolio actions, the major areas of usefulness are in the early stages of their use and for special studies done on an occasional basis. As a linear programming model is developed, it is necessary to explicitly state the bank's objective and the constraints or guidelines which the bank wants to follow in selecting actions. The need to make this information explicit brings the bank's policy to the surface and allows a useful discussion of the policies that may have been implicit and not well understood. After making the objective and constraints explicit, the linear programming model is very helpful in evaluating these elements of bank policy. Which constraints really limit the bank's actions? Which are the most costly to the bank? What could be gained by changes in some of the guidelines that were imposed? Out of the answers to these and other questions will come a better understanding of the bank's policy and perhaps some important changes in policy.

After the model has been developed and is well understood, its use for periodic decision making will produce relatively few surprises. Nevertheless it is still useful, particularly on occasional studies of special importance. Sample studies might include an evaluation of the sale or retirement of capital notes, an investigation to help determine the amount of capital losses on securities that should be realized this year, and an evaluation of significant changes in the allocation of bank funds being considered. Such studies are important enough to justify the added effort required to use a linear programming model rather than a simpler deterministic simulation model. In addition, the conclusions of these studies are less affected by the need to develop a hedging strategy. Capital notes, for example, will either be sold this year or not. Since there is no hedging strategy, a linear programming model can usefully look at the implications of selling now versus waiting under a variety of interest rate scenarios.

6

SIMULATION MODELS THAT INCORPORATE UNCERTAINTY

Deterministic simulation and linear programming models discussed in the previous two chapters are useful in exploring the implications of a portfolio strategy over a single economic scenario. Both modeling techniques require that a set of projections of relevant interest rates and other variables (the scenario) be supplied to the model. The simulation model will then compute the implications of a particular portfolio strategy specified by the user. A linear programming model selects its own strategy, but the set of portfolio actions it computes and evaluates are also based upon the single scenario supplied to it. These two modeling techniques have a number of important uses, but they do not explicitly take uncertainty into account. Fortunately there are more sophisticated forms of both of these modeling approaches that can deal directly with the uncertainty portfolio managers must face. Linear programming under uncertainty is the subject of Chapter 7 and succeeding chapters of the book. A Monte Carlo simulation model incorporating uncertainty is discussed in this chapter.

It is important to consider uncertainty because the economic scenario assumed for the simulation model (or the linear programming model) is only one of many that might actually occur. The results from the portfolio strategy under study would certainly be different if future rates differed from the assumed scenario. How badly or how well might this strategy work under the variety of possible scenarios? What is the likelihood of various outcomes if this strategy were implemented?

In addition to looking at a single portfolio strategy under a variety of assumptions about the future, it is also useful to explore different kinds of strategies. Some portfolio actions might work very well if the future behaves as expected but prove to be disastrous if rates move in unexpected directions. Other strategies might reduce the risks of bad performance but not produce very high returns regardless of which way rates move. Which kind of strategy will provide the best return consistent with the level of risk appropriate to the bank?

These are the kind of questions which Monte Carlo simulation models can help to answer. As in deterministic models, a portfolio strategy is specified for the model. It differs, though, in that the Monte Carlo model contains a process for generating a large number of future economic scenarios. When the model is used, it randomly selects one of the possible economic scenarios in a manner such that the probability of being selected corresponds to the scenario's assessed likelihood of occurrence. The specified portfolio actions are then assumed to be carried out for this scenario, and the result is computed. By repeating this process many times, the Monte Carlo model computes the results that would be obtained over a wide range of future economic events. From this information we can calculate the average performance of the strategy and construct a frequency distribution indicating the range of possible outcomes and their likelihood of occurrence.

In Chapters 4 and 5 we discussed the types of deterministic simulation models and linear programming models either commercially available or commonly used. In this chapter we adopt a different approach that allows us to both illustrate the nature of Monte Carlo simulation models and report an evaluation of alternative portfolio strategies. Here we describe a specific Monte Carlo simulation model developed to study the implications of alternative maturity structures in bank portfolios. Taking state and local government securities as an example, we explore the performance of various laddered and barbell portfolios. The questions studied include the following: Do laddered or barbell portfolios have better performance characteristics? As longer maturities are included in laddered portfolios, what happens to return and risk of the portfolio? What happens to risk and return in barbell portfolios as the percentage of the portfolio in short maturities is changed?

In the next section of the chapter we describe the Monte Carlo simulation model, providing both an overview of the model and a more detailed list of assumptions and discussion of how it works. Then the results of the simulation model are reported for both relatively long- and short-term planning horizons. Important parts of this discussion are the definition and measurement of risk since the selection of a portfolio strategy is critically affected by the way a bank views risk. Finally the implications of these results for management of bank portfolios are discussed.

DESCRIPTION OF THE SIMULATION MODEL

The model in effect simulates what would happen if a portfolio manager adopted a particular portfolio strategy and mechanically followed the specified trading rules year after year. For example, assume that he decided to adopt a laddered portfolio of tax-exempt bonds with maturities spread equally from 1 to 10 years. If we assume the starting portfolio had maturities spread in this manner, the manager with each passing year would reinvest the proceeds of the maturing bonds in new 10-year bonds. The interest received each year would be reinvested equally in a spread of new 1- to 10-year bonds, so that the portfolio would always have 10% of its maturities in each maturity category, 0–1, 1–2, 2–3, etc. Interest rates fluctuate each year, but the portfolio manager makes no attempt to anticipate or take advantage of rate swings. At the end of the planning horizon, say 10 years, the portfolio is evaluated and the return and other characteristics of this strategy are computed.

The return obtained from this strategy depends, of course, upon the particular sequence of rates assumed each year in the planning horizon. In the model we assume that municipal rates will be about as volatile in future years as they were in the late 1960s and early 1970s. The specific interest rate sequence used for each scenario is determined by a statistical process that simulates this historical behavior of rates. Since there are a large number of possible rate sequences over the period, the portfolio strategy under study is repeated many times with a new sequence of rates drawn for each scenario.

We used a process of this kind to evaluate several portfolio strategies of the laddered and barbell type. The laddered portfolios studied contained maturities spread equally over some range from 1 year to a longest maturity. For example, we studied the characteristics of portfolios laddered from 1 to 5, 1 to 10, and 1 to 15 years, among others. The barbell portfolios studied contained a spread of short and long maturities where the short bonds were divided equally among 1- to 7-year maturities and the long were spread equally from 24- to 30-year maturities. To look at the implications of changes in the average maturity of barbell portfolios we varied the percent of the portfolio allocated to the short and long end of the range.

Structure of the Model

When a portfolio strategy is specified for evaluation, the model computes its performance over each of a large number of interest rate scenarios. Each of these scenarios represents a sequence of municipal yield curves that is assumed to occur over the period under study. Evaluating the strategy for one of these scenarios is called a "trial" of the simulation model.

At the start of each simulation we assume that there is an initial portfolio containing a set of securities with a book value of $100 and a maturity structure similar to the portfolio strategy under study. Thus if the strategy to be studied is a laddered portfolio with maturities spread from 1 to 10 years, the starting portfolio would contain $10 each of 1-year, 2-year, and so forth, securities. The 10-year bond in the starting portfolio would be a bond just purchased, that is, a $10 bond purchased at par with a yield equal to the current 10-year rate. The 9-year bond in the portfolio would represent a bond purchased one year ago with an original maturity of 10 years. Similarly the one-year bond represents a 10-year bond purchased 9 years ago. This approach to structuring an initial portfolio was adopted to conform to one of the alleged advantages of laddered portfolios. Since proceeds of all maturities are reinvested in the longest bond allowed, after a while the bonds in the portfolio comprise securities that had an original maturity of the longest bond allowed. It is argued that since yield curves are normally upward sloping, reinvestment of the runoff of maturities in the longest bond will produce a high interest income. Our starting procedure gives this advantage to the laddered portfolios studied.

The model is structured into 1-year time periods, so that the portfolio is updated at the end of each year using the yield curve prevailing then. (The process that generates these yield curves is discussed below.) For the laddered portfolios the updating process involves taking the cash from maturing 1-year bonds and investing it in a new 10-year bond. The interest obtained from the portfolio is reinvested equally among the portfolio maturities so that it maintains the specified structure. Note that after this first reinvestment of interest the portfolio will contain two different 1-year bonds. One is the 10-year bond purchased 9 years earlier and the other is a small amount of a new 1-year security purchased with 10% of the interest received.

Updating a barbell portfolio is more complicated since both ends of the 1–7 and 24–30-year barbell must be maintained. Proceeds of the maturing 1-year bonds are reinvested in a new 7-year bond to maintain the 1- to 7-year maturity distribution. With the passage of 1 year, the 24-year bond has become a 23-year bond, which is now sold. After-tax proceeds from this sale are invested in a new 30-year bond to maintain the 24- to 30-year structure on the long end. There is a transaction cost on this sale, which is assumed to be 1% of the book value of the bond. This amount is approximately equal to the spread between bid and asked prices on long municipals. The tax on gains or the tax savings on losses from the sale is assumed to be 50% of the gain or loss on sale of the 23-year bonds. Finally, interest from all of the portfolio is reinvested in the same proportion as the maturities in the starting portfolio. If 5-year bonds made up 7% of the starting portfolio, for example, 7% of the interest received each year is invested in new 5-year bonds.

At the end of each trial the model computes the results of the portfolio strategy. The final market value of the portfolio is calculated, interest income is totaled, and realized and unrealized gains and losses are computed. These numbers are recorded by the model and it moves to the next scenario of interest rates for the next trial. A new initial portfolio is selected and a new trial begins.

Process for Generating Interest Rate Scenarios

One of the critical components of the simulation model is the process that generates the sequences of yield curves used to evaluate portfolio strategies. Although it is not possible to know which sequences of interest rates are possible in the future, we can make some assumption about the general behavior of municipal yield curves and then generate a large number of interest rate scenarios consistent with this behavior. The general assumption we have made for the model is that the volatility of future interest rates will be about the same as it was in the period from 1966 through 1972. This period contains two major interest rate cycles, including the credit crunch of 1966 and the tight money period of 1969–1970. At the end of this period short-term municipal rates were about the same as in the beginning. Years prior to this period were excluded because rates moved within a much narrower range, which most observers feel will not be typical of the future.*

The 1-year municipal interest rate, as defined by Salomon Brothers in the firm's "good grade" municipal rate series, is used as a key rate in the generating process. Using the same methodology as discussed in Chapter 3 for U.S. Government securities, year-to-year changes in the 1-year municipal rate are used to determine the magnitude of shifts in the yield curve that appear in each period. The distribution of changes in the 1-year rate is based on the historical changes in this rate. More specifically, the probability of a particular change in the 1-year rate from its current level is based on the frequency of this change in the period 1966–1972.

The cumulative frequency distribution of 1-year changes in the 1-year rate is shown in Figure 6.1. As can be seen in the figure, the median change

---

* This time period encompasses the enactment of the Tax Reform Act of 1969 which eliminated the low capital gains tax on security sales by commercial banks, except for a transitional period. Although this change in bank tax rates may have some impact of the behavior of municipal rates, our estimates of the relationship among rates for the four years following the tax change are very similar to the parameters estimated for the 1966–72 period.

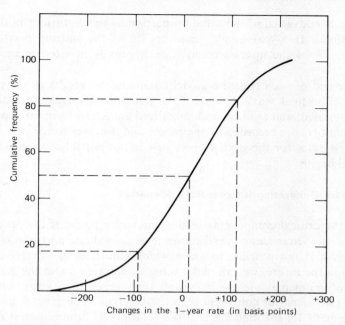

Figure 6.1. Cumulative distribution of changes in the 1-year municipal rate.

was very close to zero and 90% of the annual changes were within a range of plus or minus 200 basis points. To limit the number of possible yield curves, we approximated this distribution with three equally likely points, that is, three possible rate changes were allowed each period. To get the three points the distribution of changes was divided into thirds. The medians of these equally likely brackets are the 16⅔, 50, and 83⅓% points on the distribution and the changes in the 1-year rate corresponding to these frequencies are −98, +7, and +112 basis points, respectively. Use of these three numbers to generate interest rate scenarios would lead to an upward drift in the rates over time. To avoid this bias we centered the distribution of rate changes on zero and rounded the possible changes to 100 basis points. Thus we assume in general that the 1-year rate for the next period has an equal chance of being down 100 basis points, not changing from its current level, or increasing 100 basis points.

If we generated interest rates by this process for several periods, it is clear that the level of interest rates could rise or fall to levels not considered reasonable. To solve this problem we put upper and lower limits on the 1-year municipal rate that reflect the range of this rate in recent years. The limits selected were 1.9 and 5.9%. Since rates are assumed to move in units of 100 basis points, these limits constrain the permissible 1-year rates to five levels, 1.9%, 2.9%, and so forth.

For each of these levels a complete municipal yield curve has been defined, as shown in Figure 6.2. Curve 3, the middle curve, was selected to represent an average, or normal, curve with a 150-basis-point spread between the 30- and 1-year rates. The other yield curves are based upon changes from curve 3 that reflect typical changes in shape when interest rates rise and fall.

The procedure used to specify the other curves is similar to the methodology of Chapter 3. Regression analysis was used to estimate the magnitude of changes in intermediate- and long-term rates relative to changes in the 1-year municipal rate for the 12-month periods during 1966–1972. The results of this analysis are shown in Table 6.1.

These relative changes were used to specify several rates on each of the other yield curves. For example, the 1-year rate on Curve 4 is 100 basis points above Curve 1 and the 20-year rate is 67 basis points higher. Yields not specified by the regression equations were filled in to obtain smooth curves. Note that the volatility of interest rates declines as maturity is lengthened. This results from the tendency of yield curves to flatten as the

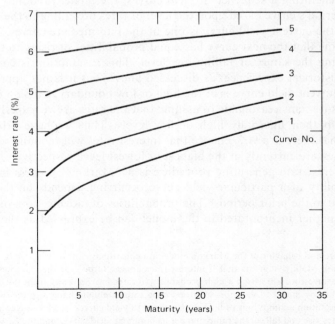

Figure 6.2. Possible yield curves in Monte Carlo simulation.

Table 6.1 Changes of Other Municipal Rates Relative to Changes in the 1-Year Rate: 1966–1972

Maturity (years)	Regression Coefficient (stated as a percent of the 1-year rate change)	Percent of Variance Explained*
2	96.0	99.4
5	89.2	96.2
10	80.5	90.1
20	67.0	71.1
30	61.2	62.1

* This is an approximate measure of how well the equation fits. The percent variance explained is not strictly defined since the constant term in the regression equation was forced to be zero.

level of interest rates rises and to become more steeply sloped as rates fall, as illustrated in Figure 6.2.

While generating a sequence of yield curves, the model randomly selects the next period's curve based upon the level of rates prevailing in the current period. If the current yield curve is one of the intermediate curves, 2, 3, or 4, we assume that the next curve has equal probabilities of rising to the next level, staying the same, or falling one level. This assumption is consistent with the historical experience, as discussed above, but it is not appropriate when the current yield curve is at the high or low boundary, Curve 5 or 1. In these cases it seems reasonable to assume that the rates are very likely to rebound from their unusually high or low levels. Thus we have arbitrarily assumed that there is a 90% chance that interest rates will rebound to Curve 4 or 2 if they are currently at the highest or lowest level, respectively.

This interest rate generating procedure is a "Markov" process in which the probability of a particular yield curve occurring depends on the curve that existed in the prior period.* The probabilities of moving from one yield curve to another incorporated in the model can be expressed as the transi-

* The structure and behavior of the Markov model are consistent with work by Malkiel [1962] and Pye [1966]. Malkiel suggests that if interest rates appear to be near the extremes of their normal range, investors will assign a high probability to rates moving away from the extremes. Pye uses a Markov model to describe investors' expectations about changes in the one-period rate. The expectation assumptions of both authors lead to yield curves which change their slope as interest rates rise and fall, in the same manner as observed yield curves and the curves in our model.

tion matrix shown in Table 6.2. This table can be used to generate as many sequences of interest rates as desired to test portfolio strategies.

Table 6.2   Yield Curve Transition Probabilities

Yield Curve in Period t	Yield Curve in Period $t + 1$				
	I	I	III	IV	V
I	.1	.9	—	—	—
II	.333	.333	.333	—	—
III	—	.333	.333	.333	—
IV	—	—	.333	.333	.333
V	—	—	—	.9	.1

The computer model randomly selects an initial curve to start the sequence. It then randomly selects the second curve according to the probabilities in the table. A third curve can then be chosen, and so on, until there is a complete sequence of yield curves, one for each year in the planning horizon. Such a sequence is one of the scenarios used to test the portfolio strategy. We randomly generated 400 such sequences of rates for the testing of portfolio strategies.

For each set of experiments we selected a specific planning horizon of up to 10 years and we simulated each portfolio strategy over the 400 randomly selected interest rate scenarios. The portfolio strategies were evaluated from the start of the simulation model, year 1, to the end of the planning horizon, but is was also necessary to generate sequences of rates for time periods prior to the start of the model in order to obtain initial portfolios. As discussed above, we assumed that the portfolio policy being simulated contains an initial portfolio consistent with this policy. For example, a strategy that maintains a laddered portfolio with maturities from 1 to 10 years requires a rate sequence begun 9 years earlier. At the start of the simulation the initial portfolio contains a 10-year bond purchased 9 years earlier, a 10-year bond purchased 8 years earlier, and so on, so that its maturities are evenly distributed from 1 to 10 years. To handle this assumption each of the interest rate sequences generated by the model cover a 40-year period, the last 10 of which were available to evaluate the policy. Sequences of this length allow an initial portfolio laddered out to a 30-year maturity, and this policy can then be tested for an additional 10 years. The same sequence of interest rates was used to test each portfolio strategy. The first 30 years of each sequence ($t = -29$ through 0) were available as needed to develop an initial portfolio, and the last 10 were available to evaluate the strategy.

Performance Measures

The simulation model computes some measures of performance, so that we can compare the effectiveness of alternative portfolio strategies. These measures help answer two important questions about each portfolio strategy tested: How well will the portfolio policy perform on average? How much risk has to be taken to achieve this return?

In order to provide a fair comparison among the strategies we have chosen to use a "total return" concept to measure the return from each portfolio policy. Each portfolio policy studied will produce some interest income and a net capital gain or loss for each trial of the simulation model. If the policy involves no trades, the gain or loss will be an unrealized amount at the horizon, but the barbell policies might also have a net realized gain or loss from the trades necessary to maintain the structure. The sum of the interest income plus the unrealized and realized net gain or loss (after tax) is the total return from a portfolio strategy for a trial of the model. This sum plus the original investment is the final market value of the portfolio (including any cash) at the horizon. Thus a portfolio policy which produces a higher market value at the horizon has produced a higher total return.

This return measure is computed for each trial of the simulation model. Since we have 400 trials for each portfolio strategy studied, the model provides 400 observations of the return that would be provided by this strategy. The mean of these returns is the "expected" return for this strategy. It can be broken into two components since this mean is the sum of the expected interest income and the expected capital gain or loss (realized plus unrealized) as stated in the following equation:

$$\text{Exp}(R) = \text{Exp}(I) + \text{Exp}(G)$$

in which R, I, and G represent return, interest, and gain, respectively.

In portfolio management it is frequently possible to obtain a higher expected return, but at the cost of taking on additional risk. To look at this aspect of portfolio performance we compute two measures of risk. The first is the traditional measure of risk used in portfolio theory, the standard of deviation of total return, which is a measure of the variability in returns from a portfolio strategy. Originally introduced by Markowitz [1959], this measure of risk or some variant of it has been a key part of much of the research on portfolio management in recent years. Its logic is that if a portfolio manager were choosing between two portfolio policies with equal expected returns, he would choose the policy that was more sure to produce the expected return. The more variability in return that might occur, the less sure he would be of achieving the expected return. The standard deviation of returns is a convenient way of measuring this variability.

In terms of the simulation model the total return from a portfolio strategy is computed for each of the 400 trials. Just as we compute a mean of these 400 returns, we also compute the standard deviation of them. The variance, the square of this measure, can be broken into three components that will be useful in the discussion of results later. The total variance is the sum of the variance of interest income, the variance of capital gains and losses, and two times the covariance of interest income and net capital gains. This is stated as an equation below:

$$\text{Var}(R) = \text{Var}(I) + \text{Var}(G) + 2 \times \text{Covar}(I,G)$$

While the standard deviation of total return is a useful measure of risk, it makes the assumption that banks do not care whether the variability of return comes from the variation in interest income or in capital gains or losses. Many banks would argue that this is not a reasonable assumption since fluctuations in realized and unrealized gains and losses have special implications. Banks are concerned about realizing net losses on the sale of securities, in part because it is a very visible direct reduction in the reported earnings per share of the bank.* In recent years banks have also been limiting bond trading activity because of their small taxable income position. Realized losses on bond sales can be treated as a deduction from taxable income and reduce the bank's taxes. Most large banks, though, have relatively small taxable income positions and hence limited ability to use the tax deductions because of other activities that reduce their tax liability, such as equipment leasing and foreign tax credits. Finally, banks desire to limit their exposure to declines in the market value of their assets, even if they do not intend to realize the loss by selling the bonds. One of the reasons is that large potential losses tend to increase their need for equity capital as perceived by regulatory authorities.

For these reasons many banks consider the "risk" of a portfolio strategy to be its potential for realized and unrealized losses in market value.† We have attempted to capture this aspect of risk by computing the total of realized and unrealized losses for each trial of the model. Then by looking at the 400 trials for each portfolio strategy we can compute a "maximum" loss position for this strategy. This maximum loss is selected so that the realized and unrealized losses on approximately 98% of the trials will be smaller, that is, total losses will be worse than the "maximum" only 2% of the time.‡

In computing the total of realized and unrealized gains and losses over

* Kane [1968] provides some empirical evidence for banks' reluctance to realize losses.
† Use of potential losses as a measure of risk is analogous to the "safety first principle" that has been used in portfolio theory and models. An example is provided by Telser [1955–1956].
‡ The 98th percentile of total losses was estimated by assuming that the distribution of total net gains (losses) is normal and computing the loss represented by the mean less two standard deviations, that is, the .023 point on the cumulative distribution.

the horizon of the model, we are assuming that banks are indifferent to the distinction between accumulated realized losses and the unrealized loss at the end of the planning horizon. Banks actually plan for and consider these two aspects of portfolio management individually, but we adopted this procedure to obtain a combined measure of risk applicable to both the laddered and barbell strategies. Use of realized losses by itself is not an appropriate measure of risk since all of the loss potential of a laddered portfolio is the unrealized amount at the horizon. Similarly, unrealized loss at the end of the horizon is a useful risk measure for some purposes, but consideration of this number alone ignores the ability of a bank to reduce unrealized loss potential by regular trading of securities. For example, the trading of the 23-year security in the barbell strategies reduces the potential buildup of unrealized losses. Thus the unrealized loss potential of barbell strategies tends to be less than that of the laddered policies.

IMPACT OF RISK MEASURE

As a first step, laddered and barbell policies were studied using a 10-year planning horizon to look at the longer-run implications of following a naive strategy. Figure 6.3 shows the risk-return characteristics of laddered portfo-

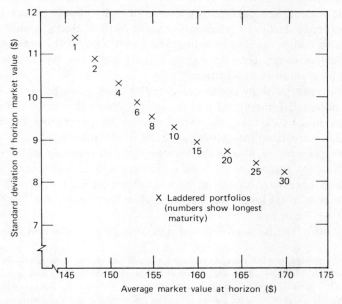

Figure 6.3. Expected return versus standard deviation for 10-year horizon.

lios of various maturity lengths. Each point in the exhibit represents a portfolio laddered from a 1-year maturity out to the maturity identified in the label. For each of these portfolios, the figure shows the expected total return as measured by the average market value of the portfolio at the horizon. Risk is shown on the vertical axis and is measured by the standard deviation of the horizon market values. The plotting of the risk and return for each of the laddered portfolios forms a "frontier" in which return increases and risk declines as the longest maturity in the ladder increases from 1 to 30 years.

It is to be expected that longer-maturity laddered portfolios would produce higher returns since they were constructed with longer term bonds. Portfolios laddered from 1 to 30 years, for example, consist of bonds that were all originally 30-year bonds. Since the 30-year rates are higher on average than other rates and there is no upward bias in the interest rate scenarios, these portfolios should produce the highest average return. It may be surprising, though, to note that this higher return can be achieved at a lower, rather than higher, risk. Most portfolio managers regard longer-term bonds more risky than short bonds. Some banks, even some very large ones, do not hold municipal securities with maturities longer than 10 to 15 years.

There are two reasons why risk declined with longer maturities. One was that standard deviation of return was used as the measure of risk, and the other was that a relatively long planning horizon was used. Here we will discuss the risk measure, leaving the issue of the length of the planning horizon to the next section.

Lengthening the maturity structure of a laddered portfolio tends to reduce the variability of interest income over the horizon because it lowers the turnover of the portfolio and longer rates are less volatile than shorter rates. As an example, consider a portfolio laddered from 1 to 10 years as compared with a portfolio laddered out 20 years. Over a 10-year horizon all of the initial securities in the 10-year ladder are completely replaced with new securities, but only 50% of the 20-year ladder turns over. Moreover, the fluctuations in the 20-year interest rate are only 83% as large as those of the 10-year municipal rate, based on the volatility of interest rates reported in Table 6.1.

Although the variability of unrealized gains and losses grows when the portfolio ladder is lengthened from 10 to 20 years, this increase is more than offset by the reduction in interest income variability. The variance components for the 10- and 20-year ladders are shown in Table 6.3.

When the definition of risk is changed to be the maximum realized plus unrealized losses, the risk-return frontier of laddered portfolios behaves more as bankers would expect. As shown in Figure 6.4, the riskiness of the portfolios increases as the length of the ladder is increased to include longer-term bonds. Thus one reason a bank might not include longer-term mu-

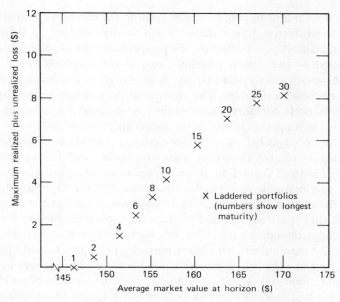

Figure 6.4. Expected return versus maximum loss for 10-year horizon.

nicipals in a laddered portfolio would be its desire to limit the unrealized loss potential of the portfolio.

One of the major purposes of experimentation with the simulation model is to see how barbell portfolios would perform in comparison with laddered portfolios if both were managed mechanically. All of the barbell portfolios studied contained an equal spread of 1- to 7-year maturities on the short end and an equal spread of 24- to 30-year maturities at the other end of the

Table 6.3   Components of Variance of Total Return: 10- and 20-Year Laddered Portfolios

	Total Variance*	Variance of Interest Income	Variance of Net Capital Gain (Loss)
10-Year ladder	87.11	71.80	5.62
20-Year ladder	76.23	44.00	18.27

* Columns do not add to total variance because 2 × covariance is not shown. It can be computed by substracting the variance of interest income and net capital gain from the total.

range. Various mixes of these two maturity groups were tried, ranging from 100% short to 100% long.

Figure 6.5 illustrates the risk-return profile of barbell portfolios when the standard deviation of return is used as the measure of risk. It can be seen that portfolio risk increases along with return as the proportion of the portfolio allocated to the long bonds is increased above 20%. Of more interest is the result that laddered portfolios are more "efficient." For a given level of return, the laddered portfolios tend to have less risk than the barbell structure. This results from the lower volatility of interest income when laddered portfolios are used. For example, the portfolio laddered from 1 to 15 years and the barbell portfolio with 70% allocated to short maturities provide about the same return. The total variance and its components for each of these two portfolio policies are shown in Table 6.4.

These two policies have similar variances of net capital gains, but the interest income of the barbell portfolio has a significantly larger variance. This stems partly from the higher turnover of the barbell portfolio, which has one-seventh of its bonds maturing or traded each year as compared to the one-fifteenth of the laddered portfolio that matures. In addition, proceeds from maturing short-term securities in the barbell portfolio are reinvested at the relatively volatile 7-year rate.

If risk is defined to be maximum loss rather than the standard deviation

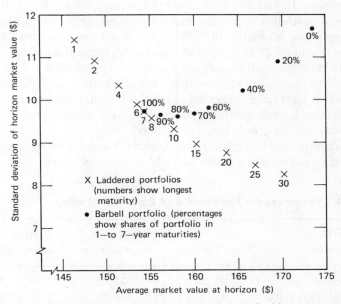

Figure 6.5. Expected return versus standard deviation for 10-year horizon.

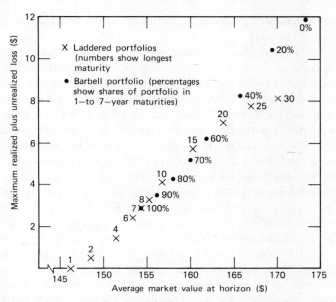

Figure 6.6. Expected return versus maximum loss for 10-year horizon.

of return, the performance of barbell portfolios relative to laddered maturities improves. In fact the barbell portfolios perform slightly better than the laddered portfolios over some maturity ranges, as shown in Figure 6.6. For example the barbell with 70% allocated to short maturities had a maximum loss of $5.22 as compared with the $5.79 maximum loss of the 1- to 15-year laddered portfolio, which provides a similar return. This may or may not be a significant improvement, but the pattern in Figure 6.6 does suggest that if banks are concerned about the potential for realized and unrealized losses, barbell portfolio policies perform competitively with laddered structures over a wide range of policies.

The barbell portfolios perform even better if the measure of risk is taken to be maximum *unrealized* losses only. Most if not all banks want to limit

Table 6.4 Variances for Laddered and Barbell Portfolios

Portfolio Strategy	Total Variance	Variance of Interest Income	Variance of Net Capital Gain (Loss)
15-Year ladder	80.49	55.75	11.76
Barbell with 70% short	93.87	71.81	11.14

realized losses each year, but some may be willing to tolerate modest losses from their trading activity. So long as realized losses are within some policy limit, the bank's major concern of a risk nature is the unrealized losses that might build up. If so, the barbell portfolio has an advantage over a mechanically managed ladder because of the regular sales necessary to maintain the structure. In the example of the previous paragraph, the 15-year ladder had a maximum unrealized loss of $5.79, while the maximum unrealized loss of the barbell with a comparable total return was $4.08. Although the annual trading activity exposed the portfolio to realized losses, the 98th percentile of the distribution of realized losses per year was a relatively modest $.60, or 0.6 of 1% of the initial book value of the portfolio.

IMPACT OF PLANNING HORIZON

The risk-return profile of laddered portfolios in Figure 6.3 suggests that banks can lower variability of returns and increase expected return over relatively long investment horizons by maintaining a laddered structure with longer maturities. Since many banks maintain ladders with relatively short maturities, this suggests that maximum loss is a more relevant measure of portfolio risk. Although there is a rationale to support this position, there is a complementary explanation of the short maturity ladders that depends upon the length of the bank's investment horizon.

Roll [1971] has pointed out that the variability of returns can be reduced in bond portfolios by holding bonds that mature both before and after the investor's horizon. The reduction in total standard deviation results from the negative correlation between the returns on bonds maturing before the horizon and the returns on those maturing after. If interest rates move in a direction so as to increase the return from the "shorter" bonds, the return on the bonds longer than the horizon will fall, lowering the impact of this rate movement on total return. This can be seen by considering a situation in which interest rates rise over the planning horizon. The bonds maturing before the horizon provide cash that can be reinvested at the higher rates occurring. On the other hand, the longer bonds will decline in value, reducing the return from this part of the portfolio. If rates were to fall, the longer securities would increase in value, but the return from the short end of the portfolio is reduced because the maturing short bonds must be reinvested at lower rates.

This negative correlation between the returns of bonds maturing before and after the investment horizon indicates that the riskiness of a particular maturity structure is dependent on the length of the investor's planning horizon. Fisher and Weil [1971] have identified an important relationship between risk, maturity structure, and investment horizon by using the concept of "duration." The duration of a bond or a portfolio has a precise mathematical definition,* but essentially it is a weighted average measure of maturity in which the weights are based on the present value of each future cash flow rather than the actual amounts maturing. Fisher and Weil have shown that under some assumptions about the behavior of interest rates, the variability of returns from a portfolio can be minimized if the duration of the portfolio is kept equal to the time remaining to the end of the investment horizon. Actual interest rates do not behave exactly as assumed, but they tested their portfolio strategies using actual corporate bond rates and found that the standard deviation of returns was kept small by equating duration and the horizon length.

Duration is an important measure of the "maturity" of a portfolio because it recognizes that not all the cash flow from a typical bond occurs at its maturity. Consider, for example, a typical 6% bond with semiannual coupons and a 10-year maturity that was purchased at par. A substantial share of the cash that will be obtained from this bond will be received before maturity so that its duration is about 7.7 years. If the bond had no coupons but was purchased at a discount to yield 6% at maturity, there would be no interim cash flows and the duration of the bond would be 10 years. For an investor with a fixed 10-year horizon, the second bond is risk free in the sense that there is no variability in its return. The bond with semiannual coupons is not risk free since it will be generating cash before the horizon that must be reinvested at uncertain rates. Thus there is some variability in the total return of this bond.

If banks had fixed investment horizons and if bonds without coupons were available, it would be relatively easy to select a portfolio having no variability of returns. For any horizon, say 10 years, the portfolio could simply consist of bonds with 10-year maturities. This portfolio would have a duration of exactly 10 years. Even though these bonds are not normally available, Fisher and Weil [1971] have shown that there is a comparable strategy of coupon bonds possessing a small variability of total return. Their

---

* The duration of a portfolio is based on the present value of future cash flows from interest and maturing bonds. Let P_t be the present value of the cash flows that will occur at the end of period t, and assume that n is the last period in which a cash flow occurs. Then the duration D is:

$$D = \frac{1P_1 + 2P_2 + 3P_3 + \cdots + nP_n}{P_1 + P_2 + P_3 + \cdots + P_n} = \frac{\sum_{t=1}^{n} tP_t}{\sum_{t=1}^{n} P_t}$$

The duration for a portfolio is affected to some extent by the choice of the discount rate used to calculate present values. In the durations for our portfolios presented later we used the average yield-to-maturity of the portfolio as the discount rate.

suggested strategy is to select coupon bonds so that the duration of the portfolio as a whole is equal to the investment horizon. To obtain this duration, at least some of the bonds will have to have maturities longer than the horizon. Although this portfolio will generate some cash before the horizon that will have to be reinvested at uncertain rates, the variability of total return is still kept small. This results from the negative correlation of returns from maturities before and after the investment horizon, which was pointed out by Roll [1971].

The concept of duration helps explain the relationship between average return and standard deviation of return from laddered portfolios over the 10-year investment horizon discussed in the previous section. As shown in Figure 6.3, increases in the maturity of the laddered portfolios led to higher average returns but also to lower variability of returns. This reduction in variability occurred because the duration of the laddered portfolios moved closer to the length of the investment horizon as the longer maturities were added to the portfolios. When the portfolio was laddered out to 30-year maturities, the duration of the portfolio finally reached 10 years because the average duration of these portfolios was about 10.4 years. Note that the addition of long bonds does not greatly increase the duration because the weighted average is based on present values, and the present value of cash flows 30 years hence is small.

If the duration concept has validity, we would not expect long-maturity laddered portfolios to be the lowest risk portfolio when the investment horizon is relatively short. This is illustrated in Figure 6.7, which shows the relationship between average return and standard deviation for a laddered portfolio over a 3-year investment horizon. The portfolio with the least variability is the one laddered out to a 6-year maturity. This portfolio has an average duration of about 3.25 years, which is very close to the length of the investment horizon. As longer bonds are added to the ladder, the average return can be increased, but only at the cost of more variability of returns.

The concept of duration does help explain the results obtained with our simulation model, even though the portfolio strategies we tested are different from the strategies studied by Fisher and Weil [1971]. They held the investment horizon fixed at some future point in time. An initial portfolio was selected so that its duration would be equal to the horizon. Then at the end of each year the portfolio was adjusted so that the duration would be one year shorter. In this manner the duration of the portfolio was kept equal to the time remaining to the fixed horizon.

In both our laddered and barbell strategies the duration of each portfolio was kept approximately constant over time, even though we evaluated the strategy at the end of a fixed horizon. The exact duration of the 6-year laddered portfolio, for example, varied because of the variability in the interest rate on new 6-year bonds added to the portfolio. However, the basic maturity structure was not altered over time. We believe this is in keeping with the way banks manage their portfolios. Although there should be a specific planning horizon in mind when a portfolio strategy is selected, this horizon is moved forward as time passes rather than held fixed.

In addition to the performance characteristics of laddered portfolios, we are also interested in the performance of barbell strategies over the 3-year investment horizon. Thus, Figure 6.7 includes average return and standard

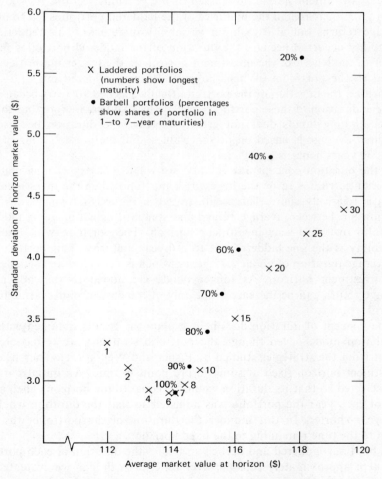

Figure 6.7. Expected return versus standard deviation for 3-year horizon.

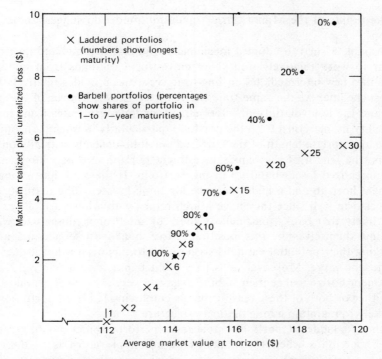

Figure 6.8. Expected return versus maximum loss for 3-year horizon.

deviation results for barbell portfolios. The conclusion remains the same as it was with the 10-year horizon. Laddered portfolios appear to be more efficient than mechanically managed barbell portfolios, providing a higher average return for the same level of variability.

As a final experiment the performance of laddered portfolios was compared to barbells over the 3-year investment horizon using maximum loss as the measure of risk. These results, shown in Figure 6.8, suggest that barbell and laddered portfolios perform comparably for portfolios with moderate to low risk. However, the maximum loss of barbells tends to increase more rapidly than that of laddered portfolios as the average maturity is increased.

IMPLICATIONS FOR MANAGEMENT OF INVESTMENT PORTFOLIOS

The major question explored in this chapter was whether barbell or laddered municipal portfolios performed better if managed mechanically over multiple time periods. This question cannot be answered unambiguously, but the results of the Monte Carlo simulation model do suggest some conclusions.

If a bank wished to adopt a mechanical trading rule, laddered portfolios appear to work relatively well. The reinvestment of funds from maturing bonds into new intermediate- or long-term securities provides relatively high interest income. At the same time the relatively slow turnover of the portfolio and the low volatility of intermediate- or long-term rates leads to low variability in the return from the portfolio, particularly in interest income.

The appropriate length of the laddered portfolio depends critically on two factors, the length of the bank's investment horizon and its willingness to have unrealized losses build up in the portfolio. If the bank has a long investment horizon and a high tolerance for capital losses, long maturity ladders perform well since they have a high return with a low variability. It is more likely that banks, particularly those of small or medium size, would not find themselves in this position. Most banks are concerned about managing their potential capital loss position to make sure that it does not become too large. Moreover, it is likely that banks have a relatively short investment horizon since their liabilities have a very short average maturity. For either or both of these reasons banks employing laddered portfolios are not likely to maintain a long maturity structure.

Although laddered portfolios appear to perform somewhat better than barbell portfolios when the standard deviation of return is used as the measure of risk, there are several reasons why a bank might wish to use a barbell portfolio strategy. Banks may be more concerned about capital loss position than they are about the variability of total return. Few if any banks even measure the variability of total return on their investment portfolios. If "maximum loss" is the more important or limiting measure of risk, barbell portfolios appear to perform about as well as laddered structures when managed mechanically. They perform even better relative to laddered portfolios if a bank is primarily concerned about the potential buildup in unrealized losses and if it is willing to tolerate up to modest amounts of realized losses each year.

Barbell portfolios also offer the advantages of more liquidity and more flexibility. The higher turnover rate of barbell portfolios does lead to more volatility of interest income, but it also provides more liquidity in that a larger percent of the portfolio is in "short" bonds and a larger volume matures each year. In an example discussed above, a portfolio laddered from 1 to 15 years provides about the same return as a barbell with 70% of its funds in the 1- to 7-year range. The barbell portfolio, however, leaves the bank in a much better position if part of the portfolio must be liquidated to meet loan demand or deposit withdrawals. Ten percent of this barbell portfolio matures within 1 year and fifty percent matures within 5 years. The laddered portfolio runs off at the rate of 6.67% per year and only one-third matures within 5 years.

The barbell portfolio also provides more flexibility for a bank that wishes to manage its portfolio more actively. With the higher turnover rate of a barbell portfolio, it is relatively easy for the portfolio manager to change the average maturity structure significantly if he wants to alter the bank's portfolio posture or take advantage of the expected interest rate swings. A comparable change in the maturity structure of a laddered portfolio requires either a longer period of time or a larger trading program, neither of which may be feasible at the time the change is desired.

In summary, barbell maturity structures do offer some significant advantages to banks that wish to manage their portfolios actively. They provide more liquidity and flexibility than laddered portfolios with the same level of return. The total return of barbell portfolios may be more volatile, but this may not be an important price to pay for some banks. On the other hand, banks not wishing to actively manage their municipal portfolio may find laddered portfolios very attractive. They can provide a comparable return with less uncertainty that the return will be achieved.

7

OPTIMIZATION MODELS THAT INCORPORATE UNCERTAINTY

In the previous three chapters we have discussed and developed various models for aiding in the evaluation and management of bank portfolios. These models have covered three important areas of management science: deterministic simulation, linear programming, and Monte Carlo simulation. In order to emphasize the area in which we are going to concentrate for the remainder of the book, we can categorize these models in a two-way table.

Most management science models can be conveniently classified along the following dimensions: (1) whether or not the model explicitly incorporates uncertainty and (2) whether the model evaluates fixed strategies determined a priori by the decision maker or generates an "optimal" strategy satisfying some limitations specified by the decision maker. For the first dimension, it is clear that of the models presented thus far only Monte Carlo simulation explicitly incorporates uncertainty. Both in the case of linear programming and deterministic simulation only one planning scenario is considered. Although these models allow for the evaluation of a number of different planning scenarios, they essentially assume that for the evaluation of a particular scenario the future is known with certainty and will correspond exactly to that scenario. For the second dimension, both deterministic and Monte Carlo simulation are methods of evaluating strategies presented by the portfolio manager. Although it is true that both types of simulation can be used to find the best strategy of those generated by the portfolio manager, neither method suggests new strategies to evaluate. On the other hand, linear programming generates an "optimal" strategy satisfying the constraints specified by the portfolio manager.

Table 7.1 Classification of Portfolio Models

	Evaluates strategies	Generates strategies
Assumes certainty	Deterministic simulation	Linear programming
Incorporates uncertainty	Monte Carlo simulation	Optimization under uncertainty

The area that has not yet been covered deals with models that explicitly incorporate uncertainty and generate an "optimal" strategy satisfying limitations specified by the portfolio manager. As indicated in Table 7.1, this latter area is referred to as optimization under uncertainty. The remainder of this book deals with these kinds of models and for the most part with a specific large scale formulation of the portfolio management problem as a linear program under uncertainty.

OPTIMIZATION MODELS UNDER UNCERTAINTY

In order to see the importance of developing optimization models under uncertainty, we will consider the various models indicated in Table 7.1 in terms of a simple example. Suppose that we have a 3-month planning horizon and can purchase only two securities, a 3-month Treasury bill or a 20-year Government bond. Suppose further that there are two planning scenarios under consideration, one involving rising interest rates and another involving falling interest rates.

A deterministic simulation model would allow us to evaluate any proposed strategy, assuming a particular planning scenario. Now suppose that we evaluated the two strategies, (1) invest all funds in the short maturity and (2) invest all funds in the long maturity, for each possible scenario. Assume that such an evaluation showed that on the falling interest rate scenario the interest income on the maturing 3-month bill was less than the interest income plus the net capital gain on the 20-year bond, and that on the rising interest rate scenario the opposite was true. The deterministic simulation model merely evaluates the strategies specified by the portfolio manager, assuming a particular known planning scenario.

There are at least two important ways that the deterministic simulation model can be generalized. First, for a given planning scenario we can construct a linear programming model that will generate an "optimal" solution. Second, for a given strategy we can explicitly introduce uncertainty into the evaluation of that strategy.

Let us first look at the implications of linear programming. In our highly simplified example our decision problem would be to determine the optimal fraction of the portfolio to invest in the long maturity, assuming the remainder is invested in the short maturity. We already know the outcome of such an analysis since the linear programming approach assumes that a particular scenario holds with certainty. For the rising interest rate scenario the optimal fraction to invest in the long maturity would be zero, while for the falling interest rate scenario the optimal fraction to invest in the long maturity would be one. Although any intermediate values for the fraction to invest in the long maturity are feasible, the extreme values are optimal to the linear programs. This results from the assumption that future interest rates are known with certainty. If we know what future interest rates will be, it is not a difficult task to select those securities that give the maximum return over the planning horizon. Since the uncertainty, which is the essence of the portfolio management problem, has been excluded, no hedging strategies will be generated by the linear program. If hedging behavior is desired it can only be obtained in the linear programming context by adding policy constraints to restrict the strategies generated. In our simple example a constraint might be added to limit the fraction invested in the long maturity to 25% of the portfolio to avoid excess exposure to possible losses. However, it should be clear how these additional constraints will affect the optimal solution. Under the falling interest rate scenario we would invest as much as possible in the long maturity (i.e., 25%), while under the rising interest rate scenario we would continue to invest zero in the long maturity. The difficulty with linear programming in this situation is that it does not give guidance as to how to set the levels of the policy constraints.

Since uncertainty is such an important aspect of the portfolio management problem, generalizing our deterministic simulation model to Monte Carlo simulation would appear to be a productive way to proceed. Assume that the two scenarios, rising interest rates and falling interest rates, have been assessed to be equally likely to occur. Now we can evaluate the performance of any particular strategy according to a number of different criteria explicitly taking into account the underlying uncertainty. For example, we might be interested in the expected return, the standard deviation of return, and some level of maximum unrealized losses, as we were in Chapter 6. Using a Monte Carlo simulation model, we could evaluate the different strategies suggested by the portfolio manager with respect to the various criteria and determine which strategies are effective hedges against the uncertainty in future interest rates. However, because of the multiple criteria there will usually be conflicts among strategies. In our simple example, investing all in the longest maturity is likely to have higher expected return, but it also has higher potential losses than investing all in the short maturity. If one were risk averse to high levels of capital losses, he would be unwilling to put all the portfolio in the long maturity. On the other hand, putting all the portfolio in the short maturity may be clearly too conservative a position with a very low expected return. Therefore, one might easily conclude that he should place part of his portfolio in the long maturity and part in the short maturity. Such hedging strategies are not even suggested by either the deterministic simulation or the linear programming model. The need for a hedging strategy would lead one to evaluate a number of strategies until one was found for which the expected return was reasonably high while the potential losses were acceptably low.

The latter idea of trying different strategies in order to find a strategy with a reasonable return and not too large potential losses leads us naturally to optimization models that incorporate uncertainty. The basic idea involved in these models is to maximize some primary criterion, such as the expected value of the portfolio at the horizon, subject to some constraints that limit exposure to risk on each scenario. In our simple example, we might constrain risk by limiting the unrealized losses on each scenario to less than 5% of the value of the portfolio. Our programming under uncertainty model will then generate the "optimal" hedging strategy that takes uncertainty explicitly into account by maximizing the expected value of the portfolio while satisfying the constraints on acceptable levels of losses.

In addition, the real power of optimization models under uncertainty is their ability to choose the optimal contingency strategy from among a potentially very large number of strategies. A contingency strategy has to indicate what the future portfolio decisions should be for every possible realization of the planning scenarios. The current portfolio decisions then can take into account these future contingency plans. If our simple example were to be extended to include a number of time periods and a large number of planning scenarios, the number of potential contingency strategies would become enormous. The large number of strategies would clearly preclude evaluating each by Monte Carlo simulation.

MODELING THE BOND PORTFOLIO PROBLEM

The bond portfolio problem can be viewed as a multiperiod decision problem in which portfolio actions are taken at successive (discrete) points in time. At each decision period, the portfolio manager has an inventory of securities and/or cash on hand. Based on present credit market conditions and his assessment of future interest rates and cash flows, the manager must decide which bonds to hold in the portfolio over the next time period, which bonds to sell, and which bonds to purchase from the marketplace. These decisions are made subject to a constraint on total portfolio size, which may be larger or smaller than the previous period's constraint depending on whether a cash inflow or outflow occurs. At the next decision period, the portfolio manager faces a new set of interest rates and a new portfolio size constraint. He must then make another set of portfolio decisions taking into account the new information. This decision making process, which is repeated over many time periods, is dynamic in the sense that the optimal first period decision depends on the actions that will be taken in each future period along each scenario.

Normative models of this decision problem, or variants of it, tend to become large and difficult to solve when many of its characteristics are taken into account. Hence most approaches to the problem have tried to limit its size by one or more of the following techniques: ignoring the dynamic structure of the problem, excluding or restricting the uncertainty, limiting the number of assets considered, and including only one or two time periods.

The initial approaches to the problem included multiple assets and time periods but ignored completely the underlying uncertainty and therefore were not dynamic in the sense of generating strategies contingent on the evolution of a scenario. These models were basically the linear programming models of Chambers and Charnes [1961] and Cohen and Hammer [1967]. These initial models and others discussed in Chapter 5 have been successfully applied to aggregate modeling of the balance sheet and income statement in a number of banks, but have not proven very useful for selecting an investment portfolio strategy.

Some authors have tried to extend the common stock portfolio theory of Markowitz [1959] to the bond portfolio management area. Cheng [1962] under restrictive assumptions, but including more than one time period, determined the expected returns and the variance-covariance matrix for a number of prespecified strategies and was then able to employ the basic results of the Markowitz theory. However, his approach was not dynamic since the strategies enumerated at the beginning of the model were not conditional on future uncertain events. A more recent extension of the Markowitz theory was carried out by Fried [1970], who added a number of policy "chance constraints" on wealth, losses, and the availability of liquid assets. Chance constraints take the form of placing limits on the probability that certain constraints hold. For example, net liquid assets not falling below a prespecified level might have to be satisfied 95% of the time.

However, Fried's models also are not dynamic since they have only one period.

Other chance-constrained models have appeared, notably those suggested by Charnes and Littlechild [1968] and Charnes and Thore [1966]. These models, which may involve more than one time period, include the uncertainty by stating that certain constraints must hold with a prespecified probability. Their drawback is that they are not dynamic since their suggested actions are not contingent upon the evolution of scenarios, and further, these models do not give any guidance as to what should be done if the outcome on some scenarios violates a constraint. The justification for these models is that they enable the portfolio manager to explicitly include uncertainty in the model in a form that is computationally tractable by most nonlinear programming algorithms. However, these models ignore the large number of contingency strategies.

Dynamic programming models that do generate contingent strategies under uncertainty have been structured and solved for only a limited number of assets. These models include the two- and three-asset models of Eppen and Fama [1968, 1971] and the two-asset and one-liability model of Daellenback and Archer [1969]. The small number of assets considered clearly limits the applicability of such models.

Two approaches, sequential decision theory and two-stage programming under uncertainty, have been used to solve multiple asset, two-period portfolio problems that explicitly incorporate uncertainty in cash flows and interest rates. The problem is amenable to these approaches, but its size grows rapidly with either approach as the number of time periods is increased. The decision theoretic approach of Wolf [1969] provided an optimal solution for only a one-period problem. In his two-period case it would be necessary to enumerate all possible portfolio strategies for the first decision period in order to guarantee an optimal solution. The linear programming under uncertainty approach, suggested by Cohen and Thore [1970] and Crane [June, 1971], can optimally and efficiently solve a two-period problem but the number of constraints is greatly increased by the addition of more periods. An extension of the Cohen and Thore application of two-stage programming under uncertainty has been given by Booth [1972].

In the remainder of this chapter we present the BONDS model, a multiple-period, multiple-asset bond portfolio model developed by the authors. An early version of this model has been discussed previously by Bradley and Crane [1972, 1973].* The computational procedures employed

* We are grateful to the publishers of *Management Science* and *Journal of Bank Research* for permission to draw upon these articles in this and subsequent chapters.

are quite efficient and permit the solution of problems that are large enough to employ as much information as portfolio managers can reasonably provide.

OVERVIEW OF THE BONDS MODEL

The need for explicitly dealing with the underlying uncertainties involving loans, deposits, and interest rates has by now been clearly established. One approach to bank planning would be to incorporate uncertainty in models addressing aggregate planning for the bank as a whole. The idea here is to generalize the models for dynamic balance sheet management, discussed in Chapter 5, to include uncertainty. Unfortunately, taking uncertainty explicitly into account will make an asset and liability management model for the entire bank computationally intractable unless it is an extremely aggregated model. The complexities of the general dynamic balance sheet management problem are such that the number of constraints and variables needed to accurately model the environment would be very large. In essence, to be solvable, optimization models for the bank as a whole that explicitly account for uncertainty in loans, deposits, and interest rates would have to be so aggregated that they would not provide enough detail to give insight into the appropriate distribution of maturities in the investment portfolio. Further, these models would tend to be so large and complex that it might be difficult to establish management confidence in their recommendations.

Hence we have chosen to develop the BONDS model that deals specifically with the investment portfolio rather than the bank as a whole. By restricting our attention to the investment portfolio, it is possible to explicitly include the effect of uncertainty in loans, deposits, and interest rates while maintaining a complete set of investment alternatives for the portfolio planner or manager at any point in time. This approach provides sufficient detail to give insight into the appropriate distribution of maturities to hold in the investment portfolio. Another reason for restricting our attention to the investment portfolio is that banks generally have separated its management in their organizational structure. Our model is therefore designed to be responsive directly to an individual in the bank, the portfolio manager.

Since the BONDS model concentrates on the investment portfolio, it must be systematically related to the planning in the rest of the bank in order to properly take into account activities of the bank outside the portfolio as well as the effect of the uncertainty in future loans and deposits. The mechanism for this decoupling of the management of the investment portfolio from the rest of the bank is scenario planning. By using consistent definitions of scenarios for all bank planning, the impact of the rest of the bank on the investment portfolio can be assessed for each scenario and incorporated in the model.

A critical element of each planning scenario is the amount of funds which will be made available to or withdrawn from the portfolio due to the combined impact of economic conditions and bank policy. This depends in part on the loan and deposit projections for each scenario as well as on the bank's judgment as to the amount of purchased funds that will be available for use if each scenario occurs. In addition, it depends on planned activities outside the portfolio, such as the level of leasing activities to be engaged in. The net of these nonportfolio sources and uses of funds can be collapsed into what we call the "net need" of the portfolio for funds. Procedures for forecasting the components of this net need that depend on general economic conditions, such as loans and deposits, are described in Chapter 3. These procedures involve making forecasts conditional on each scenario of a set of planning scenarios. The components of this net need that depend on bank policy are then also assessed conditional on the same set of planning scenarios.

There are other important elements of each scenario requiring assessment. One type of limitation on the investment strategy is imposed by the amount of risk the bank is willing to tolerate. This can be expressed in the model through limits on losses that may be realized within a tax year, as well as limits on unrealized capital losses that are allowed to build up in the portfolio over the planning horizon. Another limitation on investment strategy results from the bank's pledging requirements. The holdings of government securities as well as the holdings of some state and local bonds are affected by the levels of certain types of deposits. The fluctuations of these deposits is then also forecast for each planning scenario to indicate the minimum holdings of the securities that will satisfy the pledging requirements. The minimum holdings of government securities may also be affected by the bank's need for taxable income, although this need for taxable income also could be an element of each scenario that is directly assessed by the portfolio manager.

Scenario planning is then the key to being able to concentrate on the investment portfolio. The interface between the investment portfolio and the rest of the bank is taken into account using consistent definitions of scenarios for planning throughout the bank. For planning the investment portfolio this interface is characterized by the net need impact on the portfolio, the allowable levels of realized and unrealized losses in the portfolio, the limits on the holdings of certain broad categories of securities, as well as any other element of a scenario that the portfolio manager deems important for the planning problem being addressed. All of these elements of the scenarios are then tied to interest rate movements by using the same definitions of scenarios for forecasting yield curve movements as for assessing these elements. The procedures for using scenario definitions to assist in the forecasting of interest rates and tying these forecasts to other forecasts are presented in Chapter 3.

The structure of the portfolio model presented here assumes that decisions are made at the start of each planning period. At the beginning of each period the portfolio manager is faced with the difficult problem of deciding which securities to sell or hold in the portfolio and which to buy. This decision is difficult for two important reasons. First, he faces an uncertain future in that interest rates on securities may rise or fall and that funds may be made available to or withdrawn from the portfolio depending on external economic conditions as well as exogenous policy considerations. This uncertainty in future periods and the response of the portfolio manager to interest rates and exogenous cash flows which might occur should be taken into account in deciding upon current portfolio actions. This leads to the second problem, a very large number of possible portfolio strategies which must be evaluated.

To approach the first problem we assume that the portfolio manager is able to specify a collection of economic scenarios consisting of a sequence of specific yield curves and exogenous cash flows that might occur. Associated with each sequence is its probability of occurrence. The scenarios are complicated by the fact that the yield curve that might occur in a specific period is conditional upon the sequence of yield curves preceding it. After the first decision, for example, interest rates might rise, remain the same, or fall. Given that one of these uncertain events has occurred, rates might then rise from the new level, remain the same, or fall. Thus a scenario is not simply a sequence of continuously rising or falling rates. Other than the current yield curve, which is known, we assume in scenario planning that there are a number of different possible yield curves and exogenous cash flows that can occur in each period depending upon which scenario is specified. The particular yield curve and exogenous cash flow combination, as well as the probability of its occurrence, must be assessed by the portfolio manager conditional on an underlying scenario.

The large number of portfolio actions to be evaluated results from the need to make contingency decisions with respect to each security at the start of each period for each of the possible prior actions taken and prior uncertain events. Except for the initial decision each portfolio action is conditional upon the sequence of uncertain events and portfolio decisions preceding it, and the decision takes into account future uncertainties and possible portfolio actions.

FORMULATION OF THE BONDS MODEL

In this section we discuss the basic formulation of the BONDS model without introducing any complicated mathematical notation. In Appendix B this discussion is made more precise and rigorous by introducing notation and specifically listing the constraints. Here we structure the BONDS model by defining in general terms the decision variables, the constraints, and the objective function of a linear program under uncertainty.

For any particular analysis that the portfolio manager is considering, he must first categorize the securities to be included in the planning by general categories and then aggregate the securities available for purchase into a number of security classes within each category. The broad categories usually refer to securities described by the same yield curve, such as U.S. Government bonds or a particular grade of municipal bonds, but they may also refer to different types of securities within these categories, such as deep-discount or current coupon bonds. The aggregation of securities within these broad categories is usually by time to maturity, such as 3 months, 6 months, 1 year, 2 years, and so forth. These security classes will in general not include all maturities that are available but some appropriate aggregation of these maturities.

Usually there will be a portfolio of current holdings that will have to be accounted for. Security classes need to be defined for these holdings, and these security classes may or may not correspond to those contemplated for future purchase. For these current holdings it is usually inappropriate to define security classes for each maturity held since the number of such classes would become very large. A representative set of security classes is defined, and the coupon rate on the bonds in a particular security class is then the weighted average of the coupon rates of the bonds attributed to that class of holdings.

The critical assumptions in the formulation are that we are planning with respect to a limited number of economic scenarios and a finite number of planning periods. The scenarios are usually defined in terms of the movements of some appropriate short-term interest rate, as described in Chapter 3, while the number of planning periods is determined by the bank's planning horizon and the problem being analyzed. The possible movements of the short-term rate generate a collection of scenarios each of which consists of a particular sequence of yield curves and exogenous cash flows, as well as other properties, for each period in the planning horizon. The assumption of a finite number of scenarios results from making a discrete approximation of the continuous distribution of changes in the short-term rate, and this in turn, along with the finite number of periods, permits the formulation of an ordinary linear program that explicitly takes uncertainty into account. Associated with any particular scenario is its probability of occurrence, and this is used to structure the objective function of the linear program so as to maximize the expected horizon value of the portfolio.

The other properties of scenarios generally are policy considerations involving the interface between the investment portfolio and the rest of the bank. For each tax year in the planning horizon, the maximum amount of realized losses is usually specified for each scenario. Further, the maximum level of unrealized losses that potentially could build up in the portfolio over the planning horizon is usually specified also. In the situation where more than one broad category of securities is being analyzed, either maximum or minimum levels of the holdings of a particular category might be specified. An example of this type of constraint would be some minimum level of U.S. Government holdings that are necessary for either pledging purposes or taxable income needs.

Decision Variables

At the beginning of each period, assuming that a particular portfolio is currently held and cash is either available to or required from the portfolio, the portfolio manager must decide how much of each security class to *buy* and how much of each security class that he is currently holding to *sell* or continue to *hold*. Since the amount of capital gain or loss on a security class sold will depend on the difference between the purchase price and sales price, the portfolio manager must keep track of the amount of each security class held by its date of purchase. Further, the variables that represent decisions at the start of a particular period are conditional on the sequence of uncertain events preceding the start of that period, since the model computes the optimal set of decisions for every uncertain event sequence, or scenario.

It should be pointed out that the availability of purchased funds is also included in the model at the discretion of the planner. This allows the portfolio manager to examine the use of purchase funds within the portfolio for either financing cash outflows from the portfolio or increasing the size of the portfolio. However, since the use of purchased funds is in general a policy decision external to the investment portfolio, it was felt that an elaborate collection of liabilities was not needed. Therefore the model includes a short-term liability in each period with maturity equal to the length of that period and cost tied directly to the price of the short-term asset with the same maturity.

Constraints

In general, the model maximizes the expected value of the portfolio at the end of the planning horizon subject to five types of constraints on the decision variables as well as nonnegativity of these variables. The nonnegativity of the decision variables merely implies that short sales are not permitted. As a practical matter, short sales are uncommon in the investment portfolios of financial institutions. However, short sales could easily be included in our model by defining specific decision variables for short sales if it were thought useful to do so. The types of constraints, each of which will be discussed below, include the following: cash flow, inventory balance, current holdings, net capital loss (realized and unrealized), and broad category limits. In general, there are separate constraints for each of the planning scenarios.

Cash Flow. The model is designed on a cash accounting rather than on the accrual basis normally used by banks for reporting purposes. On balance, this is a more accurate method because it takes into account when cash is actually available for reinvestment. It is not completely accurate, however, because it ignores the tax effects of amortization of bond premiums and accretion of discounts of bonds that might be contained in the starting portfolio. If this were judged to be a significant problem, it potentially could be solved by setting up separate bond categories for each combination of maturity and initial purchase price and then adjusting the cash flow and book value.

The cash flow constraints require that the cash used for purchasing securities be equal to the sum of the cash generated from the coupon income on holdings during the previous period, cash generated from sales of securities, and exogenous cash flow. If short-term liabilities are included in the model, then these cash flow constraints will also reflect the possibility of generating additional cash by selling a one-period liability. We need to assess coefficients reflecting the income *yield* stemming from the semiannual coupon interest from holding a security and the capital *gain or loss* from selling a security, where each is expressed as a percent of initial purchase price. It is assumed that taxes are paid when income and/or gains are received, so that these coefficients are defined as after tax. Transaction costs are taken into account by adjusting the gain coefficient for the broker's commission; that is, bonds are purchased at the "asked" price and sold at the "bid" price. Finally, we also need to assess the exogenous cash flow reflecting changes in the amount of funds made available to the portfolio. The exogenous cash flow may be either positive or negative depending on whether cash is being made available to or withdrawn from the portfolio, respectively.

Apart from accretion and amortization problems, cash income from the model can be considered as an approximation to accrued income if the portfolio manager is interested in the implications of portfolio strategies for reported earnings. If periods in the model are assumed to coincide with calendar quarters and years, for example, cash income approximately equals accrued income for purchase decisions of the model. Bonds in the portfolio before the start of the model must be grouped into discrete maturity categories. Since some bonds will have coupon payments before the end of each discrete period and some after, the aggregated coupon income in each period may approximate accrued income, particularly for portfolios with a large number of issues.

Finally, the cash flow constraints hold with equality, implying that the portfolio is at all times fully invested since it is assumed that there is always a one-period, risk-free asset to purchase that has no transaction cost.

Inventory Balance. The model has what is referred to as inventory balance constraints. The commodities that need to be accounted for are the holdings of each security class purchased in a particular period. Hence these constraints state that the amount of a commodity sold plus the amount of that commodity held at the beginning of a period must equal the amount on hand at the end of the previous period. The amount on hand at the end of the previous period is either the amount purchased or the amount held at the beginning of the previous period.

It is important to point out that this formulation of the problem includes security classes that mature before the time horizon of the model. This is accomplished by setting the hold variable for a matured security to zero (actually dropping the variable from the model). This has the effect, through the inventory balance constraints, of forcing the "sale" of the security at the time the security matures. The value of the gain coefficient reflects the fact that the security matures at par with no transactions cost.

Current Holdings. The inventory balance constraints allow us to easily handle the accounting for securities held in the current portfolio. The current holdings of a particular security class are handled by setting the appropriate hold variable at time zero equal to this amount. The model will then indicate when it is best to sell or hold on to these securities. In general, there may be different security classes for the current portfolio holdings and the maturities that will be available for purchase in subsequent time periods.

Capital Loss. Theoretically, we might like to solve this problem with the objective of maximizing the bank's preference for assets at the horizon.

However, such a function would be difficult to specify since it involves preference for assets over time distinguishing both income and capital gains. In addition, problems of realistic size would be difficult to solve because such objective functions are nonlinear. Therefore, in lieu of a nonlinear preference function, we have added a set of constraints limiting the net *realized* capital loss during any year as well as the net *unrealized* capital loss over the planning horizon. This approach is similar to the "safety first principle" that some, for example Telser [1955–1956], have used in portfolio models and reflects current bank practice.

Loss constraints are particularly appropriate for banks, in part because of a general aversion to capital losses but also because of capital adequacy and tax considerations. Measures of adequate bank capital, such as that of the Federal Reserve Board of Governors, relate the amount of capital required to the amount of "risk" in the bank's assets. Thus a bank's capital position affects its willingness to hold assets with capital loss potential.

Tax regulations are also important because capital losses can be offset against taxable income to reduce the size of the after-tax loss by roughly 50%. As a result, the amount of taxable income, which is sometime relatively small in commercial banks, imposes an upper limit on losses a bank is willing to absorb.

The loss constraints sum of the gains and losses from sales of securities within each tax year and place an upper limit on net losses. Usually the loss constraints are applied so as to limit the unrealized losses in the portfolio at the horizon as well as realized losses each year. The limiting of unrealized losses at the horizon is important to insure that current coupon income and capital gains are not achieved at the expense of large holdings of unrealized losses at the horizon of the model.

Category Limits.   It may be of considerable interest to segment the portfolio into a number of broad asset categories, each of which is described by different yield curves, transaction costs, income tax rates, and distribution of maturities. There is no conceptual difficulty with this; however, some computational difficulties may arise due to problem size. Typically the investment portfolio might be segmented into Government securities and tax-exempt securities. In addition, the tax-exempt securities might be further segmented by quality such as prime-, good-, and medium-grade municipals. If such a segmentation is used, then, in general, upper or lower bound constraints on some of the asset classes might be useful. As we have already stated, a minimum level of holdings of Government securities is often needed for pledging and/or taxable income considerations. The constraints on category limits then merely state that the holdings of a particular asset category at some point in time must be above or below a level specified, conditional on each scenario.

Objective Function

Since risk aversion is contained only in the loss constraints, the objective function of this model is the maximization of the expected value of the portfolio at the end of the final period. It should be pointed out that the maximization of horizon value assumes the portfolio manager is indifferent to revenues received from interest or those received from capital gains since each add equivalent dollars to the horizon value. If desired, it would be possible to add interest income constraints to the model to assure that sufficient income would be achieved by the portfolio during each period.

The expected horizon "value" consists of the cash received in the final period from interest plus the value of securities held in the portfolio. It is not obvious, though, how the value of the portfolio should be measured since it is likely to contain some unrealized gains and losses. Should these gains or losses be calculated before or after taxes? Before or after transaction costs? At one extreme it would be possible to assume that the portfolio would be sold at the horizon so that its final value would be after taxes and transaction costs. This approach would tend to artificially encourage short maturities in the portfolio since they have low transaction costs. The alternative approach of valuing the portfolio before taxes and transaction costs is equally unrealistic. To resolve this dilemma we have assumed it is possible for portfolio managers to express an equivalent cash value that can be substituted for the expected market value of the portfolio. This value represents the cash amount the portfolio manager would be willing to receive in exchange for the final portfolio. For simplicity, we have in fact assumed that the value of the securities at the horizon is after taxes but before transaction costs.

In order to formalize the objective function, we need to define the *probability* of each scenario occurring as well as the *value* of the holdings in the final period. Then the total value of the portfolio at the horizon is the sum of the expected value of the horizon holdings plus the coupon income received in the final period.

A complete mathematical description of the model is given in Appendix B. Along with the rigorous formulation of the model, the solution procedure and comments on problem size are also presented.

ILLUSTRATING THE MODEL ON U.S. GOVERNMENT SECURITIES

The BONDS model is a general-purpose portfolio planning model with a large number of complexities. Rather than turning immediately to the more complicated policy implications of the model, in this chapter we will attempt to give the reader an understanding of some of the basic structure and implications of the model by concentrating on a particular "base case" dealing only with U.S. Government securities. We will present a base case for municipals and discuss the joint management of Governments and municipals in Chapter 9. The purpose of the remainder of this chapter is to analyze the government base case and gain an insight into the nature of the contingency strategies generated by the model.

The problem structure for the base case assumes a 3-year planning horizon divided into three 1-year periods. Buy, sell, and hold decisions are made at the start of each year. Each decision is made in the context of a particular yield curve and amounts of funds available to the portfolio, but at the time of the first decision only the current yield curve and amount of funds are known with certainty. After the first decision one of three equally likely random events occurs, each possible event being defined by a yield curve and a cash flow made available to or withdrawn from the portfolio. After the random event a new decision is made at the start of the year two. Then another one of three possible events occurs and a decision is made at the start of year three. Finally, an uncertain event occurs during year three that determines the value of the portfolio at the horizon.

For the base case it is assumed that the portfolio starts with $100,000 in cash. An initial portfolio of securities could easily be handled, but this only tends to obscure the essential properties of the optimal strategies. Initial portfolios are illustrated in Chapter 10 and Appendix C. The cash can be invested in any of nine "securities," which represent different maturity categories of U.S. Government securities. The maturities available for purchase in the first period and all subsequent periods are 1, 2, 3, 4, 5, 7, 10, 15, and 20 year. All securities are purchased at par and the coupon yield on each maturity at the start of the first period lies along a rising yield curve, as shown by the initial yield curve in Figure 7.1.

The yield curve that prevails for the second decision is uncertain. This uncertainty is represented by a random shift in the initial yield curve. With equal probabilities the yield curve may shift up, stay the same, or decline. The size and nature of these shifts was chosen to approximate the distribution of actual 12-month changes in the government yield curve that have occurred over the past several years. Analysis of these data suggests that the 3-month rate will increase 120 basis points, not change, or decrease 120 basis points with approximately equal probability. In addition, changes in the 3-year rate average about 80 percent of changes in the 3-month rate and changes in the 20-year rate average about 30 percent of the changes in the short rate. These parameters determine three points on each possible yield curve by adding the changes in the three rates to the previous yield curves.

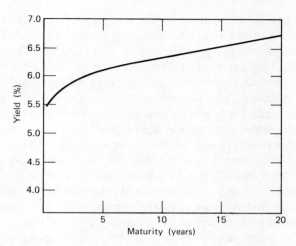

Figure 7.1.   Initial yield curve.

Yields for all other maturities are then computed from a form of the Pearson "Type III" frequency curve fitted to these three points. A description of the statistical analysis and data generation techniques has already been given in Chapter 3.

The yield curves that are possible at the decision points at the start of each period are shown in Figure 7.2. (The twenty-seven possible yield curves that might occur at the horizon have not been shown.) Note that as the yield curve moves upward, it becomes flatter and then inverted. As it moves down, the curve rises more steeply. Both of these trends occur in actual security markets as monetary conditions tighten or ease.

In keeping with the notion that rising yields imply tighter credit conditions and vice versa, the base case assumes that, if rates rise, a part of the portfolio will need to be liquidated to finance a cash outflow. A fall in the yield curve implies that extra cash is available for investment. This phenomenon is represented by a $10,000 reduction in funds available to the portfolio if rates rise, no change if rates remain stable, and a $10,000 increase in investable funds if rates fall. In effect, this means that the portfolio strategy must take into account the possibility of approximately a 10 percent change in the amount of funds available in each future decision period.

Aversion to risk in the portfolio is expressed by limits on losses resulting from sales of securities. The base case adopts a conservative approach by limiting net realized losses on sales in each year of the model to zero. At the end of the third period there is an upper limit on unrealized losses of $1000,

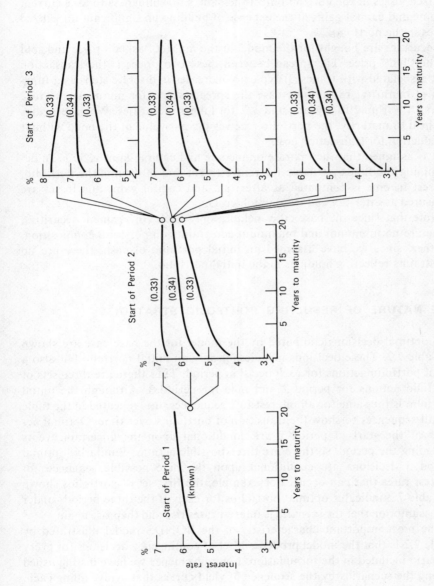

Figure 7.2. Distribution of future yield curves (probability in parentheses).

or 1 percent of the original value of the portfolio. These constraints on unrealized losses at the horizon reflect the bank's unwillingness to take current income and capital gains at the expense of building up significant unrealized losses in the portfolio.

Securities are bought for the model at the market "asked" price and sold at the "bid" price. The spread between these two prices is the transaction cost associated with trades. It typically increases in discrete steps as a function of maturity. In the base case the spread is $\frac{1}{8}$% for maturities up to 2 years, $\frac{1}{4}$% from 2 to 8 years, and $\frac{1}{2}$% for longer maturities. When securities are held to maturity, the portfolio receives the par value of the bond without a deduction for transaction costs.

It is assumed that the tax rate on income and capital gains is 50%. In determining the funds available for reinvestment and in valuing the portfolio, interest income is computed as after tax, and capital gains and losses are measured as after-tax and transaction costs.

Note that since the base case includes only U.S. Government securities, there are no minimum and maximum constraints on portfolio composition. Further, since we have assumed an initial portfolio of cash, there are no constraints reflecting holdings in the initial portfolio.

THE NATURE OF RESULTING PORTFOLIO STRATEGIES

The optimal decisions computed by the model for the base case are shown in Table 7.2. These decisions include not only an initial portfolio but also a set of portfolio actions for each decision period. Thus there are three sets of portfolio actions for period 2 and nine for period 3. Although the initial portfolio is the same for all interest rate sequences, it is repeated in the table for all sequences to show the transition of portfolios over time. Optimal actions at the start of period 2 are conditional upon the uncertain events preceding the period, so there are three possible actions. Similarly, optimal period 3 decisions are conditional upon the nine possible sequences of interest rates that can occur. For example, the first set of portfolios shown in Table 7.2 indicates optimal portfolios for each of the three periods under the assumption that the scenario is interest rates rise and then rise again.

The most important characteristic of the BONDS model illustrated by Table 7.2 is that the model produces a set of contingency decisions for every scenario included in the formulation. For convenience we have distinguished among the scenarios by the sequence of yield curves that evolve along each. It should be kept in mind that associated with each yield curve is an exogenous cash flow as well as a limit on allowable realized or unrealized losses that can occur. For each scenario the initial decisions are identical because the current actions must be taken without knowing which scenario will occur. The decisions indicated for future periods along each scenario are the decisions that should be taken if that scenario occurs. The initial decisions suggested by the model are in essence a hedge against the uncertainty as to which scenario will occur.

The optimal initial portfolio for the base case tends to be barbell-shaped with maturities concentrated at the short and long end of the maturity range. The maturities at the short end are laddered in the sense that there is a spread of maturities with some bonds maturing at the end of each decision period of the model. If rates rise and there is a cash outflow in the first year, this outflow is financed by the cash received from maturing securities and interest income. If rates rise again, the outflow is financed by the maturing 2-year securities, that were originally purchased for the initial portfolio, and interest income. The final portfolio is split between 1- and 18-year maturities. The 1-year securities mature at the horizon with no loss and the 18-year securities (17-year at the horizon) result in a maximum unrealized loss of $1000 if rates rise again.

The patterns of optimal portfolios differ over time, depending on the scenario which occurs. If rates do not change, for example, proceeds from the original 1-year securities are reinvested in new 20-year securities at the start of year 2. If rates are again stable, proceeds from maturing securities are then again invested in new 20-year securities. After this interest rate scenario, the portfolio enters the final year of the model with securities whose maturities are 1, 18, 19, and 20 years. The portfolio is laddered at the long end of the maturity range and contains the shortest maturity but includes no intermediate maturities. The portfolio is then barbell-shaped with clusters at the long and short ends of the maturity range.

In this base case the initial and all subsequent portfolios have a barbell distribution of maturities consisting of clusters of securities on the long and/or short ends of the maturity range and no intermediate maturities. This suggests that optimal portfolios in a multiperiod environment may, in general, have a barbell structure. In the next chapter we investigate the extent to which this is true by varying the underlying assumptions of the BONDS model to determine their impact on this basic portfolio structure. There we will deal exclusively with variations of the three-period base case described in this chapter.

We should reemphasize that the attributes of the base case are not those of any particular bank. These attributes are based on historical data or reflect reasonable bank practice. The yield curve movements are based on the statistical work reported in Chapter 3 with the historical upward trend

Table 7.2 Optimal Portfolios for Each Scenario: Government Base Case

Period	Sequence of Interest Rates	Amounts in Each Maturity ($)							
		1 Year	2 Years	3 Years	...	18 Years	19 Years	20 Years	Total
1	Initial curve	6,974	7,173	68,646		—	—	17,207	100,000
2	Rise	7,173	68,646	—		—	17,207	—	93,026
3	Rise	68,646	—	—		17,207	—	—	85,853
1	Initial curve	6,974	7,173	68,646		—	—	17,207	100,000
2	Rise	7,173	68,646	—		—	17,207	—	93,026
3	No change	68,646	—	—		17,207	—	10,000	95,853
1	Initial curve	6,974	7,173	68,646		—	—	17,207	100,000
2	Rise	7,173	68,646	—		—	17,207	—	93,026
3	Fall	51,357	—	—		16,160	—	38,336	105,853
1	Initial curve	6,974	7,173	68,646		—	—	17,207	100,000
2	No change	7,173	69,846	—		—	17,207	8,800	103,026
3	Rise	70,175	—	—		17,207	8,800	—	96,182

1	Initial curve	6,974	7,173	68,646	—	—	17,207	100,000
2	No change	7,173	69,846	—	—	17,207	8,800	103,026
3	No change	52,242	—	—	16,092	8,800	29,847	106,981
1	Initial curve	6,974	7,173	68,646	—	—	17,207	100,000
2	No change	7,173	69,846	—	—	17,207	8,800	103,026
3	Fall	26,835	—	—	17,207	8,800	63,564	116,406
1	Initial curve	6,974	7,173	68,646	—	—	17,207	100,000
2	Fall	—	67,610	—	—	17,207	28,253	113,070
3	Rise	79,045	—	—	—	27,504	—	106,549
1	Initial curve	6,974	7,173	68,646	—	—	17,207	100,000
2	Fall	—	67,610	—	—	17,207	28,253	113,070
3	No change	34,200	—	—	17,207	28,253	37,063	116,723
1	Initial curve	6,974	7,173	68,646	—	—	17,207	100,000
2	Fall	—	67,610	—	—	17,207	28,253	113,070
3	Fall	—	—	—	17,207	28,253	81,805	127,265

in interest rates having been removed. The initial yield curve has been selected to be typical of the rising yield curves often encountered for U.S. Government securities and roughly corresponds to yield curves in the early months of 1973. The future yield curves include both steeply rising and inverted yield curves, both of which occur periodically for this type of security. Some exogenous cash flows have been included to allow for potential changes in the size of the portfolio due to changing credit conditions. The limits on realized and unrealized losses reflect some banks' current practice. Finally, no current portfolio of holdings has been included since it was felt this only tended to conceal the essential nature of the strategy suggested by the model. When such a model is applied in a particular bank, obviously a number of characteristics of that bank as well as the actual assessments and forecasts of that bank would be included in the model. The purpose of the base case is to gain insight into the nature of the investment strategy suggested by the BONDS model in a general environment without the biases of a particular bank.

8

SCENARIO PLANNING AND PORTFOLIO STRUCTURE

As we have emphasized throughout this book, the most important aspect of planning a portfolio strategy is to take appropriately into account the portfolio manager's assessment of the uncertainties being faced. Our approach to this problem is to use the framework of scenario planning in which the attributes of a collection of possible future economic scenarios are defined and the likelihood of each scenario is assessed. The portfolio strategy that constitutes the best hedge against the uncertainties in future interest rates and needs for funds is then selected. The scenario planning framework assists the portfolio manager in assessing the attributes of his planning environment in such a way that they are consistent with the formal planning being done in the rest of the bank.

The attributes of a planning scenario consist of those that need to be forecast by the portfolio manager as well as those that are set by bank policy. For each planning scenario considered, the portfolio manager must forecast a sequence of possible future yield curves and a sequence of possible funds flows that will be added to or subtracted from the portfolio. The latter reflects use of the portfolio to meet potential liquidity needs of the bank. Further, for each planning scenario considered, the portfolio manager must establish policies with respect to the amount of losses that may be realized within any tax year and the amount of unrealized losses that are allowed to build up in the portfolio over the planning horizon. Both the forecast and policy attributes of the planning scenarios are critical in determining an optimal portfolio strategy. In this chapter we will vary each attribute of the planning scenarios by itself and examine the implications for portfolio structure.

The BONDS model, as formulated in the previous chapter, is a general purpose portfolio planning tool incorporating a great deal of complexity and a large number of options under the control of the analyst. Rather than complicating the implications of the model by dealing with a base case more complex than necessary, in this chapter we continue to concentrate on the particular base case developed in the previous chapter dealing only with U.S. Government securities. In the next chapter we will expand our analysis to include tax-exempt securities, additional asset categories, and the availability of purchased funds.

The solution of the base case given in the previous chapter suggests that optimal portfolios in a multiperiod environment have a barbell distribution of maturities consisting of clusters of securities on the long and short ends of the maturity range and no intermediate maturities. In this chapter we consider variations of this base case and examine to what extent the barbell portfolio structure is maintained. We first vary the liquidity use of the portfolio by increasing the level of funds that potentially may be withdrawn from or made available to the portfolio. Then the portfolio manager's risk aversion to both realized and unrealized losses is investigated, and guidelines for setting acceptable levels of losses are given. Next a collection of yield curves with shapes ranging from steeply rising to humped to inverted is considered. Finally, since steeply rising yield curves are often associated with expectations of rising interest rates and inverted yield curves are often associated with expectations of falling interest rates, these two cases are given special attention. In many of these variations it turns out that the basic barbell portfolio structure is maintained.

PLANNING FOR LIQUIDITY NEEDS

A good understanding of the basic nature of optimal portfolios suggested by the BONDS model can be gained by examining the manner in which the model plans for potential changes in the size of the portfolio. As has been pointed out in earlier chapters, planning for the liquidity needs of the bank is an important consideration in actively managing the portfolio. However, too often the liquidity needs of the bank are in conflict with the income needs of the bank.

In a period when interest rates are low, loan demand is generally weak and funds are available for investment in the portfolio. In such a period bank income is often low and the portfolio is looked on as a source of income to stabilize the bank's total income. This argues for investing the available funds in long-term securities to take advantage of their high coupon rate relative to short-term securities. Unfortunately, when interest rates are generally low, the portfolio manager expects them to increase in the future because interest rates tend to be cyclical. This argues for investing the available funds in relatively short-term securities to avoid the potential capital losses inherent in long-term securities in a period of rising rates. However, the short-term securities have relatively low yields. We will see in the final two sections of this chapter that the shape of the current yield curve and the portfolio manager's expectations concerning changes in future interest rates have an important influence on optimal portfolio decisions.

In this section we specifically look at the question of how the BONDS model plans for various levels of potential liquidity needs, keeping all other aspects of the base case unchanged. The base case has the generally rising yield curve pictured in Figure 7.2 and equal expectations about whether interest rates will rise, remain unchanged, or fall during all three periods of the model. We assume that if interest rates rise, funds are withdrawn from the portfolio to meet loan demand or deposit runoff; if rates remain unchanged, there is no net change in the funds available for investment; if rates fall, funds are made available to the portfolio for investment. In the base case, these potential funds flows are +$10,000, 0, and −$10,000, respectively. Here we analyze the implications of different amounts of funds flows ranging from a maximum inflow and outflow of $15,000 if rates change down to no exogenous funds flows. In the latter case the portfolio is not used at all to provide liquidity. For the purpose of this discussion, the allowable realized losses are limited to zero while the unrealized losses allowed to build up in the portfolio are limited to $1000.

The results of using the portfolio for liquidity are given in Table 8.1. First, let us comment on how the investments in long-term securities in the optimal strategy are determined. Note that in the first two periods the holdings of long-term securities, 19- and 20-year bonds, is the same for all variations of cash flows considered. The reason for this is that the holdings in the long-term securities are essentially dictated by the amount of unrealized losses that the bank will allow to build up in the portfolio. Irrespective of the cash flow forecast, it is optimal to put $17,207 in the 20-year securities in the initial portfolio. If interest rates rise three times, the potential losses associated with these holdings will build up to a level of $1000. Now if interest rates are unchanged from the first period to the second, a further investment of $8800 can be made in long-term securities since unrealized losses have not already built up in the portfolio. In fact if the interest rates have not changed there is a small unrealized capital gain associated with the 20-year securities simply from sliding down the yield curve. That is, these securities are now 19-year securities with a lower yield and correspondingly higher price because the yield curve is generally upward sloping. If the interest rates fall, considerably more funds, $28,253, are invested in long-

Table 8.1 Planning for Liquidity Needs

Period	Yield Curve	Cash Flow	Interest Income	Amounts in Each Maturity ($)					
				1 Year	2 Years	3 Years	...	19 Years	20 Years
1	Initial	100,000	0	5,769	0	77,024		—	17,207
2	Rise	0	3031	8,492	77,332	—		17,207	—
2	Unchanged	0	3031	—	77,024	—		17,207	8,800
2	Fall	0	3031	—	57,749	—		17,207	28,253
1	Initial	100,000	0	5,770	1,841	75,182		—	17,207
2	Rise	+5,000	3030	5,352	75,182	—		17,207	—
2	Unchanged	0	3030	1,841	75,182	—		17,207	8,800
2	Fall	−5,000	3030	—	62,694	—		17,207	28,253
1	Initial	100,000	0	6,974	7,173	68,646		—	17,207
2	Rise	+10,000	3026	7,173	68,646	—		17,207	—
2	Unchanged	0	3026	7,173	69,846	—		17,207	8,800
2	Fall	−10,000	3026	—	67,610	—		17,207	28,253
1	Initial	100,000	0	11,983	12,323	58,486		—	17,207
2	Rise	+15,000	3017	12,323	58,486	—		17,207	—
2	Unchanged	0	3017	12,323	64,686	—		17,207	8,800
2	Fall	−15,000	3017	—	72,616	—		17,207	28,253

term securities. This is possible without violating the unrealized loss constraint at the horizon since there is now a significant unrealized capital gain in the 20-year securities due to the falling rates.

Now look at the distribution of maturities on the short end of the portfolio. First consider the case of zero exogenous cash flow. In this case the portfolio is not being used as a liquidity buffer for the rest of the bank's operations since, regardless of interest rate changes, no funds are withdrawn from, or made available to, the portfolio. The initial portfolio still has a barbell shape consisting of 1-, 3-, and 20-year securities. The interest income from the portfolio amounts to $3031 after tax. If interest rates rise, this interest income and $5769 from the maturing 1-year securities are invested in 1- and 2-year securities. If interest rates are unchanged, these funds are invested in 20-year securities. Finally, if interest rates fall, these funds plus funds generated from the sale of some 2-year securities (initially 3-year) are invested in 20-year securities. In each instance the basic barbell character of the portfolio is maintained even though the portfolio is not used for liquidity purposes.

If we now plan for potential cash inflow or outflow of $5000 in each period, the maturity distribution of short-term securities changes somewhat. The initial portfolio now consists of 1-, 2-, 3-, and 20-year securities. The principal change is the shift of funds from 3- to 2-year securities in anticipation of possible future liquidity needs. If interest rates rise, the interest income of $3030 and the maturing 1-year securities of $5770 provide more than enough funds to cover the $5000 liquidity need. The additional funds are invested in 1-year securities. If interest rates remain unchanged, since no funds are needed for liquidity purposes, these funds are invested in 20-year securities. If interest rates fall, these funds plus funds generated from the sales of 2-year securities (initially 3-year) are invested in new 20-year securities.

Finally, if we further increase the potential cash inflow or outflow in each period to $10,000 or $15,000, significantly more funds are invested in 1- and 2-year securities in anticipation of potential liquidity needs. These funds are shifted out of the 3-year securities. In each case the interest income plus the funds from maturing securities exactly covers the cash outflow in the event that interest rates rise. If interest rates remain unchanged, as much of these funds as allowed by the loss constraints is invested in 20-year securities, with the remainder being invested in 2-year securities. In the event that interest rates fall, the funds required to invest the maximum in 20-year securities are generated from exogenous cash inflows, maturing securities, and sales of short-term securities.

In general, we conclude that the barbell structure of the optimal portfolio is maintained over a wide range of potential liquidity needs. The amount of the available funds invested in long-term securities is dictated by the bank's willingness to potentially realize losses and build up unrealized losses in the portfolio. It is not changed in response to greater or lesser use of the portfolio to meet liquidity needs. Planning for liquidity is basically accomplished by changing the maturity distribution on the short end of the portfolio in an intuitive way. Larger amounts of funds are held in 1- and 2-year securities when larger potential cash variations need to be planned for.

IMPLICATIONS OF RISK AVERSION

In the BONDS model, the portfolio manager's risk aversion is expressed by limits on the realized losses resulting from the sale of securities as well as limits on the potential unrealized losses that are allowed to build up in the portfolio over the planning horizon. In this section we look in detail at the implications for portfolio strategy of allowing various levels of realized and unrealized losses.

The base case reflects a conservative position in that it constrains the realized losses within any year to be zero. The unrealized losses that potentially could build up in the portfolio over the planning horizon are restricted to less than or equal to $1000 or approximately 1 percent of the value of the portfolio. For the base case the allowable realized and unrealized losses are limited to the same amount regardless of scenario, although, in general, different levels of losses might be allowed on different scenarios. For example, if interest rates rose steadily over a 2- or 3-year period, presumably more losses would be allowed than if interest rates fell over this same period.

Theoretically, it might be reasonable to ask a portfolio manager to assess formally a preference curve in order to quantify his attitude toward risk and then use this preference curve in analyzing the maturity structure of the portfolio. However, assessing a preference curve is a complicated task that would be quite foreign to the portfolio manager and of rather limited value. In the one effort in this direction that has been reported, Wolf [1969] was successful in having bank managers assess their preference curves as functions of total interest income and net capital gains over the planning horizon. Such a preference function leads to a nonlinear objective function, which poses some computational difficulties, but a variation of the procedures given in Appendix B can take this into account. A more important issue is whether portfolio managers believe the difficult assessment procedure is worth the effort and whether they would have confidence in results based on their use. From a theoretical standpoint some argue that the assessment procedure should go even further, asking managers to assess a preference for streams of interest income and net capital gains, both realized and unrealized. However, preference functions of this type are extremely difficult to assess and are even less likely to be acceptable to management.

Since we have found that many banks consider the risk of a portfolio to be its potential for realized and unrealized capital losses over time, we have chosen to limit these losses rather than complicate our analysis with preference theory. In making portfolio decisions, banks place a limit on the losses that they are willing to realize based on their taxable income position and other factors. They also monitor the market value of the portfolio to help insure that unrealized losses will not become too large. In general, the more losses a bank is willing to realize each year, and the larger unrealized losses the bank is willing to tolerate, the less risk averse it is considered to be.

Allowable Realized Losses

Let us first look at how the optimal portfolio strategy changes as we allow increasing amounts of realized losses within any one year. The unrealized losses at the horizon are limited to $1000 throughout this discussion. Referring to Table 8.2, we see that as increasing amounts of realized losses are allowed, more is invested in long-term securities and less is invested in the very short-term securities. The case with zero realized losses is simply the base case, where the cash outflow that occurs with an increase in rates in the second period is exactly financed with the $6974 of maturing 1-year securities and $3026 in interest income. If interest rates are unchanged and no exogenous cash flow occurs, then the funds available from interest income are invested, $1200 in 2-year securities and $8800 in 20-year securities. If interest rates fall with a corresponding $10,000 cash inflow to the portfolio, then the 2-year securities and some of the 3-year securities are sold, and $28,253 is invested in 20-year securities.

If we now increase the allowable realized losses to $100, a change in strategy occurs. If interest rates rise, with a corresponding $10,000 cash outflow, the cash outflow is financed in the second period with $2319 of maturing securities, $3059 of interest income, and the sale of 20-year securities generating $4622. The sale of the 20-year securities incurs the maximum allowable realized loss of $100. Even with these rather small levels of allowable realized losses, it becomes desirable to start with a larger share of the portfolio in long-term securities. Then, if interest rates rise, selling some of these securities provides a portion of the cash needed to finance the outflow of funds and simultaneously keeps the potential unrealized losses from rising too much. If interest rates continue to rise in subsequent periods, ad-

Table 8.2 Implications of Risk Aversion: Effects of Limits on Annual Realized Losses

Maximum Annual Losses	Yield Curve	Cash Flow	Interest Income	Amounts in Each Maturity ($)					
				1 Year	2 Years	3 Years	...	19 Years	20 Years
0	Initial	100,000	0	6,974	7,173	68,646		—	17,207
	Rise	−10,000	3026	7,173	68,656	—		17,027	—
	Unchanged	0	3026	7,173	69,856	—		17,027	8,800
	Fall	10,000	3026	—	67,610	—		17,028	28,253
100	Initial	100,000	0	2,319	4,812	68,487		—	24,382
	Rise	−10,000	3059	4,812	68,487	—		19,660	—
	Unchanged	0	3059	3,739	68,487	—		24,382	6,451
	Fall	10,000	3059	—	55,267	—		24,382	33,555
200	Initial	100,000	0	—	106	68,338		—	31,557
	Rise	−10,000	3091	2,434	68,338	—		22,113	—
	Unchanged	0	3091	—	67,432	—		31,557	4,101
	Fall	10,000	3091	—	42,912	—		31,557	38,857
300	Initial	100,000	0	—	—	61,268		—	38,732
	Rise	−10,000	3117	58	68,193	—		24,566	—
	Unchanged	0	3117	—	61,268	—		38,732	1,752
	Fall	10,000	3117	—	30,510	—		38,732	44,159

ditional amounts of these long-term securities are sold to help meet the liquidity needs and reduce the buildup of unrealized losses. The holdings of these securities must be reduced to $17,207 in order to stay within the unrealized loss constraint at the horizon in the event of three successive interest rate rises.

If we increase the allowable realized losses within each year still further to $200, the effect on the optimal strategy becomes more pronounced. The initial portfolio contains no 1-year securities and only $106 of the 2-year securities. The cash outflow from the portfolio associated with an increase in interest rates is financed by the interest income on the portfolio plus the cash generated from the sale of 20-year securities since no securities are maturing. The amount of cash generated in this manner exceeds the required $10,000 cash outflow, and the $2334 of excess funds are invested in 1-year securities. If interest rates are unchanged, all of the 2-year and small amounts of the 3-year securities are sold and reinvested in 20-year securities. If interest rates fall, with a corresponding $10,000 cash inflow, more of the 3-year securities are sold and the entire amount of $38,857 is invested in 20-year securities.

As the allowable realized losses are increased further, this basic strategy is continued. When interest rates rise, 20-year securities are sold and any excess funds beyond liquidity needs are invested in short-term securities. If rates are unchanged, the funds are invested in a barbell portfolio of short- and long-term securities similar to the initial portfolio. If rates fall, some securities are sold and the funds are invested in the long-term securities.

Essentially, increasing the allowable realized losses permits greater flexibility to meet potential cash outflows and simultaneously satisfy the unrealized loss constraints at the horizon. Additional funds can be invested in long-term securities at the outset and, in the event that interest rates rise, be sold to provide some of the funds needed to finance the cash outflow as well as reduce the buildup of unrealized losses in the portfolio. Further, as the allowable realized losses are increased, larger amounts of long-term securities can be sold in the event that interest rates rise. Since this provides funds that can be used for liquidity purposes, the short end of the portfolio is increasingly relieved of this responsibility. Hence the average maturity of the short-term securities can be increased.

Allowable Unrealized Losses

Now let us consider varying the limits on the allowable unrealized losses at the horizon. Here we limit the realized losses within any year to zero, as in the base case. The results of varying the allowable unrealized losses are given in Table 8.3. The first point to notice is that if both realized and un-

Table 8.3 Implications of Risk Aversion: Effects of Limits on Unrealized Losses at the Horizon

Maximum Unrealized Losses	Yield Curve	Cash Flow	Interest Income	Amounts in Each Maturity ($)					
				1 Year	2 Years	3 Years	⋯	19 Years	20 Years
0	Initial	100,000	0	7,037	7,234	85,725		—	—
	Rise	−10,000	2963	7,234	85,725	—		—	—
	Unchanged	0	2963	7,234	95,725	—		—	—
	Fall	10,000	2963	6,757	106,209	—		—	—
500	Initial	100,000	0	7,006	7,206	77,185		—	8,603
	Rise	−10,000	2994	7,206	77,185	—		8,603	—
	Unchanged	0	2994	7,206	82,785	—		8,603	4,400
	Fall	10,000	2994	—	84,425	—		8,603	14,126
1000	Initial	100,000	0	6,974	8,173	68,646		—	17,207
	Rise	−10,000	3026	7,173	68,646	—		17,207	—
	Unchanged	0	3026	7,173	69,846	—		17,207	8,800
	Fall	10,000	3026	—	67,610	—		17,207	28,253
1500	Initial	100,000	0	10,147	6,795	57,248		—	25,810
	Rise	−10,000	3054	9,592	57,651	—		25,810	—
	Unchanged	0	3054	6,795	57,248	—		25,810	13,200
	Fall	10,000	3054	—	45,009	—		25,810	42,379

realized losses are required to be zero on all planning scenarios, there cannot be any investment in securities that mature after the end of the planning horizon. When risk is measured by realized and unrealized capital losses, as it is in the BONDS model, only those securities that mature at or before the horizon are risk free. As soon as either some realized or unrealized losses are allowed, the portfolio can invest in long-term securities.

The optimal strategy is essentially the same as the base case for the examples given. If interest rates rise, with the associated $10,000 cash outflow from the portfolio, the cash outflow is financed by interest income and maturing securities. If interest rates remain unchanged, these funds generated to anticipate the liquidity needs can then be invested in long-term securities up to the limits imposed by the realized and unrealized loss constraints. Any remaining funds are invested in short-term securities. If interest rates fall, with the associated cash inflow to the portfolio, the available funds are again invested in long-term securities to the extent possible, with the remainder being invested in short-term securities.

As the limits on the unrealized losses at the horizon are increased, the amount invested in long-term securities also increases. This results simply from being able to hold more of the long-term securities without violating the increased loss constraint at the horizon. In these examples there is no trading out of some of the long-term securities in the event that interest rates rise. Since no net losses can be realized, the long-term securities can be traded only when there is a gain to balance against the loss. Hence increasing the unrealized losses at the horizon does not change the form of the optimal strategy but only the relative share that can be held in long-term securities.

We can summarize the effect of both the realized and unrealized loss constraints by examining the four cases given in Table 8.4. Either increasing allowable realized losses within any year or increasing allowable unrealized losses at the horizon increases the amount of funds in the initial portfolio that can be invested in the highest yielding securities. Since the yield curve is rising, the highest yielding securities are the long maturities. In comparing cases A and B and cases C and D in Table 8.4, where the allowable realized losses are increased from $0 to $100, the amount invested in the 20-year securities is increased and less is invested in 1- and 2-year securities. In comparing cases A and C and cases B and D, where the allowable unrealized losses at the horizon are increased from $500 to $1000, the amount invested in the 20-year securities is increased while the amount invested in the 3-year securities is reduced. The difference in the basic strategies comes only in subsequent periods. If some realized losses are allowed, long-term securities can be sold in future periods to help finance a portion of the bank's liquidity needs.

Table 8.4 Implications of Risk Aversion: Effects of Limits on Realized and Unrealized Losses

Case	Annual Realized Losses	Unrealized Horizon Losses	Maturities in Optimal Initial Portfolios ($)			
			1 Year	2 Years	3 Years $\cdots$	20 Years
A	0	500	7006	7206	77,185	8,603
B	100	500	2351	4844	77,027	15,778
C	0	1000	6974	7173	68,646	17,207
D	100	1000	2319	4812	68,487	24,382

Since the amount of losses that can be realized within any year depends on the taxable income of the bank as a whole, available income must be forecast before the level of allowable losses can be set. It is important to keep in mind that the BONDS model assumes that all realized losses are taken as credits against taxable income. If a bank does not anticipate sufficient taxable income on a particular scenario, the level of allowable realized losses associated with this scenario should be set to zero in most cases.

Establishing Levels of Acceptable Losses

If, as suggested in the previous section, we are to use loss constraints as surrogates for the bank's risk aversion, it would be helpful to give some assistance in deciding whether or not the allowable realized and unrealized losses are appropriate or overly restrictive. The way to answer this question is to look at the expected total earnings of the portfolio as a function of the allowable losses.

In Figure 8.1, we have graphed the expected total earnings of the portfolio over the planning horizon as a function of the allowable annual realized losses. This graph has a concave shape and consists of linear segments, as would be expected from linear programming theory. The slope of each segment represents the increase in the expected total earnings of the portfolio over the planning horizon per unit increase in the allowable realized losses. In this case the changes in slope from one linear segment to the next one are not very dramatic.

Since the base case constrains the realized losses to be zero, the slope of this curve at zero losses indicates that there is an increase in the expected earnings on the portfolio of $11.70 per dollar increase in the limits on allowable realized losses within each year. The level of allowable realized losses is often set external to the portfolio planning process; however, the marginal costs associated with these constraints should give guidance as to what levels to allow.

If we now consider varying the level of allowable unrealized losses in the portfolio, an important observation can be made from a similar analysis. In Figure 8.2 the expected total earnings of the portfolio is graphed as a function of the allowable unrealized losses at the horizon. There appears to be a clear breakpoint at an unrealized loss level of about $700. The marginal worth of relaxing the unrealized loss constraints below $700 is approximately $0.92 per dollar of allowable unrealized loss, while above $700 the marginal worth of relaxing the unrealized loss constraint drops to $0.73 per dollar of allowable unrealized loss. In an instance such as this the bank may want to insure that it allows planning for potential unrealized losses of at least $700 to take advantage of the relatively high marginal worth of relaxing these constraints over this range.

Since the realized and unrealized loss constraints are policy guidelines rather than fixed inviolable limits, it is often very useful to point out the

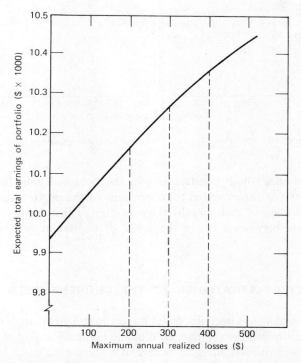

Figure 8.1. Expected portfolio earnings as a function of allowable realized losses.

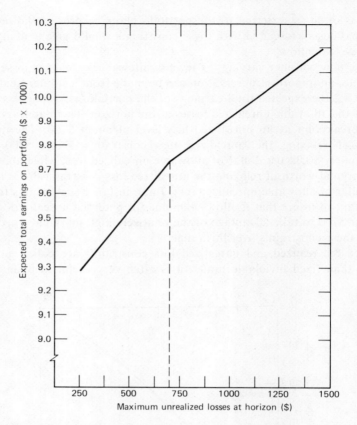

Figure 8.2. Expected portfolio earnings as a function of allowable unrealized losses.

costs of including these constraints and the potential gain from relaxing them. Looking at the expected total earnings of the portfolio as a function of allowable realized and unrealized losses gives a firm basis for discussing the trade-offs between risk, in the sense of capital losses, and expected return.

SENSITIVITY OF STRATEGIES TO THE CURRENT YIELD CURVE

The base case that has been discussed has an initial yield curve that is rising across the entire maturity range, so that the highest yielding maturities are the 20-year securities. This is, of course, not always the case. In fact in the base case there are expectations about other shaped yield curves. In Figure

7.2 of the previous chapter the yield curves that may occur in the base case are indicated. Note that if one rate increase occurs the yield curve becomes humped, while if two rate increases occur the yield curve becomes essentially inverted. On the other hand, if one rate decrease occurs the yield curve becomes steeper, and if two successive rate decreases occur the yield curve becomes steeper still. In general, even in the base case where the initial yield curve is rising there are expectations that future yield curves might be anywhere from steeply rising to humped or even inverted. It is of interest to see how the optimal strategy changes when the initial yield curve takes on one of these alternative shapes. It should be pointed out that all of these various shapes of yield curves occur from time to time as the interest rates on U.S. Government securities vary.

We shall consider the collection of yield curves depicted in Figure 8.3, where the base case yield curve is labeled B and all other yield curves have been constructed so as to have exactly the same yield for the 20-year securities. The reason for so constructing the yield curves is to fairly easily make comparisons from one curve to another. In this section we vary only the shape of the current yield curve but not the portfolio manager's expectations

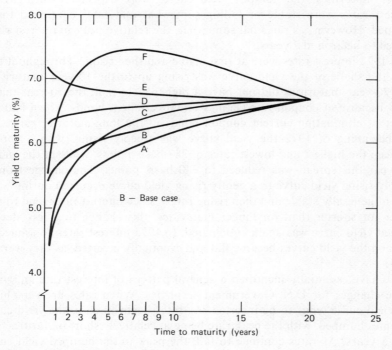

Figure 8.3.   Various initial yield curves.

of future changes in interest rates, In all cases it is assumed equally likely that the 3-month rate will rise 120 basis points, remain unchanged, or fall 120 basis points. The relationship between the shape of the current yield curve and our expectations about changes in interest rate levels is discussed in the next section.

Although these particular yield curves do not represent actual interest rates at specific points in time, their general shapes have often occurred. If we consider one cycle of interest rate fluctuations, say from the beginning of 1969 to the middle of 1973, we can gain some insight into how these various shapes follow one another. In the beginning of 1969 and in fact essentially throughout the year the yield curve was inverted with only minor exceptions. As the year progressed, rates were rising and the yield curve went from nearly flat to significantly inverted. In February 1969 the spread between the long-term and short-term rates was minus 33 basis points while in December 1969 the spread was minus 117 basis points. In 1970 the yields became generally humped with the peak in rates usually falling between the 3- and 5-year maturities. During this period rates were generally falling, and since the rates for shorter maturities tend to fall faster than the rates for longer maturities, the humped yield curves were expected. During 1971 interest rates were stable or falling somewhat and rates continued to be humped. However, as rates fell somewhat, the relative peak in interest rates tended to be around 7 years.

In 1972 interest rates were at first stable and then rising. Throughout this year the shape of the yield curve was rising up to the 10-year maturities. The 20-year maturities did not have a higher yield than the 10-year maturities because of coupon rate ceilings on Government bonds, which had the effect of eliminating current coupon bonds in the long-maturity range. In the beginning of 1972 the yield curve was steeply rising, with a spread between the highest and lowest rates of 287 basis points, while at the end of the year this spread was reduced to 140 basis points. The change from a steeply rising yield curve to a gently rising yield curve occurred during a period of generally stable and then rising rates. Since interest rates tend to rise faster for shorter than for longer maturities, this change to a less steeply shaped yield curve was again anticipated. In 1973 interest rates continued to rise and the yield curves became flat and eventually inverted, as they were in 1969.

We have essentially identified a general pattern of interest rate and yield curve changes for U.S. Government securities. When rates are very high, the yield curve tends to be inverted. As rates begin to ease, the yield curve becomes humped, with the peak rate being at relatively short maturities, say 3 to 5 years. As rates continue to fall, the peak in the humped yield curve moves toward the longer maturities, say 7 years, and then finally the yield curve becomes rising. Now as rates begin to rise again, the yield curve becomes humped again and then finally inverted. If one looks at a time series of yield curves, he observes that this general result has been repeated a number of times.

The collection of yield curves shown in Figure 8.3 is robust enough to account for the variations in yield curves that have occurred as well as to address the questions of the relative steepness of yield curves. The base case was rerun for each of the current yield cuves show in Figure 8.3, assuming that interest rates were equally likely to rise, remain unchanged, or fall. Table 8.5 gives only the optimal initial portfolios for various yield curves. It should not be thought of as the optimal composition of a particular portfolio at the point in time, but rather as the way in which new funds might be invested if they were made available while facing that particular yield curve. Clearly such an allocation would depend on the portfolio currently held, but in order to avoid complicating the interpretation of these results, we will keep our assumption for the moment that the initial portfolio consists entirely of cash. This will allow the impact of the shape of the portfolio to be examined without reference to a particular portfolio of current holdings.

In order to understand the results presented in Table 8.5 we can group them by their similarities. Consider the initial portfolios for yield curves A, B, and D. In each of these cases the yield curve is rising with increasing maturity but not extremely steeply. In each case the initial portfolio is barbell shaped with essentially a laddered collection of maturities on the short end of the portfolio and the 20-year maturity on the long end. In case D the laddering on the short end extends into 4-year maturities. Since these 4-year maturities will still be in the portfolio at the horizon, the amount invested in the 20-year maturity must be appropriately reduced to stay within the binding loss constraint. Note that in these three cases as the yield curve becomes

Table 8.5   Optimal Portfolios for Various Yield Curves

Yield Curve	Maturities in Optimal Initial Portfolios ($)						
	1 Year	2 Years	3 Years	4 Years	5 Years	$\cdots$	20 Years
A	6,746	19,264	57,602	—	—		16,388
B	6,974	7,173	68,646	—	—		17,207
C	7,026	7,209	9,901	64,769	11,095		—
D	7,179	7,359	42,342	32,550	—		10,570
E	100,000	—	—	—	—		—
F	6,374	6,581	751	86,294	—		—

less steep, the laddering on the short end of the portfolio is lengthened. It is interesting to note that when the yield curve actually becomes inverted, as in case E, the optimal portfolio shifts entirely to the shortest maturity. Apparently as the yield curve changes from generally rising to flat, there is a tendency for the portfolio to become more and more laddered on the short end. Since a truely flat yield curve can never exist, this tendency never becomes very pronounced.

Looking at cases C and F, we can now examine the question of steepness of the yield curve further. In these two cases the optimal initial portfolios are very similar. Each portfolio is laddered on the short end of the maturity range and neither have investments in the 20-year maturity. Since case F is a humped yield curve, we would not expect any investment in the 20-year maturity but rather we might expect a similar investment in the maturity with the highest yield. In this case the highest yielding securities are those of 7 years maturity. However, the optimal initial portfolio contains no 7-year maturities. Apparently the yield curves in cases C and F rise so steeply for short-term securities that investments in 4-year and 5-year maturities have a higher capital gain potential than investment in the 20-year maturity.

In each case the amounts invested in the 4- and 5-year maturities are dictated by the loss constraints since these securities are held till the horizon. Part of the high capital-gain potential from these relatively short-term securities results from the phenomenon of sliding down the yield curve. Rather than putting the available funds in 20-year maturities with the relatively high interest income guarantee and capital gain potential, it is optimal to invest these funds in 4- and 5-year maturities with a high likelihood of substantial capital gains due to the increase in price resulting simply from the securities becoming shorter term. The steepness of the yield curve in this range indicates a high capital gain potential.

Further, case A can in a sense be viewed as a very steep yield curve for maturities of 2 years and less. Note that in this case more funds are invested in the 2-year maturities than are necessary to finance a possible cash outflow in the second period. These additional funds invested in the 2-year maturities are to take advantage of the relatively high capital gain potential due to the steepness of the yield curve in this range. The funds available from these securities one period later are then put in 20-year maturities to the extent possible, dictated by the loss constraints on each particular scenario.

Finally, in case E, which has an initial yield curve that is inverted, the entire investment is made in the shortest maturity available. This is reasonable, given our expectations, since not only does this security have the highest yield but it is simultaneously the most liquid. Therefore, rather than the goals of liquidity on the one hand and high return on the other being in conflict, in case E they are in concert and the investment is made in 1-year maturities.

Throughout all of these cases we varied only the shape of the initial yield curve. In each case our expectations concerning changes in future interest rates were that it was equally likely that rates would rise, remain unchanged, or fall. As a result the strategies given in this section for Cases A and E may seem somewhat counter intuitive. We therefore examine this question in more detail in the next section.

ANTICIPATING SWINGS IN INTEREST RATES

In the previous section we assumed that it was equally likely that the 3-month rate would increase 120 basis points, remain unchanged, or decrease 120 basis points. Further, the changes in the 3-year rate were assumed to be 80 percent of the changes in the 3-month rate, while the changes in the 20-year rate were assumed to be 30 percent of the changes in the 3-month rate. These assumptions were held constant for all initial yield curves given in Figure 8.3. Many would correctly argue that these assumptions would normally be unrealistic for some of the cases considered. In particular, to most portfolio managers the inverted yield curve of Case E would indicate a high probability of falling rates. Similarly, the large difference between the 3-month and the 20-year rates of Case A would indicate a high probability of rising rates.

If a portfolio manager believed that interest rates were going to fall in the near term, he would tend to invest some of his funds in relatively long-term securities to take advantage of the expected capital gain. This is not indicated by the results of Case E since no such expectations of falling rates were incorporated in the model, even though the yield curve is inverted. Similarly, if the portfolio manager believed that interest rates were going to rise, he would tend to keep his portfolio relatively short to avoid the expected capital losses inherent in the longer-term securities in a time of rising interest rates. Again this is not indicated by the results of Case A since no such expectations were incorporated in this model. In this section we then look more closely at these two cases, varying our expectations about the changes in future interest rates and noting the impact on the optimal portfolio strategy.

There are a number of ways to incorporate in the model our expectations concerning future interest rate changes. The easiest way to think about these expectations is to leave the percentage relationships between the 3-month, 3-year, and 20-year changes in the interest rates the same but vary the cumulative probability distribution of changes in the 3-month rate. Assuming that we keep the variance of this distribution the same, we can shift the entire distribution in one direction or the other. We will assume in Case A, where the yield curve is relatively steeply rising, that we expect that interest rates will be rising. We will assume in Case F, where the yield curve is inverted, that we expect that interest rates will be falling. In order to shift the cummulative probability distribution of changes in the 3-month rate, we can either change the probabilities associated with these changes or change the magnitudes of these changes. In case A, in which we expect interest rates to rise, we have simply changed the probabilities from equally likely for the three events to .6 for an increase of 120 basis points, .3 for no change, and .1 for a decrease of 120 basis points. In case E, in which we expect interest rates to fall, we have simply changed the probabilities from equally likely for the three events to .1 for an increase of 120 basis points, .3 for no change, and .6 for a decrease of 120 basis points.

The effect of varying our expectations concerning future changes in the interest rates is given in Table 8.6. For ease of comparison, the results for cases A and E from the previous section with equal expectations of interest rates are included. The resulting portfolios in each case show a dramatic shift in the optimal strategy in the direction one would expect. In case A, in the face of a steeply rising yield curve and equal expectations concerning changes in interest rates up or down, the usual barbell portfolio strategy is indicated, with as much invested in 20-year securities as the realized and unrealized loss constraints will allow. However, when there are significant expectations that interest rates will rise, the available funds are invested entirely in short-term securities of 1 and 2 years duration. The reason for this is to avoid the potentially high capital losses from being invested in long-term securities in a period of rising rates. After one rise in interest rates, the $92,976 resulting from maturing securities and the interest income are invested in 2- and 3-year securities after satisfying the external funds

Table 8.6   Implications of Interest Rate Expectations

Rate Forecast	Yield Curve	Maturities in Optimal Initial Portfolio ($)				
		1 Year	2 Years	3 Years ⋯	15 Years ⋯	20 Years
Stable	A	6,746	19,264	57,602	—	16,388
Rising	A	92,976	7,024	—	—	—
Stable	E	100,000	—	—	—	—
Falling	E	6,581	6,811	65,486	21,122	—

needs. If interest rates are unchanged, the available funds are invested in the 1-year security. In the unlikely case that interest rates happen to fall, most of these funds are invested in short-term securities, but some are invested in 20-year securities because of the now high relative yields of these securities. The most important point is that the initial portfolio is invested in short-term securities in anticipation of the interest rate increase.

Now let us look at the case of falling interest rates. In case E, in the face of an inverted yield curve and equal expectations concerning changes in interest rates up or down, the investment strategy is to invest the entire portfolio in 1-year securities for their relatively higher yield and obvious liquidity. However, when there are significant expectations that interest rates will fall, the available funds are invested in a barbell portfolio consisting of 1-, 2-, 3-, and 15-year securities. The investment in relatively long-term securities is in anticipation of interest rates falling with the potentially high capital gains accruing from long-term securities. The choice of 15-year securities on the long end of the portfolio as opposed to 20-year securities results from a slightly higher capital gain potential, a consequence of the changing shape of the yield curve from inverted to rising with falling interest rates.

It is important to note that the nature of the optimal initial portfolio suggested by the model is rather sensitive to the shape of the current yield curve and the expectations concerning future interest rate changes. These elements must be assessed, by the portfolio manager, in conjunction with one another in order to obtain meaningful results from this type of model. Thus the scenario planning concept of assessing all the descriptors associated with a particular scenario in a consistent manner is rather important for effective planning.

9

POLICY ISSUES IN PORTFOLIO MANAGEMENT

In the previous chapter we showed that, under a variety of assumptions concerning the attributes of the planning scenarios, the optimal portfolios suggested by the BONDS model tended to have a barbell structure. There the form of the analysis was to examine a number of variations of the base case consisting only of U.S. Government securities. We examined the implications of using the portfolio to meet a portion of the bank's liquidity need, the portfolio manager's risk aversion to both realized and unrealized capital losses, the shape of the current yield curve, and the portfolio manager's expectations of future interest rate movements. The spirit of these analyses was to make specific variations in the attributes of the planning scenarios of the base case in order to better understand the strategies suggested by the BONDS model.

In this chapter we expand the concept of a base case to examine a number of other issues of portfolio management. In a certain sense this chapter is a collection of somewhat unrelated topics. It represents a group of policy issues that are representative of those that can be addressed by the BONDS model and reflects our judgment as to what is of general interest. We first look at the availability of purchased funds for use in the portfolio, both to consider expanding the size of the portfolio and to meet the liquidity needs of the bank. Next we develop a base case for good grade municipal securities and compare its optimal strategy with that of the base case for U.S. Governments. Then we combine the base case for municipals with the base case for Governments to form a portfolio of jointly managed Governments and municipals. For this jointly managed base case we first examine the implications of pledging requirements and discuss the difficulties of separately managing the Government and municipal portfolios. The need for taxable income is then considered by varying the effective tax rate imposed on the portfolio. Finally we consider the impact of the length of the bank's planning horizon.

AVAILABILITY OF PURCHASED FUNDS

Up until now we have exclusively dealt with the asset side of investment management and ignored the availability of purchased funds, that is, liabilities. In recent years commercial banks have increased their use of purchased funds both to meet the fluctuating financing needs of the bank and to increase the size of their operations. As a result the size of the investment portfolio has tended to be relatively fixed, whereas formerly it fluctuated depending on the bank's liquidity needs. In this section we examine how the availability of purchased funds can affect current portfolio decisions as well as the overall size of the portfolio.

Basically, the amount of purchased funds to utilize is a policy decision that must be made for the bank as a whole. However, we can examine the benefits of using purchased funds for the investment portfolio under two rather different assumptions. First, in some instances it is reasonable to assume that the portfolio manager is not given any direct control over the use of purchased funds. In this case the bank's use of purchased funds helps to determine exogenously both the size of the investment portfolio and the extent to which the investment portfolio is used for liquidity planning. Second, an alternative assumption is that the portfolio manager may at his discretion make direct use of purchased funds up to some specified limit consistent with the bank's overall policy for their use.

We shall first take up the case where the portfolio manager does not have the ability to directly make use of purchased funds. In this instance, the bank's policy with respect to the use of purchased funds is included in the BONDS model through the initial portfolio size and the net need for funds attribute of each scenario. The net need figure represents the combined impact on the investment portfolio of the bank's planned actions outside the portfolio as well as the bank's forecasts of loans and deposits. This combined impact either makes additional funds available to the investment portfolio or requires that funds be withdrawn from it.

If the bank's policy is to use purchased funds to meet all likely liquidity needs, the exogenous cash flows planned for by the portfolio manager are zero. On the other hand, if the investment portfolio may in some circumstances be used to meet liquidity needs, then nonzero cash flows are included in the appropriate scenarios. To see the impact on portfolio strategy of using the investment portfolio rather than purchased funds to meet a portion of the liquidity needs, we can compare the base case, which assumes a $10,000 cash outflow if interest rates rise and a $10,000 cash inflow if rates fall, with the same case assuming no exogenous cash flows. The optimal actions at the first two decision points for each case are given in Table 9.1.

We have already discussed in the previous chapter the changes in strategy depending on the use made of the investment portfolio for liquidity purposes, and this discussion will not be repeated here. However, it is useful to make a few comments comparing the two strategies. These strategies are identical with respect to investments in long-term securities. Essentially, each strategy invests the maximum amount possible, as dictated by the loss constraints, in long-term securities. The difference between the two strategies results from planning for liquidity with the relatively short-term securities. When the portfolio is used for liquidity, investments in 1-year and 2-year securities are made as a hedge against possible cash outflows in subsequent periods. When the portfolio is not used for liquidity, investments in 1-year securities are made to provide funds in the next period to invest in long-term securities in the event that interest rates remain unchanged or fall. Further, there is no investment in 2-year securities in this case. The net effect is that the short-term securities can be somewhat longer when there are no exogenous cash flows to plan for.

On the surface the strategies do not appear to be dramatically different regardless of whether potential liquidity needs are planned for or not. The natural question to ask is to what extent is the return on the portfolio affected by having to plan for possible liquidity needs? It turns out that the expected rates of return on the portfolio in the two cases are quite similar. In the base case the expected after-tax rate of return is 3.31% per year as compared with 3.33% when the portfolio is not used for liquidity. This would seem to imply that the investment portfolio can be used for liquidity purposes without seriously reducing the return on investment of the portfolio. However, this is overstating the case somewhat as all possible future cash outflows in the base case are balanced by equally likely cash inflows of similar amounts. We can conclude, though, that there are situations in which it is fairly inexpensive in terms of opportunity cost to use the investment portfolio for some portion of the potential liquidity needs. This results from the fact that the amount of long-term securities is determined by the limits on unrealized and realized losses.

Still assuming that the portfolio is used for liquidity purposes, we can address the question of the overall size of the portfolio by considering the information provided by the shadow prices on the constraints that limit

Table 9.1 Implications of Planning for Liquidity

Yield Curve	Amounts in Each Maturity ($)						Interest Income	Funds Flow
	1 Year	2 Years	3 Years	...	19 Years	20 Years		
	Portfolio Strategy When Used for Liquidity							
Initial	6974	7,173	68,646		—	17,207	0	100,000
Rise	7173	68,646	—		17,207	—	3026	−10,000
Unchanged	7173	69,846	—		17,207	8,800	3026	0
Fall	—	67,610	—		17,207	28,253	3026	10,000
	Portfolio Strategy When Not Used for Liquidity							
Initial	5769	—	77,024		—	17,207	0	100,000
Rise	8492	77,332	—		17,207	—	3031	0
Unchanged	—	77,024	—		17,207	8,800	3031	0
Fall	—	57,749	—		17,207	28,253	3031	0

available funds. The shadow prices indicate the incremental return that could be obtained by having an additional dollar of funds available. In Table 9.2 the shadow prices conditional on a particular scenario as well as the yield rates for the available 1- and 20-year maturities are given for the base case. First note that the shadow price on the funds made available in the first period is 3.13%. The interpretation of this number is that if one more dollar were made available in the first period and all subsequent periods, the expected after-tax rate of return earned on this additional dollar would be 3.13% per year over the 3 years of the planning horizon. Note that this rate of return lies between the 1-year and 20-year rates, reflecting that the optimal strategy consists of hedging between long- and short-term securities.

If interest rates rise and funds are withdrawn from the portfolio, the shadow price on additional funds at the beginning of the second period is even higher than the corresponding 20-year rate. This is due not only to the fact that an additional dollar is available for investment in the beginning of period 2, but also that funds in period 1 can be shifted out of 1-year securities and into higher yielding 3-year securities. This shift can take place because the potential liquidity need if interest rates rise has been reduced by the one dollar of additional funds. The incremental yield on this shift is 25 basis points, thus accounting for the high shadow price. The shadow prices for unchanged and falling rates lie between the 1- and 20-year rates, reflecting that the additional dollar in these two instances is merely invested in the hedging strategy. This would seem to indicate that having purchased funds available to meet liquidity needs is significantly more valuable than merely having additional funds for the portfolio at other times.

Although the rate of return on invested funds is a reasonable criterion for deciding on the size of the portfolio, an important question is raised by comparing the 3.31% rate of return on the portfolio as a whole to the

Table 9.2 Annual Return on Incremental Funds

Period	Yield Curve	Shadow Price (%)	Yield on Available Maturities (%)	
			1-Year	20-Year
1	Initial	3.13	2.85	3.34
2	Rise	3.77	3.39	3.52
2	Unchanged	2.97	2.35	3.34
2	Fall	2.82	2.31	3.16

shadow price on additional funds made available in Period 1 and all sub-sequent periods, which is 3.13%. The difference between these two rates reflects the implicit assumption in using shadow prices for decision making that all other coefficients in the model are left unchanged. If the dollar limits on the potential unrealized losses at the horizon are not increased, none of the additional funds that might be made available in the first period can be invested in the 20-year securities. Therefore the rate of return on the portfolio is somewhat misleading by itself since additional funds made available to the portfolio may not attain the same yield.

However, a bank might be willing to increase the dollar limit on un-realized losses in the investment portfolio if its size is increased. As an example, these losses might be limited to a percent of the book value of the initial portfolio. In this instance we would increase the level of losses permitted if the size of the portfolio were increased. In the base case the realized losses are set to zero, but the unrealized losses are limited to $1000, which is 1% of the initial book value of the portfolio. We can examine the value of additional funds in period 1 and all subsequent periods in this case by varying the size of the portfolio while keeping the unrealized losses less than or equal to 1% of the initial book value. We, in fact, performed this analysis letting the size of the portfolio vary from $90,000 to $120,000 while keeping the unrealized losses at the horizon less than or equal to 1% of this number. The results are given in Figure 9.1. The after-tax rate of return of funds over this range was constant, corresponding to 10.01% over the 3-year planning horizon, which on average is 3.34% per year. This is the rate on new 20-year securities, which could be purchased and held to the end of the planning horizon since the absolute dollar limit on potential unrealized losses is increased with increasing portfolio size.

We can conclude that the average rate of return on the portfolio may not be the best criterion for deciding on additional investments in the portfolio. In the Government base case the average rate of return on the portfolio is 3.31%; however, if potential unrealized losses at the horizon are held constant, the value of incremental funds drops to 3.13%. If these potential unrealized losses are a percent of book value, this rate rises to 3.34%. Only if all constraint limits are increased proportionally will the rate of return on additional funds be equal to the average rate of return on the portfolio.

Now let us turn to the case where the portfolio manager may at his dis-cretion make use of purchased funds up to some specified limit consistent with the bank's overall policy for their use. Although the methodology of the BONDS model could easily be extended to include a full range of lia-bilities, including a range of maturities for some types of funds, this was not in fact done. Since the bulk of purchased funds are short-term and the cost of these funds are highly correlated with each other, we felt that a bank's

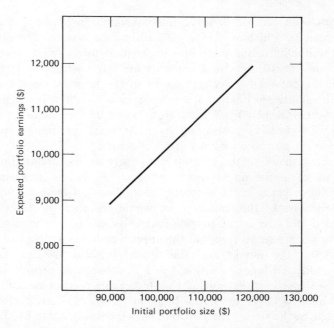

Figure 9.1. Expected portfolio earnings assuming losses are a percent of portfolio size.

use of purchased liabilities could be approximated by inclusion of a single short-term liability in the BONDS model. The cost of this liability is tied to the scenario planning structure, and it represents an average of the costs of the various liabilities a bank might use.

The BONDS model allows the option of using purchased funds in any period. The maturity of these funds is equal to the length of the period in which they are used, and their cost is specified as a spread above the return on the asset of the same maturity. Clearly, if the cost of the purchased funds was less than the return on the asset of the same maturity, we would have an arbitrage situation in which all of the liability available could be purchased and invested in the asset with the same maturity. We have not limited the amount of purchased funds used, but we have kept their cost sufficiently high to avoid this arbitrage situation.

In Table 9.3 we present some results for the case where the portfolio is used for liquidity purposes and purchased funds are available at the discretion of the portfolio manager. The three cases correspond to spreads between the cost of the purchased funds and the asset of the same maturity of 75, 50, and 25 basis points. In the first case the strategy differs only slightly from that given in Table 9.1, when no purchased funds were

Table 9.3 Availability of Purchased Funds: Effects of the cost of the Liability

Liability Spread (bp)	Yield Curve	Amounts in Each Maturity ($)						Liability Sold	Interest Income	Funds Flow
		1 Year	2 Years	3 Years	...	19 Years	20 Years			
75	Initial	6974	5,644	70,175		—	17,207	—	0	100,000
	Rise	5644	70,175	—		17,207	—	—	3026	−10,000
	Unchanged	6844	70,175	—		17,027	8,800	—	3026	0
	Fall	—	67,617	—		17,207	28,253	—	3026	10,000
50	Initial	5769	—	77,024		—	17,207	—	0	100,000
	Rise	—	77,337	—		17,207	—	1,513	3031	−10,000
	Unchanged	—	77,024	—		17,207	8,800	—	3031	0
	Fall	—	77,024	—		17,207	28,253	9,452	3031	10,000
25	Initial	—	—	82,793		—	17,207	—	0	100,000
	Rise	—	82,793	—		17,207	—	6,962	3038	−10,000
	Unchanged	—	82,793	—		17,207	8,800	5,762	3038	0
	Fall	—	82,793	—		17,207	28,253	15,215	3038	10,000

available, since only minor use is made of these funds. As the purchased funds become less and less expensive, more use is made of them. In all cases the amount of funds invested in the long-term securities is the same and is essentially dictated by the allowable levels of realized and unrealized losses. However, the distribution of maturities on the short end of the portfolio changes significantly, which implies that the manner in which the liquidity need of the bank is met also changes.

Consider the case of a 50 basis-point spread for the purchased funds. The initial portfolio consists of 1-, 3-, and 20-year securities but no 2-year securities. If the interest rates rise, the $10,000 cash outflow is financed by $5769 in maturing securities, $3031 in interest income, and $1513 in purchased funds. A sum of $313 is left over and invested in 2-year securities. If interest rates are unchanged and there is no change in cash made available, no use is made of purchased funds. Funds held to meet the potential outflow can now be invested in long-term securities. If interest rates fall, and a $10,000 cash outflow occurs, an additional $9452 in purchased funds is used. The maturing securities, interest income, additional cash flow, and the purchased funds are all invested in long-term securities up to the maximum allowed by the limits on losses. If the cost of the purchased funds is reduced further to a spread of 25 basis points, then even more use is made of purchased funds. Clearly, as the purchased funds become less expensive, it is better to use them to generate the funds to invest in the long-term securities in the event that rates either remain unchanged or fall. For larger spreads it is less expensive for the portfolio to generate these funds internally by selling short-term securities if rates remain unchanged or fall.

The key point to note is that the availability of purchased funds allows the short end of the investment portfolio to be invested in longer securities, thus increasing the yield on the portfolio. The lower the spread between the cost of purchased funds and the return on the security of the same maturity, the longer the short end of the portfolio can be made. This is the same observation that we made when purchased funds were not available within the portfolio, but the portfolio was not used for liquidity purposes either. It is rather interesting to note that the optimal decisions in the first period for the case where the liability spread is 50 basis points are identical with those for the case given in Table 9.1, where the portfolio is not used for liquidity. For the base case we can conclude that freeing the investment portfolio from being used for liquidity purposes has essentially the same effect as permitting discretionary use of purchased funds within the portfolio if the cost of these funds is about 50 basis points above the return on the short-term asset.

Eventually, if the cost of purchased funds continues to decrease, it will be optimal to increase the size of the portfolio in the initial period. When this point is reached it will always be optimal to borrow as much of these funds as is permitted by overall bank policy. On the other hand, if the cost of the purchased funds continues to increase, eventually none of these funds will be used and the optimal strategy will be identical to that of the base case when no purchased funds are available. We can get a measure of the value of having purchased funds available at various costs by graphing the expected portfolio earnings over the planning horizon as a function of the liability spread. This graph is given in Figure 9.2. The shape of the graph is convex, which is the usual result when a linear program is considered as a function of the coefficients of its objective function. Since the expected after-tax rate of return on the portfolio is 3.31% per year, we can conclude that the availability of purchased funds within the portfolio can improve on this but not significantly. Its return is only 3.33% at a spread of 50 basis points.

In recent years banks have increased their use of purchased funds to meet their liquidity needs, with the effect that the investment portfolio has been more stable in size. Our analysis suggests that this increased availability of purchased funds does not indicate a significant change in the basic strategy for managing the portfolio. Since the amount of long-term securities that can be held is dictated by the allowable levels of realized and unrealized losses, any additional funds made available without corresponding increases in these limits cannot be invested in long-term securities. The effect of the

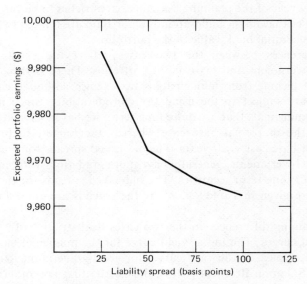

Figure 9.2.   Impact of the cost of purchased funds.

increased availability of purchased funds is only to permit the securities that mature before the horizon to have a somewhat longer average maturity.

CONTRASTING GOVERNMENTS AND MUNICIPALS

In general, most large commercial banks have tended to shift as much of the assets of their investment portfolio out of U.S. Government securities and into higher yielding tax-exempt securities as possible. Since our results up until now have been stated for a base case consisting of all Government securities, the question that naturally arises is to what extent do the conclusions reached for Governments also hold for tax-exempt securities? In this section we present a base case for municipal bonds with many of the same attributes as the base case for Governments and compare their essential characteristics. In subsequent sections we combine these two base cases into a jointly managed portfolio of Governments and municipals and investigate some issues involving the management of the entire investment portfolio.

In order to make comparisons between a base case for municipals and one for Governments, we have made the two cases as similar as possible. Each consists of three 1-year periods with three uncertain events per period. The size of the initial portfolio is $100,000, and cash outflows of $10,000 occur in each of the first two periods if interest rates rise, while corresponding cash inflows of $10,000 occur if interest rates fall. In both cases the realized losses in any year of the planning horizon are restricted to be zero, while unrealized losses that might build up in the portfolio are limited to $1000, or 1 percent of the initial book value of the portfolio.

The differences between the two cases reflect the usual differences between Government and tax-exempt portfolios. There is the obvious difference that income from municipals is tax-exempt, although capital gains and losses are subject to the usual tax considerations. Since most banks hold some municipals that are quite long term, we have included 30-year securities in the municipal base case whereas the longest maturity in the Government base case is 20-years. The bid-asked spreads for municipals, as opposed to Governments, generally have more gradations with maturity and are larger for long-term securities. The bid-asked spreads for the municipal base case are given in Table 9.4, where the spreads are quoted in terms of $100 per bond.

The remaining differences in the two cases deal strictly with the generation of yield curves. The initial yield curve for the municipal base case was chosen to be typical of the yield curves for good grade municipal bonds, as defined by Salomon Brothers [1974], during the first few months of 1973. The yield curve for the Government base case was chosen similarly. The two

Table 9.4   Bid-Asked Spreads for Municipals

Less than 2 years	0.125
2 to 3 years	0.25
3 to 7 years	0.375
7 to 11 years	0.625
11 years or greater	0.75

base case yield curves are given in Figure 9.3. The difference in the shape of these two yield curves is that the municipal yield curve appears to rise more rapidly than the Government yield curve. This seems to be true on average inasmuch as the yield spread between the 10-year bond and the 1-year bond has been about 80 basis points for municipals and about 30 for Governments, based on the data for 1965 through 1972.

In Chapter 7 we investigated the impact of the shape of the initial yield curve on optimal portfolio strategies, and that discussion will not be repeated here. However, there is an important difference in the behavior of municipal interest rates as compared to Government rates that needs to be captured in any yield-curve generating process. Whereas yield curves for Government securities are often inverted, in the sense that the short-term rates are higher than the long-term, the yield curves for municipal securities seldom exhibit this phenomenon. Yield curves for individual bond issues have been inverted from time to time. However, the Salomon Brothers yield curve for good grade municipal bonds has not been observed to be inverted for any significant period of time.

We can explain this phenomenon by examining the changes in various interest rates as a function of the changes in the short-term rate defining the scenarios. For the Government base case, the 1-year changes in the 3-month rate were used to define the various scenarios. In Figure 9.4 the changes in Government rates and the changes in municipal rates are plotted as fractions of the observed changes in the 3-month Government rate. The interesting point to note is that changes in the municipal rates as a percent of the changes in the 3-month Government rate are smaller than the corresponding changes for Government rates on short-term bonds and larger than the corresponding changes for Government rates on longer-term bonds. One conclusion that can be drawn from this exhibit is that short-term rates for Governments are relatively more volatile than short-term rates for municipals, while long-term rates for Governments are relatively less volatile than long-term rates for municipals.

Another conclusion can be drawn from a consideration of the shapes of

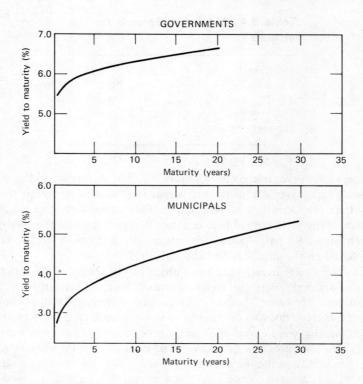

Figure 9.3.   Initial yield curves for government and municipal base cases.

these curves, ignoring their absolute levels. The change curve for municipals is relatively flat in Figure 9.4, indicating that the municipal yield curves tend to move up and down, generally keeping the same shape. One possible explanation of this relatively flat curve for municipals is that the default risk on these securities rises for longer-term bonds as interest rates rise generally. For whatever reason, the long- and short-term municipal rates tend to move more closely than the corresponding Government rates. In the case of Governments the variation of long-term relative to short-term rates produces some very steeply rising as well as inverted yield curves.

Although the same basic yield curve generation process is used for the municipal base case as is used for the Government base case, none of the possible future municipal yield curves are inverted. This simply results from the fact that the rate generating process is based on the relative changes in interest rates as a function of maturity, as given in Figure 9.4. The yield-curve generation process for the municipal base case assumes that the 1-

year rate is equally likely to rise 100 basis points, remain unchanged, or fall 100 basis points over the course of a year. The changes in the 20-year rate and the 30-year rate were taken to be 67 and 61% of the changes in the 1-year rate, respectively.* The rest of the yield curve was filled in using the functional form developed in Chapter 3.

In Table 9.5 the optimal strategy for the municipal base case is given. In order to facilitate an easy comparison with the results for the Government base case given in Chapter 7, we have given the optimal sequence of actions for each possible scenario. The important thing to note is that the form of the strategy is essentially the same. The initial portfolio consists of the maximum amount permitted by the loss constraints invested in the longest maturity, with the remaining funds being laddered in securities that mature at or before the end of the planning horizon. For all periods of the model the basic strategy is a barbell consisting of a balance between long-term and short-term securities with the absence of intermediate maturities.

We will not repeat here any of the analysis, given in Chapter 8, of how

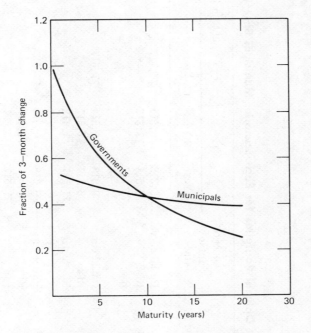

Figure 9.4. Contrasting governments and municipals.

---

* These parameters are based on the behavior of municipal yield curves in the period 1965–1972, as described in chapter 6.

Table 9.5 Optimal Portfolios for Each Scenario: Municipal Base Case

Period	Sequence of Interest Rates	Amounts in Each Maturity ($)							
		1 Year	2 Years	3 Years	...	28 Years	29 Years	30 Years	Total
1	Initial curve	6,318	6,514	77,517		—	—	9,651	100,000
2	Rise	6,514	77,517	—		—	9,651	—	93,682
3	Rise	77,517	—	—		9651	—	—	87,168
1	Initial curve	6,318	6,514	77,517		—	—	9,651	100,000
2	Rise	6,514	77,517	—		—	9,651	—	93,682
3	No change	77,517	1,412	—		9651	—	8,588	97,168
1	Initial curve	6,318	6,514	77,517		—	—	9,651	100,000
2	Rise	6,514	77,517	—		—	9,651	—	93,682
3	Fall	77,517	2,591	—		9651	—	17,408	107,167
1	Initial curve	6,318	6,514	77,517		—	—	9,651	100,000
2	No change	6,092	77,517	6,703		—	9,651	3,720	103,683
3	Rise	77,517	6,703	—		9651	3,720	—	97,591

1	Initial curve	6,318	6,514	77,517	—	—	9,651		100,000
2	No change	6,092	77,517	6,703	—	9,651	3,720		103,683
3	No change	73,731	6,703	—	9651	3,720	13,791		107,596
1	Initial curve	6,318	6,514	77,517	—	—	9,651		100,000
2	No change	6,092	77,517	6,703	—	9,651	3,720		103,683
3	Fall	65,828	6,703	—	9651	3,720	27,738		117,640
1	Initial curve	6,318	6,514	77,517	—	—	9,651		100,000
2	Fall	6,514	78,698	2,699	—	9,651	16,120		113,682
3	Rise	92,665	2,699	—	9651	12,668	—		108,032
1	Initial curve	6,318	6,514	77,517	—	—	9,651		100,000
2	Fall	6,514	78,698	2,699	—	9,651	16,120		113,682
3	No change	77,516	2,699	—	9651	16,120	12,046		118,032
1	Initial curve	6,318	6,514	77,517	—	—	9,651		100,000
2	Fall	6,514	78,698	2,699	—	9,651	16,120		113,682
3	Fall	60,506	2,699	—	9651	16,120	39,257		128,233

the basic strategy changes when attributes of the scenario of the base case are varied. The conclusions reached there will generally hold for the municipal base case. However, the section of Chapter 8 devoted to the shape of the initial yield curve may be of particular relevance. To the extent that the municipal yield curve is relatively steeper than the corresponding yield curve for Governments, there is more of a tendency with municipals to have the investment in those securities that mature after the end of the planning horizon be in relatively short-term securities.

Finally, we can compare the rates of return on the two portfolios because they are designed to reflect the same environment. The expected after-tax rate of return for the municipal portfolio is 4.04% per year as compared with an expected after-tax rate of return for the comparable Government portfolio of 3.31% per year. This is certainly not surprising and merely reflects the fact that portfolios of municipals generally have higher after-tax yields than Governments. Since most banks hold Governments for reasons other than earnings, in the next two sections we examine some of the issues that arise in the joint management of Government and municipal portfolios.

DECENTRALIZED PORTFOLIO MANAGEMENT

Although in most banks responsibility for management of the investment portfolio generally falls under a single individual, often the actual management of the portfolio is more decentralized. In these instances the investment portfolio is divided into separate pools of funds for Governments, tax-exempts, and possibly a liquid asset pool. These pools of funds are then managed as separate portfolios subject to some overall guidelines. In this section we compare managing a single portfolio of Government and municipal securities with managing two separate portfolios consisting of only Governments and only municipals.

To form a joint base case including both Government and municipal securities, we have simply combined the investment opportunities of the two existing cases and maintained the other attributes of these cases, such as overall portfolio size, funds flow, allowable realized and unrealized losses, and so forth. Somewhat arbitrarily we limited the holdings of U.S. Government securities to be at least $40,000 on all scenarios at all times.

In order to examine the question of jointly managing a single portfolio of Governments and municipals as compared with individually managing two separate portfolios, we have had to allocate the properties of the joint portfolio to the two separate portfolios. The easiest allocation scheme is to simply prorate all constraints of the individual base cases by a fixed fraction reflecting the percent holdings of that type of security. Hence the initial portfolio size, the funds flow, and the unrealized losses for the separate Government portfolio are 40% of those for the joint case, while these figures are 60% for the separate municipal portfolio. A comparison of the suggested strategies in the first period for the individually managed portfolios as well as the jointly managed portfolio is given in Table 9.6. It should be pointed out that the strategies suggested for the separate Government and municipal portfolios are exactly 40 and 60% of those given in their respective base cases. This result stems from our particular allocation scheme.

The jointly managed portfolio has the same fundamental strategy that we have seen in both the Government and municipal base cases. The maximum amount possible is invested in the long-term municipal securities, which have the highest after-tax yield, and the remaining funds are invested in securities that mature before the end of the planning horizon. The minimum amount of Government securities is held even though the model was free to invest more in Governments if this had been promising. The net impact of the separately managed portfolios is similar to the jointly managed portfolio except that no 20-year Government securities are purchased in the jointly managed case. These funds are invested in a combination of 30-year municipals and 3-year Governments.

Since the sum of the actions taken in the separately managed portfolios is an allowable strategy for the joint case but was not selected by the model, it must not be an optimal solution. This must, in fact, be the case since the expected after-tax rate of return on the sum of the separately managed portfolios is 3.75% per year, while the expected after-tax rate of return on the jointly managed portfolio is 3.93%, a difference of 18 basis points per year. Therefore, although managing the Government and municipal portfolios separately may have a number of desirable properties from an organizational point of view, the bank is still foregoing some additional return on its investment, even if the individual portfolios are managed optimally. This suggests that we should look more closely at jointly managing the entire investment portfolio.

For banks that want to maintain separate government and municipal portfolios for whatever reasons, the question that naturally arises is what general bank guidelines can be established to force the separately managed portfolios to behave as nearly as possible like the jointly managed portfolio. By considering the nature of the optimal strategy suggested by the joint case, we can offer a few guidelines. The major recommendation is that realized losses in any period and unrealized losses at the horizon should not be allowed in the Government portfolio. The impact of this is that no Government securities will have maturities longer than the planning ho-

Table 9.6 Joint Management of Governments and Municipals

Portfolio	Maturities In Optimal Initial Portfolio ($)						
	1 Year	2 Years	3 Years	...	20 Years	30 Years	Total	Annual Return
Governments only	2790	2869	27,458		6883	N.A.	40,000	
Municipals only	3791	3908	46,510		–	5791	60,000	
	6581	6777	73,968		6883	5791	100,000	3.75%
Joint portfolio								
Governments	–	–	40,000		–	N.A.	40,000	
Municipals	6549	6752	37,048		–	9651	60,000	
	6549	6752	77,048		–	9651	100,000	3.93%

rizon. This allows the full amount of unrealized losses the bank is willing to tolerate to be allocated to the municipal portfolio, and permits the maximum amount to be invested in high-yielding long-term municipals.

The joint management results also suggest that if the investment portfolios are used for liquidity purposes, the potential funds inflows and outflows might best be planned for in the municipal portfolio. Although banks do use short-term municipal notes to some extent for liquidity purposes, the model's results would be difficult to implement and might not be appropriate in actual practice. Short-term Governments are more marketable in times of stress than are municipals. Furthermore, there exists an active market for Government security repurchase agreements that makes these securities particularly attractive for liquidity purposes.

To study the implications of using Governments rather than municipals to meet liquidity needs, we set up separately managed portfolios under two sets of assumptions. In one case the Government portfolio was used for liquidity purposes and in the other case the municipal portfolio was used. In both cases the portfolio used for liquidity faced potential outflows of $10,000 if rates rose and possible increases in funds of $10,000 if rates fell. The Government portfolio was allocated $40,000 and was restricted to zero realized and unrealized losses. The municipal portfolio was allocated $60,000 and was restricted to zero realized losses but was permitted the entire $1000 unrealized loss potential at the horizon. The resulting optimal decisions for the separate portfolios are given in Table 9.7 for each case.

These results suggest that when portfolios are managed separately, total earnings from the portfolios are relatively unaffected by a choice between use of Governments and municipals for liquidity. The rate of return when Governments are used is 3.81% as compared with 3.79% for the municipal case. This slightly higher return for the Government case results from the fact that more interest income is given up when part of the short-term securities in the municipal portfolio is shifted to 1 and 2-year maturities than when Governments are shifted to these maturities.

It is interesting to note that both of the individually managed cases in Table 9.7 produce annual rates of return significantly under the 3.93% of the jointly managed case. In the joint case interest income from Governments is reinvested in municipals, but this income goes into Governments when the portfolios are separately managed. Although this suggests one more way to improve the combined return from separately managed portfolios, it is probably going too far to maintain the fiction that the portfolios are being managed independently if the earnings of one are withdrawn and invested in the other. If separate management of the Government and municipal portfolios is necessary for organizational or other reasons, guidelines such as those suggested above will probably do as well as possible.

Table 9.7 Separate Management of Governments and Municipals

Portfolio	Maturities In Optimal Initial Portfolio ($)							Annual Return
	1 Year	2 Years	3 Years	...	20 Years	30 Years	Total	
Government	7746	—	40,000		—	N.A.	40,000	
Municipal*	7746	7,987	34,616		—	9651	60,000	
	7746	7,987	74,616		—	9651	100,000	3.79%
Government*	8825	9,077	22,098		—	N.A.	40,000	
Municipal	—	3,774	46,575		—	9651	60,000	
	8825	12,851	68,673		—	9651	100,000	3.81%

* Used for liquidity needs.

However, some return on investment is bound to be foregone by this decentralized approach.

NEED FOR TAXABLE INCOME

In many banks, holdings of U.S. Governments have been reduced to minimums required for pledging and cosmetic purposes. This shift out of taxable income-producing securities into tax-exempt municipals has contributed to a shortage of taxable income that has developed in recent years for many banks. Initially it was not a problem, but the expansion of banks into leasing and the growth of foreign activities have created the shortage. Leasing activities generate large depreciation tax shields as well as investment tax credits, and international activities lead to foreign tax credits. Both activities are profitable, but both require taxable income to absorb the deductions and credits. Some banks may have reached the point where it would be profitable to shift funds back into Governments from municipals to generate additional taxable income.

In this section we examine the jointly managed portfolio of Governments and municipals to attempt to understand whether the basic strategy given in the previous section should change, given a need for additional taxable income. To do this we leave unchanged all of the attributes of the jointly managed portfolio of Governments and municipals, and vary the effective income tax rate on the portfolio. The usual definition of the effective tax rate is the ratio of actual tax paid to pretax earnings. Tax-exempt earnings, investment tax credits from leasing activities, and foreign tax credits all act to reduce the effective tax rate of the bank. Suppose that the bank is considering engaging in more leasing activities, which would generate a sizeable depreciation tax shield, resulting in a net loss for this year and also produce investment tax credits that need to be taken this year. Then both the depreciation tax shield and investment tax credits will tend to reduce the actual tax paid unless some of the investment portfolio is shifted into Government securities. Therefore, if the level of taxes paid is thought of as determined outside this analysis, then pursuing the increased leasing activity will have the same impact as reducing the effective tax rate on the portfolio. We can, therefore, use the effective tax rate on the portfolio as a surrogate for activities outside the portfolio that reduce taxable income.

In Table 9.8 we have indicated the optimal decisions in the first period for a jointly managed portfolio of Governments and municipals wherein the effective tax rate on income is varied. The results are not very surprising. The results of the jointly managed base case correspond to the 50% effective rate. The minimum is invested in Governments in 3-year maturities, which

Table 9.8   Need for Taxable Income: Impact of Effective Tax Rate on Joint Portfolios

Effective Tax Rate	Maturities in Optimal Initial Portfolios ($)				
	1 Year	2 Years	3 Years · · ·	30 Years	Total
50%					
Governments	—	—	40,000	—	40,000
Municipals	6549	6752	37,048	9651	60,000
					100,000
40%					
Governments	6280	6495	40,000	—	52,775
Municipals	—	—	37,574	9651	47,225
					100,000
30%					
Governments	5735	5964	78,650	—	90,349
Municipals	—	—	—	9651	9,651
					100,000

are held to the horizon. When the effective tax rate is reduced to 40%, there is a shift in the portfolio in the direction of Governments. At this effective tax rate the liquidity needs of the portfolio are financed by interest income and maturing Government securities. When the effective tax rate is reduced to 30%, there is a further shift in the portfolio toward Government securities. In this case the entire short end of the portfolio is held in Government securities, and only the long-term investment portion is held in municipals. If we continued to reduce the effective tax rate of the portfolio even further, the long-term municipals would be dropped and replaced by long-term Governments.

The effective tax rate is not a perfect surrogate for other investment opportunities in the bank. However, the analysis suggests that if the bank thought it attractive to pursue more activities that generate tax deductions and credits, it might well be justified in moving to an investment portfolio in which more of its short-term securities were Governments. A careful analysis within the bank would, of course, be required to determine if this shift were actually beneficial.

IMPACT OF THE PLANNING HORIZON

As discussed in Chapter 6, the length of the bank's planning horizon affects the riskiness of securities held in the portfolio. If risk is defined as the variability in the total return of the portfolio, the only risk-free security is one that has no interest coupons and that matures at the horizon. Any receipts from maturing securities or interest income before the end of the planning horizon would have to be reinvested at currently uncertain yields. Any securities that mature after the end of the horizon would have an uncertain value at the end of the investment planning period. When risk is considered to be the potential for capital losses, as it is in the BONDS model and in some of the analyses of Chapter 6, maturity is still an important element of risk, but more bonds are risk-free. Under this definition of risk, securities maturing on or before the end of the planning horizon are risk-free if proceeds from interest income and maturing securities are reinvested in securities that mature on or before the horizon. Securities that mature after the horizon are "risky" since they have the potential of producing unrealized losses at the horizon. Thus, we would expect the bank's planning horizon to have an important impact on the strategies suggested by the BONDS model.

In Table 9.9 we have indicated the optimal first-period decisions for a group of cases that have from 1 to 4 years for their planning horizons and contain one period for each year. The structure of the one- and two-period models is very much like the three-period base case for Government securities. Their planning horizons have been made 1 and 2 years, respectively, and the allowable unrealized losses have been made one-third and two-thirds those of the 3-year horizon, respectively. Further, since exogenous funds flows are not permitted at the horizon, the 1-year model does not plan for any changes in portfolio size. The 3-year model is the Government base case.

Table 9.9   Impact of Planning Horizon

Horizon Length	Maturities in Optimal Initial Portfolios ($)				
	1 Year	2 Years	3 Years	4 Years	20 Years
1	82,154	—	—	—	17,856
2	15,776	66,802	—	—	17,422
3	6,974	7,173	68,646	—	17,207
4	6,961	11,843	7,322	58,563	15,311

In order to limit the size of the problem that had to be solved, the four-period case does not have exactly the same structures as the other cases. As in the three-period base case, there are three uncertain events that can occur after period 1 and 2 decisions, but in periods 3 and 4 the distribution of interest rates is approximated by two uncertain events rather than three. Thus yield curves could rise or fall with equal probability following each of the last two decisions. Further, in the four-period case the unrealized losses are limited to be equal to those of the three-period case.

The first thing to note is that the amount invested in the long-term securities is approximately the same in all cases. This is due to the fact that the unrealized losses allowed to build up in the portfolio were limited roughly to correspond to the length of the planning horizon. In each case the model invested as much in the long-term security as the realized and unrealized loss constraints would allow.

The most obvious property of the cases given in Table 9.9 is that as the length of the planning horizon is extended, the length of the longest short-term security corresponds to the length of the planning horizon. This results from the fact that if realized and unrealized losses are the measure of risk aversion, only the bonds that mature before the end of the planning horizon can be risk-free. The intermediate maturities were not selected by the model because, in this example, the long-term security has the best interest income and potential for capital gain at the horizon.

The results of Table 9.9 might suggest that as the planning horizon is lengthened, a bank's short-term securities should become longer also. However, this is not a realistic conclusion. These longer shorter-term securities can lead to potential unrealized losses, before the end of the horizon, that are clearly unacceptable to a bank. To illustrate this point and suggest an easy resolution, we will compare a model with a 5-year planning horizon with one with a 3-year planning horizon.

In order to make the two models as directly comparable as possible, we limited the possible fluctuations in interest rates to the same magnitude. The 3-year model is merely the base case for municipals. The 5-year model is identical to the 3-year model except that it consists of a 1-year period and two 2-year periods. The maximum increase or decrease in interest rates is the same in both cases, and the allowable unrealized losses at the horizon are also the same. The resulting optimal solution for the 5-year planning horizon is given in Table 9.10. Note that the nature of the solution is as expected. The maximum is invested in long-term securities while the largest investment on the short end is made in the 5-year securities, which mature at the end of the planning horizon. The absence of 2-year and 4-year securities in the optimal strategy results merely from the length of the periods used.

Table 9.10   Optimal Decisions for 5-Year Planning Horizon

	Amounts In Each Maturity ($)							
	1 Year	2 Years	3 Years	4 Years	5 Years	⋯	29 Years	30 Years
Initial	6090	—	2557	—	81,089		—	10,264
Rise	—	2557	—	81,089	—		10,264	—
Unchanged	—	1819	—	91,828	—		10,264	—
Fall	—	1454	—	102,204	—		10,264	—

To illustrate the practical difficulty of employing a 5-year planning horizon, we have computed the unrealized losses that build up in the portfolio on the high interest rate scenario at intermediate points in time. The losses at the end of 1 year and 3 years are shown in Table 9.11. On the assumption that the limit on unrealized losses in the portfolio is $1000 at all times, as in the 3-year horizon model, the unrealized losses that can build up in the 5-year model are clearly unacceptable. Even at the end of only 1 year these potential losses amount to $1523, while at the end of 3 years they have risen to $2849.

A way to eliminate this difficulty is to put constraints on the unrealized losses as well as the realized losses throughout the model. This will undoubtedly solve the problem but significantly increase the number of constraints. It turns out that adding these constraints is unnecessary since we already know their impact. Limiting the unrealized loss constraints at the end of 3 years will reduce the amount invested in the long-term security to $9651 and eliminate the holdings of 4- and 5-year securities since they are lower yielding and contribute to these unrealized losses. The funds that were invested in the 4- and 5-year securities will then be invested in 1- to 3-year securities, just as in the 3-year base case for municipals.

The unrealized loss constraints at the end of 3 years are more binding than the unrealized loss constraints at the end of the 5-year horizon. Essentially, we can conclude that adding constraints on intermediate levels of unrealized losses has the same effect as shortening the time horizon until the unrealized loss constraint at the horizon is binding. Therefore it is not necessary to have long planning horizons inasmuch as shorter term considerations tend to dictate the nature of the solution.

A similar phenomenon occurs if risk is measured by the variability of total return. As shown in Chapter 6, a portfolio laddered out to a 30-year maturity has the least return variability of the laddered portfolios. This

Table 9.11   Intermediate Unrealized Losses

Year	Maturity (Yrs.)	Amount ($)	Coupon Rate (%)	Yield Rate (%)	A/T Loss Rate (%)	Unrealized Loss ($)
1	2	2,557	3.55	4.31	0.72	18
	4	81,089	3.80	4.55	1.36	1103
	29	10,269	5.35	5.92	3.91	402
						1523
3	2	81,089	3.80	6.20	2.20	1784
	27	10,264	5.35	7.08	10.38	1065
						2849

strategy, however, produces a very high volatility of returns over a 3-year horizon that is unlikely to be acceptable. Thus long planning horizons do not appear to be very useful. Actually this result is fortuitous since accurately forecasting interest rates for long planning horizons is clearly rather difficult.

10

MANAGEMENT OF THE PORTFOLIO OVER TIME

The simulation results presented in Chapter 6 compare the performance of various mechanically managed laddered and barbell portfolio strategies in terms of their expected return and exposure to risk. The basic conclusion reached there is that laddered portfolios work well for banks that wish to adopt mechanical trading rules, while barbell portfolios offer significant advantages to banks that wish to manage their portfolios more actively. Barbell portfolios provide more liquidity and flexibility to anticipate swings in interest rates than do laddered portfolios. However, these advantages come at the cost of possible increased volatility of returns for the same expected return.

The advantages of using a barbell strategy in managing a portfolio are reinforced by the analyses presented in Chapters 7, 8 and 9 based on the BONDS model. In addressing a number of different questions under a variety of assumptions, the results presented in these chapters tend to have barbell portfolios for the optimal strategies. Since the BONDS model is not restricted to either laddered or barbell portfolios, although these are both admissible strategies, these results strongly support the use of barbell portfolios. However, in these analyses the BONDS model was run as of one particular point in time. Is a barbell portfolio still desirable if managed over time? One might conjecture that it would not, in general, be advantageous to regularly trade out of long-term securities and that over time the barbell portfolios suggested by the BONDS model would evolve into laddered portfolios.

In this chapter we address the question of what portfolio strategy should be adopted over time by using the BONDS model to "manage" a hypothetical portfolio of municipal securities over a 10-year period. The important advantage derived from using such a model to aid in planning the portfolio maturity structure is that it gives the portfolio manager the opportunity to take explicitly into account the characteristics of the current portfolio as well as expected interest rate swings, liquidity needs, programs for realized losses, and exposure to unrealized losses. By and large, the model purchased and maintained a barbell structure for our hypothetical portfolio.

Ideally we would like to use the BONDS model in a Monte Carlo simulation with the same basic methodology as was employed in Chapter 6, where laddered and barbell strategies were compared. There we assumed a finite set of states in the form of particular yield curves that could occur and specified the transition probabilities of going from a particular state at one period to some other state at the next period. The simulation involved approximately 400 trials, wherein each trial consisted of updating the portfolio according to the strategy being evaluated for each year over the number of years in the simulation horizon.

If we were to apply the same simulation approach using an optimization model to make portfolio decisions at each stage, it would be prohibitively expensive from the standpoint of both computer and researcher time. To do so would involve running 400 trials, in which each trial modifies the portfolio by buying and selling securities at the beginning of each of 10 years. Thus for one such simulation experiment there are 4000 portfolio modifications that must take place. To apply this simulation methodology we would have to update and run the BONDS model 4000 times, which is clearly impossible.

However, in spite of the difficulty of carrying out a Monte Carlo simulation, it is still extremely important to see how stochastic programming models, such as the BONDS model, perform over time. As an alternative to the Monte Carlo simulation it is possible to perform a historical simulation. By this we mean we could look at how interest rates behaved over a particular period of time and attempt to plan a portfolio strategy that could have been followed over this period. To implement this we have chosen to take the 10-year historical period starting January 1, 1964. In order to keep the simulation simple, portfolio decisions were allowed to be made once a year and the resulting portfolio was held for the entire year. We clearly do not suggest that any bank would have followed the strategy proposed by the model for the entire year; however it can be considered as a rough approximation of such a strategy over the 10-year period.

If we compare this procedure for a historical simulation with the Monte Carlo simulation procedure of Chapter 6, we see that the historical simulation involves only running the optimization model ten times, once for each time the portfolio can be modified, instead of 4000 times. In essence, such a historical simulation is the same as running *one* trial of a Monte Carlo simulation.

It should be strongly emphasized that it is difficult to draw firm conclusions from the results of a historical simulation against one particular realization of interest rates. A strategy that performed well against that particular sequence of rates might have performed poorly against some other sequence of rates that had a relatively high likelihood of occurring. The opposite is, of course, also true. Nevertheless, it does allow us to make comparisons between strategies for a particular sequence of interest rates that indeed did occur.

In what follows, we first describe the simulation environment. The historical interest rates are presented and the actual yield curves used in the simulation are given. Then the procedure for assessing the portfolio manager's expectations about future yield curves for each period in the simulation is developed in such a way that there is no chance of using information that the portfolio manager would not have had at his disposal at the time. Next the rollover procedure used in the simulation is given. Finally, the results of the simulation are given, and the performance of the BONDS model is compared with that of various mechanically managed laddered and barbell portfolio strategies.

THE SIMULATION ENVIRONMENT

Let us look at the actual interest rates over the period of the simulation. Our hypothetical portfolio of securities is based on the Salomon Brothers time series of good-grade municipal-bond yields covering the period January 1957 to January 1974. The actual "management" of our portfolio covers only the period January 1964 to January 1974, a period of 10 years, but we have included a number of years of history prior to the beginning of this simulation period because we needed to assess interest rate expectations for a portfolio manager at the beginning of 1964. It is clear that these expectations should be based on the interest rate history immediately preceding the beginning of the simulation. In Figure 10.1 the yields on 1-, 10- and 30-year maturities are given for good-grade municipal bonds covering the indicated time period.

The early part of the interest rate series, prior to 1960, was a period of sharp interest rate fluctuations. This was a time of economic cycles during which the Federal Reserve played an active role in offsetting both booms and recessions. In addition, during this period there was a slow trend toward

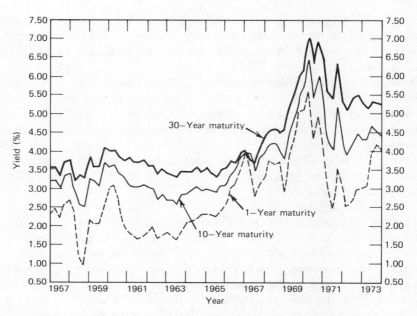

Figure 10.1.   Yields of good-grade municipals. (Source: Salomon Brothers [1974].)

higher interest rates in general but no particular trend in the spread between long- and short-term rates.

The years 1961 and 1962 were a time of very stable rates, exhibiting essentially no trend in either level or spread between long- and short-term rates. Then as the buildup in Vietnam began to be felt, interest rates started their steady rise beginning in 1963 and lasting through 1969, except for a turndown lasting only 6 months following the credit crunch of 1966. During the period of rising rates prior to 1966, the spread between long- and short-term rates continued to decrease until the yield curve became essentially flat in late 1966. Following the subsequent fall in interest rates, beginning in 1967 rates generally rose through 1969, with minor variations keeping the spread between long- and short-term rates roughly unchanged.

The years 1970 and 1971 saw a great drop in interest rates with some very large fluctuations. The large fluctuations provided the opportunity for significant capital gains resulting from actively trading the portfolio. The years 1972 and 1973 saw the beginning of another significant rise in interest rates with the spread between long- and short-term rates once again decreasing.

For the historical simulation covering January 1964 through December 1973, the time series of interest rates is dominated by rising rates and rising inflation resulting from the Vietnam War. Major credit crunches occurred in both 1966 and 1969. Following the credit crunch of 1966 the variability of interest rates became much more pronounced than it had been, significantly exceeding the variability exhibited from 1953 through 1960.

It should be emphasized that the historical simulation was performed in such a way that only ten 1-year time periods were considered. In fact this means that trading of the portfolio was allowed only at the beginning of each year and not at any other time during the year. Hence, although some years exhibited a great deal of variation within a year and thus provided a potential for improving performance via an active trading policy, these variations were not considered. The actual yields used in the simulation for the 1-, 10- and 30-year maturities are given in Table 10.1.

Note that these sequences are essentially rising for all maturities until January 1970. After that time there were two successive interest rate drops and then two successive interest rate increases. These representative yields indicate the amount of interest rate fluctuation that was actually allowed in the simulation.

In order to have prices for all the maturities that could be purchased in the simulation, the eleven yield curves that actually occurred had to be determined. Data were available for the actual yield curves covering maturities of 1, 2, 5, 10, 20, and 30 years. These data could have been used directly employing a linear interpolation for the intermediate maturities needed, but since yield curves are generally considered to be smooth curves, they were fit-

Table 10.1 Actual Yields Used in the Simulation

| Year | Maturity | | |
	1 Year	10 Years	30 Years
1964	2.15%	3.02%	3.45%
1965	2.30	2.86	3.40
1966	3.00	3.41	3.75
1967	3.60	3.69	3.80
1968	3.75	4.28	4.55
1969	3.85	4.54	5.20
1970	5.42	6.57	7.00
1971	2.92	4.45	5.65
1972	2.38	4.05	5.10
1973	3.10	4.45	5.20
1974	4.10	4.40	5.25

ted with the functional form of the yield curve reported in Chapter 3. Hence, letting R_m be the yield on securities with m years to maturity, the function

$$R_m = am^b e^{cm}$$

was fitted to the existing data points to get a smooth curve that could be used to determine the yield to maturity of any available security.

All of the actual yield curves were fitted in this way except the final one. The yield curve on January 1, 1974 was essentially S-shaped, and therefore our functional form was not a very good fit. Since this curve was merely used for evaluating the final portfolio and not for planning future portfolios, a simple linear interpolation was used. The particular yield curves used in the simulation are shown in Figure 10.2.

ASSESSING FUTURE INTEREST RATES

Now let us consider how to manage our hypothetical portfolio. If we are starting to make portfolio decisions in January 1964, it is important that in our historical simulation we do not use any information that was not available to a portfolio manager at that time. If we consider our data estimating techniques as discussed in Chapter 3, it is clear that we cannot use

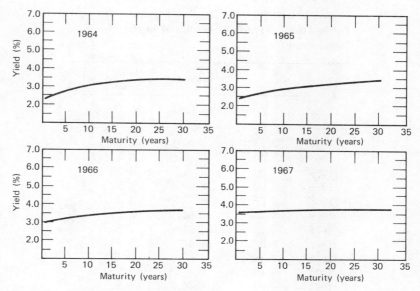

Figure 10.2.   Yield curves used in the simulation.

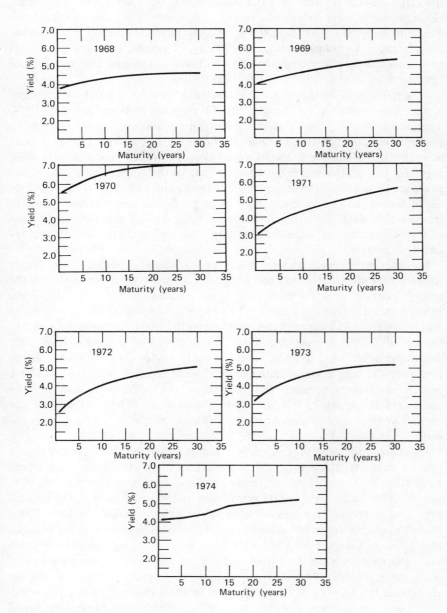

Figure 10.2 (Continued)

the estimates for interest rate fluctuations that were developed there since those estimates were based on a recent 7-year history of interest rates from 1966 through 1973. This period was used to estimate interest rate fluctuations because we believed that the volatility of interest rates present in this period would probably continue into the future. However, the volatility of interest rates prior to 1964 was significantly less.

It is difficult to imagine or reconstruct exactly what a portfolio manager would have forecast for future interest rate changes in January 1964. Therefore, for the purpose of this historical simulation, we have based the portfolio manager's interest rate assessments on the previous 7 years of data at each stage where the BONDS model is used to modify the portfolio holdings. That is, at the beginning of each year in the simulation the portfolio manager knows the current actual yield curve, and he bases his expectations about future yield curve movements at that time on the previous 7 years of interest rate data. By using this methodology we are not biasing the historical simulation by using information that we have gained with twenty-twenty hindsight.

In order to estimate the portfolio manager's expectations about future interest rate fluctuations at the beginning of each year, we analyzed the prior 7 years of data for each year in the simulation. We started with the interest rate data for the years 1957 through and including 1963, and, based on these data, yield curves corresponding to the portfolio manager's expectations of future interest rate fluctuations were constructed. These yield curves were then used to make portfolio decisions for the year 1964. For the next year the data corresponding to 1957 were dropped from the data base and the data corresponding to 1964 were added to the data base, and the analysis was repeated. For each subsequent year of the simulation the earliest year of data was dropped and the most recent year of data was added.

Estimating the tree of yield curves representing the portfolio manager's interest rate expectations at the beginning of each of the 10 years of the simulation consisted of two separate analyses. First, the distributions of 1-year changes in the 1-year rate were estimated for each year in the simulation. The mean and standard deviation of each distribution is given in Table 10.2. The procedure used for estimating these distributions was the same as that given in Chapter 3. A monthly time series covering the prior 7 years was used to determine the actual distribution. Second, the changes in two other rates, the 20- and 30-year rates, were forecast conditional on the changes in the 1-year rate. Then, given a forecast change in the 1-year rate, three points on the corresponding forecast future yield curve were determined by adding the current levels for these rates to the forecast changes in these

Table 10.2 Distribution of 1-Year Changes in the 1-Year Rate

Year	Mean (basis points)	Standard Deviation (basis points)
1964	−0.2	74.6
1965	−3.3	72.4
1966	12.4	59.8
1967	15.2	61.9
1968	11.6	59.0
1969	24.4	52.3
1970	41.9	68.6
1971	37.7	83.5
1972	11.2	109.5
1973	6.7	110.5

rates. The new levels for 1-, 20- and 30-year rates then determined the parameters for the functional form of the yield curve given above.

To forecast the changes in the 20- and 30-year rates conditional on the changes in the 1-year rate, two regressions were performed for each year in the simulation. The changes in each of these two rates were separately regressed against changes in the 1-year rate. The two regression equations were used to compute the changes in these rates as deterministic functions of the changes in the 1-year rate. This is the same procedure for generating a scenario as described in Chapter 3, and it reduces all the uncertainty to the distribution of changes in the 1-year rate.

The means and standard deviations of the regression coefficients as well as an R-square-like measure corresponding to the percent of variance explained by the regression equation are given in Table 10.3. The mean of the regression coefficient gives the change in the 20-year rate or the change in the 30-year rate as a fraction of the change in the 1-year rate.

Since a constant term was not included in these regressions, technically R-square cannot be computed. However, the "R-square" measure reported has approximately the same interpretation as the percent of variance explained, and is based on comparing the variance of the dependent variable, either the changes in the 20-year rate or the changes in the 30-year rate, with the variance of the residuals of the appropriate regression equation. This measure indicates that the conditional forecasts of the changes in

Table 10.3   Changes in the 20- and 30-Year Rates as a Fraction of the Changes in the 1-Year Rate

| Year | 20-Year Fraction | | | 30-Year Fraction | | |
	Mean	Standard Deviation	"R-square"	Mean	Standard Deviation	"R-square"
1964	.3615	.0416	85.6	.3289	.0398	86.8
1965	.2820	.0312	91.9	.2473	.0274	93.7
1966	.3010	.0354	89.1	.2762	.0298	92.3
1967	.3862	.0331	90.4	.3222	.0261	94.0
1968	.3578	.0399	86.3	.2792	.0358	88.9
1969	.4413	.0501	74.7	.3609	.0504	74.3
1970	.6753	.0421	79.8	.6187	.0478	74.0
1971	.6777	.0507	74.3	.6176	.0549	69.8
1972	.6585	.0431	84.4	.6004	.0468	81.6
1973	.6702	.0437	84.1	.6119	.0478	81.0

the 20- and 30-year rates are reasonably good, so that our disregard of the uncertainty associated with these forecasts is a reasonable first approximation.

The remaining question to address regarding the assessment of future interest rate scenarios for each year of the simulation concerns the handling of the time trend in the interest rate data. In Table 10.2 the mean of the distribution of 1-year changes in the 1-year rate is almost always positive, indicating increasing rates on the average. Would a portfolio manager have assumed that interest rates would continue to increase according to these historical means when forecasting future rates at the beginning of each year of the simulation? We assumed that a portfolio manager would have initially forecast the upward drift in rates prior to 1970 corresponding to the mean based on the previous 7 years of data. In 1969 rates dropped precipitously, and uncertainty about the direction of future changes increased. Hence from 1970 until the end of the simulation we assumed that the portfolio manager would have forecast no net drift in interest rates, but would have had a variance of that forecast corresponding to that observed in the previous 7 years.

The forecasting procedure assumed for the manager of our hypothetical portfolio is really very naive. We can indicate just how naive by considering the errors that resulted from the forecasts of the changes in the 1-year rate. In Table 10.4 we give the mean change in the 1-year rate based on the prior

Table 10.4   Errors in Forecasting the 1-Year Rate

Year	Mean of Past 7 Years (bp)	Mean Change Forecast (bp)	Actual Change (bp)	Error (bp)
1964	−0.2	0	15.0	15.0
1965	−3.3	0	70.0	70.0
1966	12.4	12.4	60.0	47.6
1967	15.2	15.2	15.0	−0.2
1968	11.6	11.6	10.0	−1.6
1969	24.4	24.4	157.0	132.6
1970	41.9	0	−250.0	−250.0
1971	37.7	0	−54.0	−54.0
1972	11.2	0	72.0	72.0
1973	6.7	0	100.0	100.0

7 years, the change in the 1-year rate forecast by our portfolio manager, the actual change that occurred, and the observed error in the forecast. It is interesting to note that in 6 of the 10 years the forecast was for no change in the 1-year rate, indicating no attempt even to predict the direction of rate changes. The average absolute error in the forecast of the 1-year rate was 74 basis points, not very accurate forecasting. We can conclude that an actual portfolio manager at the time would probably have been able to improve on this significantly. However, this forecasting procedure was used since it does not depend on any information that would not have been available at the time the forecasts had to be made.

THE ROLLOVER PROCEDURE

We have described in the previous section how the actual yield curves were fit and how the portfolio manager's expectations about variations in future interest rates were modeled. In this section we describe the remaining assumptions made and the procedure for rolling over the BONDS model.

The only securities under consideration in this simulation are good grade municipal bonds. The actual yield curves used in the simulation are given in Figure 10.2. We allow the purchase of nine different maturities—1, 2, 3, 4, 5, 10, 15, 20, and 30 years. This is a robust enough collection to see how the model behaves, although at times some of the maturities that were not included might have been slightly preferable.

The planning horizon for the bank is taken to be 3 years. Since this is a yearly simulation, three 1-year periods were then used in structuring the model. It should be pointed out that assuming a 3-year horizon for planning purposes indicates that the bank is willing to say that its objective is to maximize the value of the portfolio at the end of 3 years. As each year passes the bank moves its horizon out one more year. Therefore at any point in time the bank is planning as if it wants to maximize its portfolio value at the end of the next 3 years, but, in fact, it is always rolling over the horizon, so the end is never reached. We believe the 3-year horizon is a reasonable assumption, but individual banks might have chosen a shorter or longer period.

Next we have the problem of assessing the tree of scenarios with respect to which the bank chooses to do its planning. For ease in computation we assumed a particularly easy structure, which is essentially the same as the base case of Chapter 7. That is, we assumed that there were three uncertain events that could occur during each period in the planning horizon. This is equivalent to assuming that the distribution of 1-year changes in the 1-year rate was approximated by three bracket medians. We have assumed for computational convenience that the distribution of 1-year changes in the 1-year rate is approximately normal. This allows us to approximate the upper bracket median, which should correspond to the .833 fractile, by the mean plus one standard deviation, which actually corresponds to the .841 fractile. This difference is well within the other approximations used in the simulation.

By approximating the distribution of 1-year changes in the 1-year rate with three bracket medians, the number of branches on the scenario planning tree is three in the first period, nine in the second period, and twenty-seven in the third period. A yield curve is generated for each branch in the planning tree by the process described in the previous section. Normally the remaining part of the scenario would be the exogenous cash flow either to or from the portfolio. However, since we are interested in evaluating the performance of the portfolio and since liquidity needs depend on the environment of a particular bank, we have assumed that all cash generated by the portfolio is reinvested and there is no net cash either made available to or withdrawn from the portfolio.

There are a few other assumptions that are held constant for the entire simulation and should be pointed out. The trading of securities involves a cost, which is paid at the point of sale of the securities and amounts to the spread between the bid and asked prices of the market. For bond prices quoted in terms of $100 per bond the bid-asked spreads assumed in the simulation are given in Table 10.5. Since the securities in the simulation are municipal bonds, the income tax rate is assumed to be zero and the capital gains rate is assumed to be 50%.

Since the objective of the bank is taken to be the maximization of the

Table 10.5   Bid-Asked Spreads by Maturity

Maturity Range	Spread
Less than 2 years	0.125
2 to 3 years	0.25
3 to 7 years	0.375
7 to 11 years	0.625
11 years or greater	0.75

portfolio value at the end of the planning horizon, some comments on this evaluation should be made. The securities held in the portfolio at the horizon are clearly worth somewhere between their bid and asked prices. Theoretically, we could assess a value between bid and asked price that correctly reflects the bank's expectations of the discounted selling cost of each security in the future, but this seems an unnecessary refinement. The value of the securities held in the portfolio at the horizon is simply taken to be the bid price, but after taxes.

Throughout the simulation the limit on realized losses within any one year on any scenario was held to 0.5% of the initial book value of the portfolio. That is, at the beginning of each year in the simulation the current book value of the portfolio was computed, and the losses that were allowed to be realized that year and planned for over each of the years of the planning horizon were limited to 0.5% of this value.

The unrealized losses, on the other hand, were handled differently. Since the actual interest rates rose over the course of the simulation, fairly large amounts of unrealized losses tended to build up in the portfolio. We contrained the potential unrealized losses to be the same for all scenarios and assumed that the level of these unrealized losses under moderately adverse circumstances should be kept as small as possible. With this view, the limits on potential unrealized losses were as low as 1% and as high as 5% depending on how much interest rates had risen to data. In the first year of the simulation the allowable unrealized losses on all scenarios at the end of the 3 years in the planning horizon were limited to 1% of the initial book value.

THE RESULTS OF THE SIMULATION

Let us first look at the sequence of portfolio decisions in the historical simulation. In Table 10.6 we show for January 1 of each year in the simula-

Table 10.6 Portfolio Holdings During Simulation

Year	Maturity (Years)	Purchases ($)	Portfolio ($)	Coupon (%)	Yield (%)
1964	3	19,915	19,915	2.5387	2.5387
	5	28,300	28,300	2.7373	2.7373
	15	23,636	23,636	3.1854	3.1854
	20	28,149	28,149	3.3	3.3
1965	2		9,819	2.5387	2.4357
	4		28,300	2.7373	2.5911
	14		23,636	3.1854	2.9831
	19		28,149	3.3	3.1235
	30	13,056	13,056	3.4	3.4
1966	2	33,676	33,676	2.9601*	3.1063
	3		28,300	2.7373	3.173
	18		25,358	3.3	3.5667
	29		13,056	3.4	3.7355
	30	5,149	5,149	3.75	3.75
1967	1	73,332	73,332	3.6	3.6
	17		21,939	3.3	3.7341
	28		13,056	3.4	3.7903
1968	2	50,149	50,149	3.903	3.903
	3	23,288	23,288	3.995	3.995
	16		13,469	3.3	4.3951
	27		13,056	3.4	4.524
	30	11,613	11,613	4.55	4.55
1969	1		50,149	3.9032	3.85
	2	2,972	26,260	3.998*	4.0214
	15		6,235	3.3	4.7333
	26		13,056	3.4	5.0834
	29		11,613	4.55	5.1712
	30	7,986	7,986	5.2	5.2
1970	1		26,260	3.998*	5.4226
	2	7,795	7,794	5.75	5.75
	3	17,841	17,841	5.9473	5.9473
	4	33,760	33,760	6.089	6.089
	14		6,235	3.3	6.6955
	25		13,056	3.4	6.9368
	28		11,613	4.55	6.977
	29		2,740	5.2	6.9889

* Weighted average.

Table 10.6   (Continued)

Year	Maturity (Years)	Purchases ($)	Portfolio ($)	Coupon (%)	Yield (%)
1971	2	24,132	24,132	3.3	3.3
	3		12,387	6.089	3.5496
	4	47,016	47,016	3.7406	3.7406
	13		6,235	3.3	4.6912
	24		3,132	3.4	5.3577
	27		3,897	4.55	5.5079
	28		2,740	5.2	5.5561
	30	25,070	25,070	5.65	5.65
1972	2		12,387	6.089	2.8
	3	27,123	74,139	3.498*	3.0775
	23		3,037	3.4	4.8388
	27		2,740	5.2	4.9965
	29		25,070	5.65	5.0667
	30	12,258	12,258	5.1	5.1
1973	1		12,387	6.089	3.1
	2		15,319	3.7406	3.4627
	3	54,555	54,555	3.6926	3.6926
	5	13,871	13,871	4.0009	4.0009
	26		2,740	5.2	5.1031
	28		25,070	5.65	5.1535
	30	10,786	10,786	5.2	5.2

tion the maturities held, the amount just purchased, the resulting portfolio holdings, the coupon rate, and the yield rate of each of the securities in the portfolio. For this simulation all purchases were made at par—that is, there were no purchases of discounted or premium-priced securities.

The initial portfolio consisted of $100,000 of cash, and in 1964 maturities of 3, 5, 15, and 20 years were purchased in roughly equal proportions. Normally we would expect more of a barbell structure when investing only cash, as seen in Chapter 8, but this emphasizes the point that for a particular current yield curve and expectations about future rates, it is certainly possible to purchase other than a barbell structure of maturities. At that time the municipal yield curve was relatively flat, so that the return from long maturities was not sufficient to justify the added risk. However, as the simulation progresses, it will be clear that there is a tendency for the model to trade out of the intermediate maturities.

Table 10.6 explicitly gives only the purchases of securities and the resulting portfolio. However, we can easily deduce the implied sales in dollars of book value from successive years in the table. In 1965 a sum of $13,056 was invested in 30-year maturities. These funds resulted from selling $10,096 of a 2-year maturity (3-year maturity in 1964) plus interest income of $2962, as given in Table 10.7.

In 1966 all of the 1-year maturity (2-year maturity in 1965) amounting to $9819, all of the 13-year maturity (14-year maturity in 1965) amounting to $23,636 and $2791 of the 18-year maturity (19-year maturity in 1965) were sold. The amount sold was limited by the allowable realized losses within any year. Throughout the simulation this amount was 0.5% of the book value of the portfolio, and the dollar amount is indicated in Table 10.7. The resulting cash plus interest income of $3150 was invested in 2-year and 30-year maturities at the level of $33,676 and $5,149, respectively. The amount invested in the 30-year maturity was essentially dictated by the unrealized loss constraints at the horizon. On all scenarios the limit of unrealized losses 3 years hence was 1.5% of the current total book value. This limit was raised from 1.0% due to the increased unrealized losses currently held in the portfolio as a result of rising interest rates. Note that for intermediate maturities all of the 13-year maturity and as much of the 18-year maturity as the realized loss constraints would allow were sold.

In 1967 the yield curve became very flat, almost inverted. Many portfolio managers would have correctly forecasted a drop in rates at this point in time. However, in this simulation we employed a rather naive model for expectations of future interest rate changes in order not to take advantage of twenty-twenty hindsight. We forecast a continuing upward trend in rates with a median change in the 1-year rate one year hence of 15.2 basis points (see Table 10.4). It turned out that, although there was a significant drop within 1967, in January 1968 the entire yield curve had risen somewhat, with long-term rates rising more rapidly than short-term rates. With this upward forecast in January 1967, the model shortened up the portfolio, as would be expected. A sum of $73,332 was invested in 1-year maturities, the cash being generated by selling everything but the 28-year maturity (29-year maturity in 1966) and some of the 17-year maturity (18-year maturity in 1966). More of the 17-year maturity would have been sold except for the limit on realized losses within any one year. The model clearly was trying to divest itself of any intermediate maturities.

In 1968 and 1969 the trading patterns were similar. Expected increases in the short-term rates were forecast to be 11.6 and 24.4 basis points, respectively. Further, actual increases in interest rates tended to limit the flexibility for trading since most of the securities in the portfolio were building up significant losses as a result of these increases. In each of these years as

Table 10.7   Portfolio Characteristics for Each Year

Year	Beginning Book Value ($)	Interest Income ($)	Interest Return on Book Value (%)	Realized Net Losses ($)	Potential Horizon Unrealized Losses (%)
1964	100,000	2962	2.96	0	1.0
1965	102,959	3150	3.06	3	1.0
1966	105,578	3296	3.12	531*	1.5
1967	108,327	3808	3.52	547*	1.5
1968	111,574	4305	3.86	561*	2.0
1969	115,300	4601	3.99	579*	2.5
1970	119,301	5935	4.97	600*	5.0
1971	124,610	5358	4.30	626*	2.5
1972	129,631	5635	4.35	337	2.5
1973	134,730	6017	4.47	537	2.5
		45,067		3,517	

* Maximum allowable realized losses taken.

much of the intermediate maturity (16-year in 1968 and 15-year in 1969) as possible was sold, subject only to the limit on realized losses within a year. In addition, as much was invested in the 30-year maturity as the limit on potential unrealized losses 3 years hence would allow.

In January 1970 interest rates peaked for the simulation. Although extrapolating the historical data on short-term rates forecast a 41.9 basis-point increase, it was clear that no portfolio manager would have made such a forecast. In fact most portfolio managers forecast a drop in rates. However, again not to take advantage of knowledge acquired later, our portfolio manager forecast rates to be unchanged. Further, over the last 4 years of the simulation our portfolio manager continued to forecast short-term rates to be unchanged. The distribution of changes in short-term rates was taken to have zero mean and the standard deviation given in Table 10.2 over this period.

The portfolio actions over the last 4 years of the simulation appear to be similar in nature. In each of these years roughly 30 percent of the portfolio is invested in intermediate- and long-term maturities (greater than 10 years), and this amount is dictated by the limit on potential unrealized losses 3 years hence. The only intermediate securities held in this period were $6235 of the 20-year maturities purchased in 1964. These were finally sold in 1972 when they were 12-year maturities. In each instance of a sale of these intermediate securities, they were always sold at a loss for tax purposes, with the proceeds being reinvested. Since interest rates peaked in 1970 of this simulation, during the last 3 years there were significant gains to offset realized losses from trading. In fact in 1971 and 1972 the current realized loss constraint was not binding, as indicated in Table 10.7.

In Figure 10.3 we have given the holdings of the portfolio over time in broad maturity categories. It is interesting to note the extent to which a roughly barbell portfolio strategy is maintained. Initially some intermediate maturities (15- and 20-year) were purchased. However, the 15-year maturity was sold off as soon as the program for realized losses would allow. No other investments in intermediate securities were made during the simulation. The final portfolio was clearly a barbell structure with 1-, 2-, 3- and 5-year maturities on the short end and 26-, 28- and 30-year maturities on the long end.

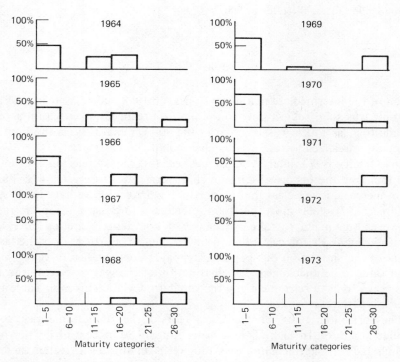

Figure 10.3.   Maturity distributions of managed portfolios.

If we now look more closely at Table 10.7 we can get some idea of the time sequence of increasing portfolio value. It should be pointed out that the period of the simulation shows a very large increase in interest rates in general, and therefore a potential for large capital losses for programs involving active trading of securities. The generally high interest income exhibited by the portfolio is not completely reflected in the increased book value of the portfolio the next year because losses resulting from trading have reduced the book value. Note that interest return on book value peaked in 1970 following the extremely large interest rate increases that occurred in 1969. The increasing return on book value figure prior to this stems completely from the generally rising interest rates. After 1970 the return figure decreases considerably and then increases in 1973 as interest rates start to rise again.

In Table 10.7 the column labeled Potential Horizon Unrealized Losses gives the limit on unrealized losses at the planning horizon, in percent of current book value, that had to be allowed. In 1970 interest rates peaked and the current holdings of unrealized losses were large. These losses, given in Table 10.8, amounted to 4.9% of the after tax book value of the portfolio. Essentially the BONDS model was able to manage the portfolio so as not to increase the potential unrealized losses at the planning horizon, 3 years hence, above the level already existing in the current holdings.

The final market value of the portfolio in January 1974, including cash received, was $141,269, which is broken down by categories in Table 10.9. The unrealized gain in the portfolio is taken after tax, but before transaction costs. This total value corresponds to a compound aftertax rate of

Table 10.8   Unrealized Losses, January 1, 1970

Maturity (Years)	Coupon (%)	Yield (%)	Price/ $100	Book Value ($)	Market Value ($)	Unrealized Loss ($)
1	3.9980	5.4226	98.6313	26,260	25,901	359
2	5.7500	5.75	100	7,794	7,794	0
3	5.9473	5.9473	100	17,841	17,841	0
4	6.089	6.089	100	33,760	33,760	0
14	3.3	6.6955	69.4562	6,235	4,331	1,904
25	3.4	6.9368	58.2836	13,056	7,610	5,446
28	4.55	6.9770	70.3128	11,613	8,165	3,448
29	5.2	6.9889	77.895	2,740	2,134	606
				119,299	107,536	11,763

Table 10.9   Final Value of the Portfolio

Book value	$122,342
Aftertax gain	523
Interest income	6,017
Maturities	12,387
Total Value	$141,269

return on the initial investment of 3.52% per year. Given the large increase in interest rates with the potential for losses, this is a respectable return. For example, the strategy of investing only in 1-year maturities, which would have been a reasonable strategy in a period of rising rates, would have resulted in a final value of $137,596 for a return on investment of 3.28% per year. The BONDS model, then, outperformed this strategy by 24 basis points per year, which on a $500 million portfolio amounts of $1.2 million per year after tax. In the next section we compare the performance of the BONDS model to that of a number of different portfolio strategies for the same history of interest rates.

COMPARING VARIOUS STRATEGIES

Now that we have seen the performance of the BONDS model applied in a somewhat naive manner, we can compare these results with other strategies. In this section we look at the results of applying various laddered and barbell strategies to the same historical interest rate sequence used to evaluate the BONDS model.

These alternative portfolio strategies were implemented essentially in the same way as the BONDS model, except that no forecasting procedure was needed since the strategies were applied in a mechanical manner. For the laddered portfolios, at the beginning of each year of the simulation the funds from maturing securities were reinvested in the longest securities allowed in the ladder, and the coupon income was distributed equally among all maturities to keep the proportions in each fixed. For the barbell portfolios, at the beginning of each year of the simulation the shortest securities in the long end of the barbell were sold and reinvested in the longest securities allowed. Similarly, the maturing securities were reinvested in the longest securities allowed on the short end. The coupon income was allocated between the long and short ends of the barbell to maintain the stated proportions, and within either end it was distributed equally among the maturities included.

Before discussing the specific results of historical simulations employing other strategies, it is important to reemphasize that drawing conclusions from a historical simulation is somewhat dangerous. A historical simulation such as carried out in this chapter amounts to essentially *one* Monte Carlo simulation trial. These comparisons tell how a particular strategy performed against that specific sequence of interest rates, but they do not say how a strategy would perform against other equally likely sequences of interest rates. However, since the sequence of rates used in the historical simulation actually occurred, it is of interest to see what strategies performed best against this one particular realization.

First let us consider some laddered portfolio strategies. The results of applying these strategies in the historical simulation are given in Table 10.10. The strategies consisted of from one to ten maturities equally spaced at 1-year intervals. Each strategy was applied to the historical interest rate sequence by always reinvesting any maturing securities in the longest maturity allowed in the ladder. The interest income each year was then spread equally over the maturities in the ladder to keep the proportions of the portfolio invested in each maturity equal.

Note that the highest final value results from the ladder consisting of five maturities. This final value results from having the highest interest income offset by a relatively minor unrealized loss at the horizon. The 3- and 5-year ladders both exhibit a final unrealized loss due to the increasing interest rates in the last 2 years of the simulation. The longer ladders, on the other hand, exhibit gains since they had built up significant unrealized gains from the large drop in interest rates following 1969, and they reinvest less than the shorter ladders in each time period. Of course there are no realized

Table 10.10 Laddered Portfolio Strategies

Strategy	Total Interest ($)	Total Realized Losses, A/T ($)	Final Unrealized Gain, A/T ($)	Final Value ($)	Compound Rate of Return (%)
1–10	39,775	0	642	140,416	3.45
1–7	40,553	0	345	140,898	3.49
1–5	41,355	0	−175	141,180	3.51
1–3	41,043	0	−409	140,634	3.47
1	37,596	0	0	137,596	3.24

losses or transaction costs with any laddered strategy since all securities are
held to maturity.

Any of these relatively short ladders would seem to be a good strategy
against the rising interest rate sequence. The 5-year ladder gives the highest
final value, which is slightly less than that obtained by the BONDS model,
reported in the previous section to be $141,269, corresponding to a 3.52%
compound rate of return. However, had the interest rate sequence been
decreasing or shown more fluctuation, the BONDS model would have
performed significantly better than the 5-year ladder by being able to
balance capital losses against gains in each period while maintaining a relatively large proportion of the portfolio in longer maturities with higher
interest income.

Now let us look at the performance of various barbell strategies. The
results of applying these strategies in the historical simulation are given in
Table 10.11. The first column, called Strategy, gives the maturities held in
the portfolio at all times and the percentage of the portfolio that is invested
in the long end of the barbell. For example 1–7, 24–30, 20% means a barbell
portfolio structure with seven bonds on the short end and seven on the long
end, but with only 20% of the total value of the portfolio being invested in
the long end.

It is useful to compare laddered portfolios with barbell portfolios having
the same number of bonds on the short end. It is clear that for this

Table 10.11   Barbell Portfolio Strategies

Strategy	Total Interest ($)	Total Realized Losses, A/T ($)	Final Unrealized Gain, A/T ($)	Final Value ($)	Compound Rate of Return (%)
1–10, 21–30, 20%	40,949	1723	189	139,415	3.38
40	42,135	3456	−266	138,413	3.30
1–7, 24–30, 20	41,879	2579	635	139,935	3.42
40	43,220	5178	931	138,973	3.35
1–5, 26–30, 20	42,835	2953	458	140,340	3.45
40	44,334	5933	1102	139,503	3.39
1–3, 28–30, 20	42,896	2422	−415	140,059	3.43
40	44,775	4865	−420	139,490	3.38
1, 30, 20	40,242	3020	0	137,222	3.21
40	42,941	6066	0	136,875	3.19

particular realization of interest rates the laddered portfolios did better than the comparable barbell portfolios. This is due to the fact that although the barbell portfolios had higher interest incomes, these were offset by having to realize losses from selling a relatively long-term security during a period of increasing interest rates. If interest rates had fallen, the barbell portfolios would still have had higher average interest incomes than the ladders but would have realized capital gains rather than losses. Hence, for this historical simulation in a rising period of rates the laddered portfolios did better than the barbell.

If we now look within any barbell structure at the percent of the portfolio invested in the long end, we see that the more that was invested in the long end the worse the performance was. This is again due to the fact that the realized losses were so large over this period of rising interest rates. A greater amount invested in the long end produced a greater total interest income because the yield curves were generally increasing with maturity. However, the increased interest income was not sufficient to offset the capital losses incurred in trading.

Finally, we can comment on the riskiness of the portfolio strategies by looking at the amount of unrealized losses that had built up under each strategy in the year of peak interest rates, 1970. In Table 10.12 the book value, market value, and unrealized aftertax losses as a percent of book value are given for the strategy followed by the BONDS model and for various laddered and barbell strategies. In a period of rising rates strategies that keep most of their assets in short-term securities will have lower unrealized losses. In the extreme case, a ladder consisting of only the 1-year maturity would have zero unrealized losses at all times in the simulation since the entire portfolio would mature each period.

On this dimension the strategy followed by the BONDS model builds up significant losses, roughly comparable to a 10-year ladder or a barbell with five maturities on each end and, say, thirty percent of the portfolio value invested in the long end. However, this general level of unrealized losses in the credit crunch of 1969 might have been considered very reasonable. Any strategy that places a significant proportion of its assets in relatively short-term securities will not develop unrealized losses. Nevertheless, just as there is potential for losses with any strategy there is also potential for similar gains.

We can sum up the performance of the BONDS model by comparing it with the best of the mechanically managed laddered or barbell strategies. The performance of the 5-year laddered portfolio was almost as good as that of the BONDS model against the particular sequence of interest rates that occurred. However, it should be pointed out that a portfolio laddered only out to 5 years is a very conservative strategy, rather unlikely to be

Table 10.12   Unrealized Losses, January 1, 1970

	Book Value ($)	Market Value ($)	Unrealized Aftertax Losses (%)
Bonds	119,299	107,536	4.93
Ladder 1–5	119,198	115,252	1.66
1–10	119,403	113,958	4.56
Barbell 1–5, 26–30, 20%	118,051	113,688	3.70
1–5, 26–30, 40%	116,889	110,107	5.80
Barbell 1–10, 21–30, 20%	119,222	111,200	6.73
1–10, 21–30, 40%	119,039	108,415	8.92

followed in practice. It happened to turn out after the fact, that this was a good strategy to have adopted; but it is not clear that any portfolio manager would have been motivated to adopt such a conservative strategy consistently over the period of the simulation.

Although the performance of the BONDS model was slightly better than the 5-year laddered portfolio, it also turns out that the BONDS model had a somewhat greater exposure to risk in the sense of maximum unrealized losses that built up in the portfolio. The continually rising sequence of interest rates worked to the disadvantage of any strategy that invested significant amounts in long-term securities. This is why all of the mechanically managed barbell portfolios performed relatively poorly. On the other hand, the conservative 5-year laddered portfolio was exposed to only a modest amount of risk in this environment.

Finally, we should point out that, had interest rates been level or falling, the BONDS model would certainly have outperformed the 5-year ladder. In these instances some other laddered or barbell portfolio might perform competitively with the BONDS model. However, the important characteristic of the BONDS model is that is produces a strategy that is adaptive to the environment over time. The BONDS model should perform well against *any* interest rate sequence, whereas a particular laddered or barbell portfolio will perform well for some realizations of interest rates and poorly for others. In actual practice, the portfolio manager would be actively forecasting interest rates, and the BONDS model provides a method of systematically taking advantage of these forecasts.

11

SELECTION AND IMPLEMENTATION OF A PORTFOLIO MANAGEMENT APPROACH

Scenario planning is a useful way of approaching some of the problems posed by bond portfolio management in an uncertain world. This planning process involves an assessment of future portfolio environments that might occur and an evaluation of alternative portfolio actions that might be taken in these environments. The object is to select a strategy providing a good return while hedging against uncertainty about future interest rates and available funds. Although straightforward in concept, scenario planning can pose a burden of analysis not normally undertaken in many banks. A major purpose of our research work has therefore been to develop statistical aids and computer models to assist in this aspect of portfolio management.

A second important objective of the research was to provide information to help a portfolio manager select a basic maturity structure. To accomplish this purpose we used the computer models developed in the project to analyze the characteristics of alternative portfolio strategies. In addition, we were able to study a number of current portfolio issues, such as the implications of greater use of purchased liabilities for management of investment portfolios.

After first reviewing some important issues in portfolio management, we summarize the results of our study of alternative portfolio policies. We then discuss how scenario planning can be used in the continuing management of portfolios and how the techniques described in this book can be brought to bear in this process. Particular exphasis is placed on the selection of analytical techniques appropriate to the bank's needs and resources.

ISSUES IN BANK PORTFOLIO MANAGEMENT

Bank assets expanded rapidly in the late 1960s and early 1970s as banks took advantage of opportunities to meet growing demands for credit from customers and to expand into new areas. Holdings of securities did not keep pace with this expansion because these assets did not have either the current or the long-run profit potential of other investment alternatives. This decline in the relative size of security portfolios was aided in large part by the greater availability and use of purchased funds such as CDs, Eurodollars, and commercial paper. With the advent of these sources of funds, banks had less need to build up a store of assets to provide liquidity for later use when loan demand grew or deposits ran off. Thus bank portfolios are now much more stable in size and less subject to undesired liquidation.

In this new environment there has been a substantial shift out of U.S. Treasury securities into tax-exempt state and local government bonds. Treasuries are regarded as the more liquid of the two security types, but as liquidity became a less important criterion, banks shifted to the higher aftertax yields of tax-exempt securities. This shift has now stopped, partly because Treasury securities reached minimums required for pledging and other purposes. In addition, the shift to tax-exempt securities lowered taxable income, a commodity already in short supply. Such income is needed to take full advantage of tax deductions and tax credits from other profitable ventures, such as leasing and foreign operations.

This shortage of taxable income has had other impacts on bank portfolio management as well. It has limited the amount of bond trading banks undertake in their investment accounts. It used to be common for banks to undertake trading programs in which losses would be realized and the tax savings from these losses would then be reinvested in new securities to improve the return to the bank. Passage of the Tax Reform Act of 1969 removed a substantial incentive for such trading programs when it increased the tax rate on bank capital gains, treating gains as ordinary income. The shortage of taxable income has added a further impediment since losses on the sale of securities reduce the taxable income available for other desirable tax deductions.

In spite of these changes, many of the old problems of bank portfolio management remain. One of these is the traditional conflict between the desire to improve the return from portfolio assets while limiting the exposure to risk. Short-term securities have little risk of fluctuation in market value, but they normally provide lower interest income. Besides, the return from these holdings tends to be volatile because of the rapid turnover of short securities and the fact that short-term interest rates tend to fluctuate more than long-term rates. Securities with longer maturities frequently offer the opportunity for higher returns and more stable income, but at the cost of more risk of fluctuations in market value.

It would be relatively easy to resolve this conflict if it were possible to accurately forecast future interest rates. Unfortunately, this is another of the old portfolio problems remaining. In spite of the improvements in forecasting techniques, future interest rates are still uncertain. They may be even more uncertain, given the greater volatility of rates in recent years. Thus banks must choose some mix of short- and longer-term securities that will provide a satisfactory balance between expected return from the portfolio and the risk stemming from uncertain returns and potential capital losses.

Much of the discussion about appropriate portfolio mixes has revolved around two basic strategies, laddered portfolios and barbell portfolios. Laddered portfolios are the more traditional strategy and they are much more frequently used. In this approach to portfolio management the securities held in the portfolio are spread relatively evenly across maturity categories, ranging from short-term securities out to the longest maturity considered appropriate by the bank. This maturity structure is easy to manage because it can be maintained by simply reinvesting the proceeds from maturing securities in new bonds with the longest maturity. In addition to this virtue, many banks feel the laddered approach also produces relatively high interest income. Long-term rates are normally higher than short, so that the bonds purchased each year tend to have relatively high interest rates.

In recent years the research literature has recommended, and a few banks have adopted, the alternative barbell approach to portfolio management. These portfolios tend to have their maturities concentrated in short- and longer-term securities with little or no intermediate maturities. They require more active management since the long end of the barbell becomes short with the passage of time unless bonds are periodically traded and the proceeds invested in new long-term bonds. However, some have argued that this portfolio structure provides a higher return than a laddered portfolio for an equivalent exposure to risk. The argument is that a combination of short and long bonds will provide better performance than the intermediate securities held in a laddered portfolio. At the time of each portfolio decision there is some chance that interest rates will rise over the planning horizon and some chance that they will fall. If rates do in fact fall, the long-term securities will provide the largest capital gain and will also maintain their high interest income over the period. On the other hand, if rates rise, short-term securities will provide the least capital loss, and their maturities will provide funds that can be reinvested at the higher rates. In most instances intermediate-term securities do not provide the interest income and capital gain potential of the long maturities, nor do they provide the protection against capital loss of the short security. This suggests that a combination of short-

and long-term securities may be the most efficient way of obtaining return at a given level of risk.

Each of these two portfolio structures has its advocates, but previously published research on the strategies has not been particularly helpful to portfolio managers trying to choose which maturity structure to develop and maintain. Changes in the portfolio management environment, such as the greater use of purchased liabilities, have also posed some questions worthy of consideration. Thus in our research we have attempted to answer a number of questions concerning the old problem of balancing risk and return and the new problems posed by the changing environment:

1.   What basic portfolio structure is likely to provide the best balance between return and risk?

2.   How should the level of risk a bank is willing to tolerate affect the maturity structure of its portfolios?

3.   If a portfolio is not to be used for liquidity purposes, so that its size is relatively constant, how does this affect the choice of a maturity structure?

4.   How does the availability of purchased funds affect portfolio strategy?

5.   How are the maturity structures of U.S. Treasury and tax-exempt securities affected when the total return and risk of the two portfolios are considered jointly?

6.   What is an appropriate planning horizon for a bank to use in selecting a set of portfolio actions?

THE RESEARCH METHODOLOGY

To help answer these questions we needed to examine the performance characteristics of several portfolio strategies. One approach is to see how various strategies would have worked during a historical period. This is an example of "deterministic simulation," in which a portfolio policy is simulated over one scenario of interest rates, in this case a historical sequence of rates. While such an approach provides useful information about the performance of a strategy, the past pattern of interest rates represents only one of the many possible interest rate scenarios. Strategies that worked well in the secularly rising rate period of 1950–1970 may not work well in the future.

The essence of the portfolio management problem is that decisions have to be made in the face of uncertainty about future rate trends. Thus, from the portfolio manager's viewpoint, it is important to evaluate portfolio alternatives against a variety of interest rate scenarios that might occur rather than against the one pattern of rates that did occur. Because of this need, a part of our research effort has been devoted to the development of statistical models capable of assisting a manager in specifying likely sequences of future interest rates.

These same models can be used in an experimental manner to generate realistic sequences of interest rates for use in our study of portfolio strategies. The major assumption underlying these interest rate scenarios is that interest rates in the future will be about as volatile as they were in the late 1960s and early 1970s. In addition, as the level of rates rises and falls, the shapes of the yield curves will change in the same manner as they did in this period. Yield curves for Treasury securities, for example, develop a "hump" and then become inverted, or downward sloping, during a period of rising interest rates. When interest rates fall, short-term rates fall faster than long rates so that yield curves develop a steep upward slope.

Having developed procedures for generating realistic sequences of interest rates, we then developed models to generate and evaluate various portfolio strategies. One of the models is a "Monte Carlo" simulation model that evaluates a portfolio strategy over a large sample of interest rate scenarios, rather than over a single sequence of interest rates, as a deterministic simulation does. By studying a specific portfolio strategy over a large sample of rate scenarios, we were able to obtain a profile of its performance characteristics, including its expected annual return, the volatility of its return, and its potential for realized and unrealized capital losses. Thus the Monte Carlo simulation model allowed us to compare specific portfolio strategies in terms of their expected return and their exposure to potential risk.

We also developed an "optimization" model. It differs from the simulation model in that it selects a portfolio strategy that performs best according to some well defined criteria instead of analyzing a strategy specified by a planner or portfolio manager. Optimization models have been used in banks, but these models generally ignore uncertainty by selecting a set of portfolio actions based on one assumed interest rate scenario. Our model recognizes the fact that future interest rates are uncertain. It selects the portfolio strategy providing the highest expected return over a sample of interest rate scenarios that might occur. The strategy selected takes into account a number of factors, including the securities already held in the portfolio, limits a bank might wish to impose on losses realized from trades, and limits on the potential buildup of unrealized losses. Additional restrictions can also be imposed, such as a minimum on the holdings of U.S. Treasuries based on pledging requirements. These characteristics of the optimization model allowed us to study the impact of various factors on the selection of a portfolio strategy, including the bank's desire to limit capital loss potential.

SUMMARY OF MAJOR FINDINGS

Using our statistical models to generate realistic interest rate scenarios and the portfolio models to analyze alternative policies, we were able to explore issues raised in the questions above. Our conclusions on these issues are summarized below and then discussed more fully.

1.   For banks not wishing to manage their portfolios very actively, laddered portfolio structures have some desirable characteristics. In addition to being relatively easy to manage, these portfolios tend to provide reasonably high returns that are relatively stable over time. Banks wishing to manage their portfolios more actively can probably obtain better performance with barbell portfolios. They tend to provide higher returns within the limits on capital losses that might be set by a bank, if the bank is willing to realize a small amount of losses periodically to maintain the barbell structure. The allocation of funds within a barbell portfolio is dependent on the shape of the current yield curves. Thus a rigid allocation of funds to short- and long-term securities is not always appropriate.

2.   An important measure of risk is the potential for realized and unrealized losses stemming from a portfolio strategy. A bank's willingness and ability to tolerate the potential buildup of unrealized losses has an important impact on the average maturity of desirable portfolios, whether laddered or barbell. For example, the greater the ability to tolerate unrealized losses if interest rates rise, the larger the proportion of a barbell portfolio that can be placed in long maturities. In addition, the share that can be placed in long maturities is increased if the bank is able to absorb more realized losses on trades each year.

3.   Even if a bank does not intend for security holdings to provide liquidity for the remainder of the bank, a large share of the portfolio should be held in short maturities because of the bank's limited tolerance for losses and perhaps because of the desire to have some flexibility to take advantage of interest rates swings. In a barbell portfolio, for example, the proportion of funds in the short and long ends of the portfolio is relatively unaffected by a decision not to use the portfolio for liquidity purposes. However, a decreased use of the portfolio for liquidity does allow the short-term securities to have longer average maturity.

4.   The availability of purchased funds affects the way in which liquidity needs are financed, but it normally will have little effect on the size of the bank's portfolio or on the basic allocation of funds between short and long maturities.

5.   The maturity structure of U.S. Treasury and municipal securities in U.S. banks should be considered jointly. Normally Treasury holdings are

kept to the minimum needed for pledging and cosmetic purposes, except for securities held for repurchase agreements. Banks that have a need for additional taxable income, though, may find it worthwhile to hold more than the minimum amount of Treasuries. Whatever the amount, these holdings should be kept in short maturities since long-term municipals tend to provide a higher return for the amount of risk. This leads to a barbell structure across Treasuries and tax-exempts in which the short securities are a mixture of both security types but any longer bonds held are all municipals.

6. Even though banks hold some long-term securities, a planning horizon of 2 to 3 years is probably adequate. More specifically, the bank's concern about volatility of returns and unrealized losses that might build up over the next 2 to 3 years dominates the impact longer-term considerations might have on the selection of a strategy.

In analyzing the performance characteristics of portfolio policies we looked at both the return and risk of each strategy studied. Two measures of risk were used, the volatility of the return on the portfolio and the potential for realized and unrealized capital losses resulting from the strategy. The first measure is concerned with the degree of certainty that a desired return might be achieved. This measure, which is commonly used in the research literature, assumes that a portfolio manager would like to have a stable and predictable return from the portfolio each year. The second measure is one more frequently used in banks, since they are specifically concerned about the realized and unrealized capital losses that might stem from their security holdings. Most banks pay close attention to this element of risk.

Laddered portfolio strategies performed reasonably well according to both risk criteria, particularly the volatility of return. Consider, for example, a municipal portfolio with maturities laddered out to a maximum of 15 years. As time passes, the proceeds from maturities are used to purchase new 15-year securities. Since yields on municipal securities are normally higher for longer maturities, this regular purchase of intermediate securities provides a relatively high interest income each year. At the same time, the return is reasonably stable because only one-fifteenth of the portfolio turns over each year and because the interest rate on new 15-year securities tends to fluctuate less than the yield on shorter-term bonds. As a result of these phenomena, laddered portfolios are attractive to banks, particularly those that do not wish to actively manage their portfolios.

The choice of the longest maturity to include in a laddered portfolio depends on the bank's tolerance for volatility in the return from the portfolio and for the potential buildup of unrealized losses. As discussed in Chapter 6, laddered portfolios containing only short maturities have volatile returns because of the rapid turnover of the portfolio and the high variability of short-term rates. When the ladder is lengthened to include longer-term bonds, the volatility of return declines up to a point. If the portfolio is then lengthened further, it becomes riskier according to this measure because of the variability in market value of the longer bonds. This point of minimum volatility occurs with portfolios laddered out to maturities of 6 years in the case of the 3-year investment horizon shown in Chapter 6. The relationship between length of a ladder and the potential for unrealized losses is much simpler. Any increase in the maturities of a laddered portfolio increases the potential for unrealized losses.

Although most banks using a barbell approach manage their portfolios more actively, it is possible to establish some trading rules that maintain the barbell structure and then use these rules mechanically, as can be done with laddered portfolios. We tried out a set of such rules in our research to provide a basis of comparison with the laddered strategies. Our results suggest that a barbell approach works about as well as the laddered approach over reasonable maturity ranges, but it has different risk characteristics. For portfolios with comparable return, barbells have higher volatility of returns as a result of the rapid turnover of short maturities in the barbell. The potential for unrealized losses is less than that of laddered portfolios because some of the potential losses are realized when bonds are traded to maintain the barbell structure. However, the total of realized and unrealized losses over an investment horizon in mechanically managed portfolios is about the same for both barbell and laddered portfolios.

One conclusion to be reached from our comparison of mechanically managed portfolios is that barbell portfolios have little to offer banks not wishing to actively manage their portfolios that is not already provided by the more traditional laddered approach. For other banks the barbell approach has some advantages. One feature is that its more rapid turnover of securities makes it easier for a portfolio manager to alter the bank's maturity structure to take advantage of some characteristic of current yield curves or his expectations about future rates. More importantly, active management of barbell portfolios can improve their performance relative to laddered portfolios. Our work with the optimization model suggests that careful selection of maturities in a barbell portfolio provides the highest return while limiting the bank's exposure to realized losses each year and to unrealized losses over the planning horizon. In most environments studied, desirable portfolios selected by the model contained a spread of short-term securities and some long maturities. This was true for both U.S. Treasury and municipal securities.

Although the model had a strong tendency to select barbell portfolios, the specific maturities chosen depended upon the shape of the current yield curve and expectations about future rates. For example, there were occasions when intermediate maturities were attractive. One such instance occurred when the Treasury yield curve was "humped" so that intermediate maturities had a higher yield to maturity than either short or long maturities. In this situation the intermediate maturities were very attractive. They provided higher current income and the likely possibility of capital gains as the hump in the curve disappeared over time. Another example occurred when the current yield curve sloped upward very steeply and we assigned a high probability to a rate increase. There was substantial incentive in this environment to keep the portfolio as short as possible and wait to see if rates rise before buying long-term bonds.

To see how the optimization model and its recommended portfolios would work through a series of actual yield curve changes, we used the model to manage a hypothetical portfolio of municipal securities during the period 1964 through 1973. The computer selected an initial portfolio in January 1964, based on the general assumption that municipal rates in 1965, 1966, and 1967 were uncertain but that they would be about as volatile as they were in the previous 7 years. In January 1965 the model updated the existing portfolio, taking into account the new municipal yield curve, limits on realized losses, and updated assessments about future rate volatility over the next 3 years. This process was continued for each year through January 1973, and the final portfolio was evaluated as of January 1974. The maturity distribution which resulted from each portfolio decision made by the model is presented in Chapter 10.

By and large, the model purchased and maintained a barbell structure. As the long maturities became shorter, and as limits on realized losses permitted, it sold these bonds and reinvested the funds in new long-term bonds. Occasionally funds were put into intermediate maturities, as the model did in its initial portfolio decision in January 1964. At that time the municipal yield curve was relatively flat so that the return from long maturities was not sufficient to justify the added risk. As time passed, the model sold these maturities, but limits on losses restricted the rate at which the model could trade out of these bonds. The total return obtained over the 10-year historical period with the portfolios selected by the model was higher than those we obtained by simulating the performance of various laddered and "unmanaged" barbell portfolios.

In both laddered and barbell portfolio strategies our research indicates that the average maturity of desirable portfolios is critically affected by two factors, (1) the amount of unrealized losses the bank is willing to tolerate if interest rates rise and (2) the length of the bank's planning horizon. The potential amount of unrealized loss is directly increased by the lengthening of a laddered portfolio to include longer maturities and by putting a larger share of a barbell portfolio in long maturities. Thus a bank should give careful consideration to the highest interest rate scenario it wishes to plan for and to the amount of unrealized losses it is willing to tolerate if this scenario occurs.

It is less obvious that the length of a bank's planning horizon affects its choice of portfolio strategy, but this length of time has an important effect. If a bank decides to select a long planning horizon, say, 10 years, long-term bonds are not very risky. A 20-year bond will provide stable income over the period, reducing the variability of return over the 10 years. In addition, it has only a moderate risk of unrealized loss at the horizon since at that time it will only be a 10-year bond. Because of these phenomena long planning horizons encourage longer portfolio maturities. Such horizons may be appropriate for some banks, but the market value of these long bonds can fluctuate considerably in intervening years. This exposes the bank to uncertain returns and large amounts of unrealized losses in the near future even though the horizon is many years away. Thus it is probably more appropriate for banks to use investment horizons of 2 to 3 years. This is about as far as banks can make assessments of future interest rates, and it provides a sufficiently long planning period for the bank to evaluate the implications of a high interest rate scenario if it occurred.

Because of the critical role played by limits on unrealized losses in the selection of a portfolio strategy, the availability and use of purchased funds should have little impact on the basic maturity structure. Purchased funds do lessen the need for liquidity from security portfolios, and they offer the possibility of expanding the size of portfolios. Although a lessened liquidity need might allow for a larger share of the portfolio to be placed in long-term securities, a bank's limit on the potential for unrealized losses constrains its ability to add long-maturity bonds. As a result, the only significant impact of a smaller liquidity need is that the short end of the portfolio can have a longer average maturity. Short-term purchased liabilities could be used to buy more securities, but normally there is no profit to be made by investing these funds in short-term securities and no ability to absorb the increased loss potential of additional long-term securities.

The final issue we addressed in our analysis of portfolio strategies was the implication of joint management of U.S. Treasury and tax-exempt portfolios. Although most banks maintain separate portfolios of these securities, there should be, and normally there is, some attempt to look at the total risk and return of the two portfolios taken together. The size of the Treasury portfolio is usually dictated by noninterest rate factors, such as the pledging needs of the bank. These put a floor or minimum on the size of this portfolio. In some banks there is enough need for taxable income that it will pay to shift funds out of tax-exempt securities into Treasuries. This reduces the aftertax return from security holdings, but it provides taxable income that might be needed to use tax deductions and credits from high yielding activities, such as leasing. Whatever the size of the Treasury portfolio, our research suggests that it be kept in relatively short-term securities. Long-term municipals appear to provide higher return relative to their risk, so that they are a better means of "using up" the risk a bank is willing to have in its portfolios. This allocation of funds leads to a barbell structure across Treasuries and tax-exempts, with the short end of the barbell containing some of each security type and the long end containing only municipals.

ISSUES IN THE CONTINUING MANAGEMENT OF PORTFOLIOS

This evaluation of alternative portfolio policies had the objective of helping a banking institution select a basic portfolio structure. After this decision has been made, though, there are still a number of strategic and tactical choices that have to be made in the continuing management of the portfolio. A potential benefit of selecting the laddered approach is the need for less active management, but there is still the need to select the longest maturity of the ladder and there is some room for ongoing management initiative. For example, should funds from maturing securities be reinvested in new long maturities now or should the manager wait for a while? This choice is particularly difficult if long rates have a good chance of rising or if the yield curve is inverted so that higher income can be obtained, at least temporarily, by purchasing some short-term securities.

If a barbell structure is selected, there are a number of continuing decisions that have to be made in addition to the strategic choice of how to allocate funds between short and long maturities. The portfolio manager must decide, for example, when to trade out of the "shorter" long maturities to maintain the barbell structure. This decision should take into account the overall tax position of the bank and expectations about future interest rates. Similarly, continuing consideration needs to be given to the maturities of new securities being purchased. There will be times when the shape of the current yield curve and the bank's expectations about future interest rates indicate that intermediate maturities are attractive purchases or that the distribution of short-term maturities should be changed.

Answering these and other questions involved in the management of portfolios places a continuing burden of judgment on the portfolio manager. This judgment can be better informed if scenario planning is used in an ongoing manner to help select appropriate portfolio actions. The planning process involves two steps. First, it is necessary to assess and describe economic environments that might occur over the planning horizon of the bank. Once these economic scenarios have been specified, the second step is to evaluate the implications of these environments for alternative portfolio decisions and select a set of actions providing an appropriate balance between expected return and risk. This planning process adds to the amount of analysis that must be undertaken, but statistical aids and computer models can be of significant help. A major purpose of our research was to develop such analytical tools to assist in portfolio management.

THE SCENARIO PLANNING PROCESS

Scenario planning is something many banks do already, but it is not normally called by this name and it frequently is not carried out in a manner very helpful to a portfolio manager. The most common example of such planning is the annual planning and budgeting cycle conducted by banks. This planning process is normally conducted each fall with the objective of projecting bank assets, liabilities, and income statement items for the coming year. The resulting plan is intended to represent forecasts and bank decisions consistent with the economic environment projected by the bank.

Portfolio managers play a part in this planning process by providing information about the size and revenues of the portfolios. However, the planning document is frequently of little help in making decisions. This results in part because the length of time required to complete the plan causes it to become rapidly outdated. Another important problem is that the plan is based on a single scenario of the future economic environment. The implications of this environment provide important information to a portfolio manager, but he cannot select a set of portfolio actions based on the assumption that this is the only economic scenario that can occur. His evaluation of alternatives should take into account the fact that any of a number of scenarios are possible.

If the portfolio manager and others in the bank assess a range of possible future environments, a much more thorough analysis of alternative portfolio actions can be done. What portfolio action is appropriate in each of the possible environments? What is the cost of selecting a portfolio strategy for one environment and having one of the others occur? By exploring these questions and trying out alternative ideas, the portfolio manager can select a set of actions likely to provide a reasonable return while limiting the risk.

Assessing Economic Scenarios

Some banks have gone beyond preparation of the annual "plan" to regularly prepare descriptions of possible future economic environments. Each scenario is based on some critical assumptions concerning the direction of fiscal and monetary policy and other factors affecting the future direction of the economy. Assessments are made of how the economy will react to these influences to arrive at a projection of several key variables for each set of underlying assumptions. The result is a set of economic forecasts, one for each set of underlying assumptions.

There is a variety of sources for such projections. In larger banks internal economic staffs would be involved in preparing the underlying assumptions and projections of the economic variables. Some commercial forecasting services also prepare several economic scenarios for their customers. These can be used either as an alternative to internally prepared projections or as a source of information to bank economists who prepare their own scenarios.

Whatever the source of scenarios, it is helpful to have a management committee within the institution involved in the final selection and definition of economic environments to be considered in the bank's planning. Such a committee should include senior officers who have responsibility for asset and liability management, as well as those involved more directly in economic analysis and forecasting. One reason for involving several people is to help insure that a wide range of alternative economic environments get considered in the bank's planning. A second important reason is to bring the judgment of the bank's senior people to bear in assessing the likelihood of the alternative scenarios. These assessments can have a significant impact on the direction of bank policy.

The result of this process is a set of projections of key economic variables, including some interest rates. These interest rates projections, though, are not normally detailed enough to permit complete evaluation of alternative portfolio actions. For each scenario projected, the portfolio manager needs a yield curve for each type of security for each period in the planning horizon. Fortunately, movements in the various interest rates are highly correlated with each other, so that statistical techniques can be used to generate detailed projections based on the small number of interest rates specified in each scenario. In Chapter 3 we illustrated how a projected path of the 3-month Treasury bill rate could be used to specify other short-term rates. It could also be used to forecast rates of longer-term securities, but if the economic scenarios contain projections of at least one long rate, it is probably better to use this rate to specify other long-term rates. Once these statistical techniques have been used to specify interest rates on a few different maturities of, say, Treasury securities, curve-fitting techniques can be used to fill in the remainder of the yield curve.

Models for Portfolio Evaluation

After defining scenarios of interest rates and other factors in the portfolio environment, the next step is to generate and evaluate alternative portfolio actions. Some simple analysis can be done by manual calculations, but the range of alternatives that can be explored is very limited. Relatively simple computer models can easily be used to explore many more alternatives in a more complete manner. Although there is some additional cost, sophisticated computer models make it possible to go even further in providing information useful in making portfolio management decisions.

In our research we have drawn on some existing computer models and developed some new models that can provide assistance to portfolio managers in the evaluation of alternative strategies. These models can be categorized along two dimensions: (1) whether the model assumes a future scenario will occur with certainty or explicitly incorporates uncertainty about future events, and (2) whether the model evaluates strategies provided by the portfolio manager or generates its own strategy that is "optimal" according to some well defined criteria. The four basic model types discussed in this book can be classified as shown in the table below.

The deterministic simulation models discussed in Chapter 4 and the linear programming models of Chapter 5 both evaluate a portfolio strategy over one economic scenario at a time. In effect, the evaluation assumes that the scenario specified by the planner will occur with certainty. The other models, Monte Carlo simulation and optimization models under uncertainty (Chapters 6 and 7), take into account the fact that there are several economic scenarios that might occur. Looking at the other dimension, both types of simulation models evaluate portfolio strategies provided to them. The linear programming and optimization models, on the other hand, will generate portfolio actions that satisfy constraints provided by the portfolio manager and are optimal according to his criterion. Each of these modeling types has its strengths and weaknesses.

Deterministic Simulation. The deterministic simulation models are the most frequently used class of model for portfolio management, in large part

Table 11.1 Classification of Portfolio Models

	Strategy evaluation	Strategy generation
Assumes certainty	Deterministic simulation	Linear programming
Recognizes uncertainty	Monte Carlo simulation	Optimization under uncertainty

because they are relatively easy to implement and use. A number of such models have been developed, some for proprietary use within individual banks and others available to banks generally on a commercial basis. The basic structure of most of these models is quite similar. The bank planner or portfolio manager supplies three types of information to the model: (1) data describing the current financial position of the bank, including information about its portfolios; (2) assumptions about future trends of loans, deposits, interest rates, and other relevant items; (3) a set of actions to be evaluated. The computer model then simulates what would happen if the assumed scenario occurred and the proposed decisions were implemented. The results of this simulation are then displayed, most commonly as pro forma balance sheets and income statements, or other financial reports.

The virtues of deterministic simulation models stem from their relative simplicity. They are easy to use and to understand without the benefit of sophisticated, management science professionals. Furthermore, since models are readily available from commercial vendors or other banks, the start-up cost is very modest. The portfolio manager or bank planner knows what assumptions have been given to the model and he can understand the results.

While the ease of use is an important virtue, most of the weaknesses of deterministic models stem from the same characteristic. Many of the available simulation models use rather broad categories of assets and liabilities, which limits their usefulness for detailed evaluation of portfolio actions. In addition, the planner can only evaluate a strategy over one scenario at a time. This is one of the traits of deterministic simulation models, but some of the more complex versions of these models make it relatively easy to alter both portfolio decisions and scenarios, so that the interaction of strategies and future environments can be studied efficiently. This is helpful when studying questions such as, What is the cost of adopting a particular strategy if the high interest rate scenario occurs?

These simulation models are a good first step for a bank beginning to use computer models. Although many of the readily available models have limited flexibility, they provide an easy beginning. As time passes and the bank acquires more analytical sophistication, it is possible to add the flexibility and the detail needed to make the model more useful in evaluating portfolio strategies. Such deterministic simulation models retain their usefulness for portfolio planning even though more complex models have been developed.

Monte Carlo Simulation Models. Monte Carlo models have the same basic structure as the deterministic models, but with a major addition. As with deterministic simulation, the portfolio strategy to be studied is specified by the planner. The difference is that the strategy is simulated over a very large number of scenarios, selected to correspond to the variety and likelihood of economic environments that might occur. These results obtained over a large number of scenarios provide information not obtainable from a deterministic model. For example, the results provide data on the variability of interest income that might result from the strategy, and they provide estimates of the likelihood of unrealized losses of specific amounts. Such additional results are obtained at some increase in cost. A more sophisticated model is required since a probability model must be developed to generate the economic scenarios to be used in the Monte Carlo simulation. The probability model, in effect, is a simulation of a real world process that generates actual interest rates.

The primary usefulness of these models is in the investigation of broad strategic questions, as was done in Chapter 6. It is helpful in studying, for example, what share of a barbell portfolio should normally be allocated to the short- and long-maturity ranges. Once a broad strategy has been adopted, they are less useful in analyzing specific tactical questions on an ongoing basis. As an example, a portfolio manager might want to consider whether intermediate maturities are attractive purchases at the present time. This decision depends on the shape of the current yield curve and the manager's assessments of yield curves in future periods. Monte Carlo simulation models are not very helpful in this decision because they are not normally designed to accept and analyze specific assessments about future events. One could be designed to help in such decisions, but the benefits obtained would probably not be worth the costs.

Linear Programming. The deterministic and Monte Carlo simulation models provide useful ways of evaluating portfolio strategies specified by the portfolio manager, but neither will generate a new strategy for consideration. Linear programming models provide this capability. To use such a model, the portfolio manager must provide some of the same information he provides a simulation model, including data about the current position of the bank and a forecast or scenario of future conditions. He must also specify some information not required by simulation models. This includes an objective for the model and some policy and other guidelines, such as limits on the use of purchased funds and constraints stemming from the bank's capital position. An objective might be, for example, to maximize the bank's net worth at the end of the planning horizon. The linear programming model will find the portfolio strategy that will provide the maximum net worth for the specified scenario, while staying within all the limits specified.

Linear programming models can suggest innovative strategies that may not have been considered by the portfolio manager. In addition, the strategy selection process considers more factors and interrelationships than an individual can when thinking through alternatives. For example, the model takes into account the impact current decisions have on the ability of the bank to take advantage of future investment opportunities. The price paid for these benefits is a more complicated model usually requiring the talents of a professional management scientist in both its development and use.

The need for management science skills results partly from the more complicated mathematics of the model, but the behavior of this kind of model is also more complex than that of a simulation model. The ability to generate desirable portfolio strategies gives a linear programming model a "mind of its own" in some ways, while the simulation model only does what it is told. In the linear programming model's selection of an attractive policy, it can go too far and end up with an unrealistic set of suggested actions. As an example, it might liquidate all of the Treasury portfolio and invest the proceeds in higher yielding tax-exempts. This particular problem can be easily handled by specifying a minimum limit on the size of the Treasury portfolio based on pledging and other requirements of the bank. However, the example illustrates the fact that constraints specified by the planner play an important role in the strategy selected by the model.

With proper study these limits or constraints can provide very useful information. As the model is developed, an attempt is made to incorporate the bank's portfolio policy in the model through the use of these constraints. Then, by experimenting with the model, it is possible to identify the limits that are important in selecting a set of portfolio actions and perhaps find some policy constraints that were being used but never explicitly defined. The model can also provide information about the benefits of relaxing some of these policy constraints. A sample question that could be studied would be, How much could profit be improved if a larger share of the portfolio were allowed to be placed in longer maturities?

The major problem with linear programming models is that they consider only one scenario at a time and assume that this economic environment will occur with certainty. Thus if interest rates are projected to fall off sharply in the scenario specified, the model will tend to invest as much as allowed in long-maturity bonds. Since it assumes that the falling rates will occur for sure, there is no need to hedge and keep some funds in short securities. The only hedging done by the model is that forced upon it by the policy constraints. It is possible to use a linear programming model to explore the implications of various hedging constraints by experimenting with the model over a variety of scenarios, but this is an indirect and not wholly satisfactory approach.

In summary, linear programming models are a helpful research tool that can be used to evaluate alternative bank policies and help develop new port-folio strategies. They are particularly useful for special studies of a strategic nature. Although they are also helpful in tactical decision making, linear programming models are relatively complicated to use. The major draw-back of linear programming models is that they do not take uncertainty about future environments into account.

Optimization Models under Uncertainty. Optimization models incorporat-ing uncertainty have existed for some time, but most of these models have not been very practical because some other important element of the port-folio problem has had to be ignored in order for the model to be computa-tionally feasible. The model and solution procedure reported in this book have overcome this difficulty, making it possible to retain the critical fea-tures of the problem and still explicitly account for uncertainty about future events. The modeling approach developed in Chapter 7 is similar to the linear programming models, except that several economic scenarios are considered at the same time rather than just one.

To use such a model, the portfolio planner or manager specifies a number of economic scenarios considered to be possible and assesses the probability of each occurring. The model then takes all of this information into account when selecting a set of portfolio actions for the current period. These ac-tions recognize that there is some likelihood that interest rates will fall, in which case long-term bonds would be attractive investments. On the other hand, short-term securities will be better investments if the high interest rate scenario occurs. By considering the probability of these and other scenarios, the model selects a hedging strategy to balance expected return with the potential losses that might occur. This strategy also plans for changes in funds available to the portfolio that might have been specified for some scenarios.

Optimization models under uncertainty are the most complex and so-phisticated of the modeling approaches discussed, but they go much farther than the others in incorporating the critical elements of the portfolio problem. To get these benefits the portfolio manager must provide the model with more information. The most difficult are defining the attributes of future economic scenarios and assessing the probability of each. This is an important step to take even if an optimization model under uncertainty is not used. If a simple deterministic simulation model is used, it is still helpful to try alternative portfolio strategies in all of the likely environments to see what returns and losses would result. This analysis is necessary to develop an appropriate hedging strategy with a simulation model.

The power of the optimization model under uncertainty comes into play because of the very large number of potential strategies and contingencies that need to be considered. The model selects a set of portfolio actions for each of the possible environments and then works back from these strategies to recommend portfolio actions for the current period. Because of the complexity of using one of these models, it is not likely to be used on a continuing basis each week or month. Nevertheless, it is likely to be of substantial benefit when used to review the portfolio structure periodically or when any major change in portfolio strategy is being considered.

Although knowledge of current bond market conditions has been and will continue to be critical in portfolio management, it is also very important to bring a planning perspective to the problem. This perspective involves careful attention to the economic environments that might occur in the future, consideration of what the bank's overall policy would be in these environments, and evaluation of alternative portfolio strategies that takes cognizance of these future events and bank policy. The scenario planning approach developed in this book provides a framework for integrating these planning activities. The optimization model under uncertainty is a comprehensive model designed to help implement this method of planning. However, the scenario planning framework can be very useful regardless of the approach used to select and evaluate portfolio decisions.

ESTIMATING THE RELATIONSHIP BETWEEN SHORT- AND LONG-TERM INTEREST RATES

Chapter 3 discusses some statistical procedures that are useful in making the detailed projections associated with economic scenarios. One suggestion made in the chapter is to include a short-term interest rate, such as the 3-month Treasury bill rate, in the definition of each scenario. Then projections of other rates can be based on the forecast path of this key rate. For example, Table 3.5 shows that the behavior of the 10-year Government rate can be described by an equation that includes last period's 10-year rate and the change in the 3-month bill rate. Although this equation is relatively simple, it performs almost as well as more complex equations, and its accuracy is probably sufficient for use in planning. The purpose of this appendix is to show the relationship between the type of equations used in Chapter 3 and the more complex interest rate equations used in the research literature.

The theory of the term structure of interest rates asserts that there should be some relationship between long- and short-term interest rates. This relationship is based primarily on the assumption that a sufficient number of investors operate in both the short- and long-term credit markets that returns on long-term securities cannot be determined independently from short-term interest rates. Since investors are free to purchase either a series of short-term securities or a long-term bond, long-term interest rates are kept in line with expectations about future short-term rates. If the market, for example, expects rates to rise, investors cannot be induced to buy long bonds unless their yield is sufficiently high to cover the average of the increasing returns expected to be available in the short-term market. This phenomenon is a major cause of the steeply sloped yield curves that occur when investors expect rates to rise. A similar market phenomenon can cause the yield curve to become inverted when investors expect short-term rates to fall. In this situation they are willing to buy lower yielding long-term bonds because they expect the return over their holding period to equal or exceed that obtained from rolling over a series of short-term investments. Thus the current long-term rate is determined to a significant extent by the market's expectations about future short-term rates.

In the pure form of the expectations theory, stated by Meiselman [1962] among others, these expectations completely determine the relationship between short and long interest rates. However, many researchers believe that there are additional variables having an important influence on the shape of the yield curve. Some believe, for example, that there is a liquidity premium in the term structure or yield curve. They argue that long-term securities are riskier than short because of their potential for capital loss, so that investors must be paid a premium above the returns expected from a rollover of short-term securities. As a result, the yield to maturity of a long bond will be larger than it would be if the rate were based only on expectations about future short-term interest rates.

Modigliani and Sutch [1966] have proposed a variant of the liquidity premium theory that recognizes that rolling over a series of short-term securities poses a risk of uncertain interest income, even if this strategy avoids the risk of capital loss on long-term bonds. They argue that many investors have a natural preference for a particular maturity range of assets, based in part upon the maturity structure of their liabilities. Some of these investors might have a preference for long maturities to avoid the income risk of short-term securities. Whatever their natural preference, it is argued that investors will have to receive some premium to get them to purchase maturities outside their desired maturity range. If this is true, there may be other premiums in the yield curve.

For the purpose of assessing future interest rates we do not need to choose from among the conflicting theories. If there are liquidity or other premiums in the interest-rate structure, they will not be detrimental to forecasting equations as long as the size of any premium is relatively stable over time. If the premium for a particular maturity were constant, changes in the yield on this maturity would still be based upon changes in expectations. The difficulty in establishing the relationship between long-term interest rates and expectations is that we cannot directly observe the market's expectations. It is reasonable to assume, though, as several researchers have done, that investors' expectations about the future are based on current and past rates. If so, and if expectations affect the shape of the yield curve, then theoretically there should be some relationship between current long rates and current and past short-term rates.

One of the most comprehensive models of this relationship was initially specified by de Leeuw [1965] and then refined by Modigliani and Sutch [1966]. Their basic hypothesis is that the expected short-term interest rate is determined by a weighted average of recent short rates. This weighted average reflects a combination of two phenomena. On the one hand, the market expects rates to return to some normal level determined by an average of past rates. Working against this phenomenon is an extrapolative expectation that assumes that recent uptrends or downtrends will continue. Modigliani and Sutch argue that the combination of these two forces results in expectations about future short rates that are based on a weighted average of past short-term rates, where the weights initially rise and then fall in magnitude. That is, interest rates that occurred most recently and those that occurred farthest in the past receive the least weight in the weighted average of past rates.

This formulation of interest rate expectations leads to an equation in which the current long-term rate depends on a weighted average of current and past short-term interest rates. Modigliani and Sutch [1966, 1967, 1969] have reported a substantial volume of empirical research based on such equations. Their results show that a large share of variation in long U.S. Government interest rates can be explained by a weighted average of 3-month rates for the current and 16 to 19 past quarters.

There is a statistical problem in estimating a regression equation of their type because the explanatory variables consist of the current 3-month rate and a large number of its lagged values used to compute the weighted average. It is not possible to estimate directly the best weights for each of the past interest rates since these values are highly correlated with each other. To solve this multicollinearity problem Modigliani and Sutch used a distributed lag estimating technique developed by Almon [1965]. In this technique it is assumed that the weights on past values lie along a polynomial function. The regression model then estimates the parameters of the function, and the weights for each lagged value are computed from the polynomial equation. Modigliani and Sutch assumed that the weights would lie along a third-degree polynomial. This allowed the model to select a set of weights that have the shape of an inverted "U". Such weights are consistent with their theory of expectations, which argues that recent and distant 3-month rates should receive the least weight.

To illustrate their approach we estimated the relationship between the 20-year and 3-month Government rates as reported by Salomon Brothers. The current and 19 lagged quarterly values of the 3-month rate were used as the explanatory variables. Following the approach of Modigliani and Sutch, coefficients on these lagged values were constrained to fit a third-degree polynomial and to have approximately zero weight on the most distant value of the 3-month rate.* The equation was fitted over a 7-year period starting in 1965, with data for 1961–1964 used to provide initial values for the lagged interest rates. The following equation resulted:

$$R_{20,t} = .813 + .340r_t + \sum_{i=1}^{19} \beta_i r_{t-i} + u_{20,t}$$

$$\begin{array}{cc} (.234) & (.080) \end{array}$$

$$(\Sigma \beta_i = .593 \text{ [standard error} = .124], \quad (1)$$

$$R^2 = .953,\dagger \quad SE = 20.0 \text{ basis points})$$

In this equation $R_{20,t}$ is the current 20-year rate, r_t is the current 3-month rate, the r_{t-i} represent past values of the 3-month rate, and $u_{20,t}$ represents the error term, that is, the difference between the actual 20-year rate and the rate estimated by the equation for the tth period. Numbers shown in parentheses are the standard errors of estimate of the coefficients. The summation term in (1) is the weighted average of past 3-month rates, where the coefficients, β_i, represent the weights on each past value. The individual weights are not shown, but they had the inverted "U" shape, as expected by Modigliani and Sutch. Overall, the equation performed well inasmuch as it explained 95.3% of the variance in the 20-year rate and the standard error of the residuals was only 20 basis points.

While the Modigliani-Sutch approach is consistent with their theory and works well, Hamburger and Latta [1969] have proposed an alternative method that works about as well. Their approach starts with the simple relationship between the current long- and short-term interest rates. For example, the regression equation below estimates the relationship between the 20-year and 3-month rates.

$$R_{20,t} = 2.308 + .594r_t + u_{20,t} \qquad (R^2 = .599, \quad SE = 57.4 \text{ basis points})$$

$$\begin{array}{cc} (.508) & (.094) \end{array}$$

$$(2)$$

This equation indicates a significant relation between the long- and short-term interest rates, but it does not perform nearly as well as the Modigliani-Sutch equation, which includes lagged values of the 3-month rate. Hamburger and Latta believe that this difference in performance results from the correlation among the error terms in the simpler equation. Equation (2) tends to under- or over-estimate the 20-year rate for a number of time periods in succession, consequently the error in one period tends to be

---

* See Modigliana and Sutch [1966] for a complete description of their approach.
† All R^2 in the Appendix are adjusted for degrees of freedom.

highly correlated with that of the next period. This problem of autocorrelation can be solved by estimating the relationship among the residuals and then transforming the data as shown below.

The correlation between successive residuals in equation (2) can be estimated by least-squares analysis, with the result shown in equation (3).

$$u_{20,t} = .947\ u_{20,t-1} + e_{20,t} \tag{3}$$

In this equation .947 is the autoregression coefficient, which is normally identified as ρ, and $e_{20,t}$ represents the error term.

The autoregression coefficient is used to transform both the 20-year and 3-month rates by subtracting the coefficient times the past observation of the rate from the current observation. Then the regression equation is recomputed from the transformed data.*

$$R_{20,t} - .947R_{20,t-1} = \begin{array}{cc} .279 & + & .269 \\ (.047) & & (.062) \end{array} (r_t - .947\ r_{t-1})$$

$$(R^2 = .941, \quad SE = 21.5 \text{ basis points}) \tag{4}$$

It is sometimes necessary to repeat the cycle by estimating the structure of the residuals of equation (4) and transforming the variables again. However, in this case one transformation removed the significant autocorrelation.

This procedure led to a major improvement in the ability of the 3-month rate to explain movements in the 20-year rate. The percentage of variance explained rose to 94.1% and the standard error of the residuals was reduced to 21.5 basis points, results commensurate with the Modigliani-Sutch approach. It should not be surprising that the results are similar. In the Modigliani-Sutch equation the current long-term rate depends on current and past short-term rates, r_t through r_{t-19}. Rather than include all these short-term rates, Hamburger and Latta [1969] include last period's long rate, $R_{20,t-1}$, in their equation. According to the Modigliani-Sutch model, $R_{20,t-1}$ can be estimated by its current and lagged 3-month rates, r_{t-1} through r_{t-20}. Thus including $R_{20,\ t-1}$ in the equation incorporates almost the same effect as the lagged short-term rates.

The simple regression approach we propose in Chapter 3 builds on the same logic and on the fact that the regression coefficient between successive error terms tends to have a value close to one. If it were equal to one, equations having the form of (4) would be identical with the regression equations estimated in Chapter 3. Assume that ρ, the autoregression coefficient of equation (2), is equal to one and that we want to estimate an equation similar to (3). The equation to be estimated would then have the following

---

* This approach to reducing the problem of autocorrelation is described in a number of econometric textbooks. For example, see Johnston [1963].

form:

$$R_{20,t} - R_{20,t-1} = \alpha + \beta(r_t - r_{t-1}) \qquad (5)$$

With rearrangement of terms this equation is equal to:

$$R_{20,t} = \alpha + R_{20,t-1} + \beta(r_t - r_{t-1}) \qquad (6)$$

This is the form of the equation in Chapter 3. In that chapter we did not force the coefficient of the lagged long-term rate to equal one, as it is shown for $R_{20,t-1}$ in equation (6), but the regression model still selected coefficients very close to this value.

To illustrate, the results for the 10-year Government rate from Table 3.5 are presented below. The initial regression between the 10-year and 3-month rates is:

$$R_{10,t} = 3.065 + .518r_t + u_{10,t} \qquad (R^2 = .382, \quad SE = 78 \text{ basis points})$$
$$\phantom{R_{10,t} = }(.600) \quad (.115)$$

$$(7)$$

The correlation between successive residuals is given in (8).

$$u_{10,t} = .966\, u_{10,t-1} + e_{10,t} \qquad (8)$$

After transforming the original data, the regression results of (9) are obtained.

$$R_{10,t} - .966R_{10,t-1} = .119 + .435\,(r_t - .966r_{t-1})$$
$$\phantom{R_{10,t} - .966R_{10,t-1} = }(.035) \quad (.078)$$

$$(R^2 = .904, \quad SE = 30.7 \text{ basis points}) \quad (9)$$

If we set $\rho = 1$ as was done in Chapter 3, we can get equation (10), which is essentially the same as the result in Table 3.5.

$$R_{10,t} - R_{10,t-1} = .034 + .433\,(r_t - r_{t-1})$$
$$\phantom{R_{10,t} - R_{10,t-1} = }(.021) \quad (.077)$$

$$(R^2 = .904, \quad SE = 30.8 \text{ basis points}) \quad (10)$$

The Table 3.5 result is slightly different because for that equation we estimated $R_{10,t}$ directly as a function of $R_{10,t-1}$ and $(r_t - r_{t-1})$. We also forced the constant term to be zero, so the coefficient of $R_{10,t-1}$ was slightly larger than 1.0, as shown below:

$$R_{10,t} = 1.009R_{10,t-1} + .433\,(r_{1,t} - r_{1,t-1})$$
$$\phantom{R_{10,t} = }(.009) \quad (.077)$$

$$(R^2 = .900, \quad SE = 30.9 \text{ basis points}) \quad (11)$$

In these situations where the autoregression coefficient ρ is very close to one, the relatively simple approach taken in this book is about as good as the more complex model of Modigliani and Sutch. It is an easy approach to implement since the estimation procedure requires only a normal regression program, and no extra data are required to provide initial values of the lagged rates. The results are very easy to interpret and the method is probably accurate enough for the purpose of scenario planning. In some banks, though, use of the Modigliani-Sutch or Hamburger-Latta approach poses no special problems. Some commercial computer programs incorporate the distributed lag and autocorrelation estimation procedures, so either approach could be implemented mechanically. Some commercial services also provide historical data bases, so that sufficient past data are readily available. In these cases, the slightly greater accuracy of the more complex procedures can be obtained at a relatively small cost.

MATHEMATICS OF THE BONDS MODEL

The purpose of this appendix is to present the mathematical formulation of the BONDS model and describe the solution procedure developed in Bradley and Crane [1972]. This discussion is quite technical and is intended only for the interested management scientist. It is included mainly for completeness, as the remainder of the book is independent of the material presented here.

We first give the mathematical formulation of the model, omitting any justification of the underlying assumptions, as this has been given in detail in Chapter 7. Next the size of various models in terms of the number of constraints is illustrated and the general structure of the model presented. The decomposition approach for dealing with problems having this general structure is then developed. Finally, an efficient procedure is given for solving the subproblems created in the decomposition solution approach.

MATHEMATICAL FORMULATION

The critical assumption in the formulation of the BONDS model is that we are planning with respect to a limited number of economic scenarios. Each scenario is defined by a particular sequence of yield curves and exogenous cash flows. The assumption of a finite number of scenarios results from making discrete approximations to the continuous distributions of yield curves and cash flows, and this in turn permits formulating a deterministic equivalent linear program for the stochastic program.

In general, the model may include a number of broad categories of securities, such as U.S. Governments or various grades of municipals. Within any of these broad categories we assume that the portfolio manager is able to aggregate the securities available for purchase into a number of maturity classes $k = 1,2, \ldots ,K$, such as 3 months, 6 months, 1 year, and so forth. There may be an initial portfolio of holdings of some maturity classes, as well as cash available for investment, or a requirement for cash that must be withdrawn from the portfolio.

At the beginning of each planning period, assuming that a particular portfolio is currently held and cash is either available to or required from the portfolio, the portfolio manager must decide how much of each security class to buy, $b_n^k(e_n)$, and how much of each security class that he is currently holding to sell, $s_{m,n}^k(e_n)$, or continue to hold, $h_{m,n}^k(e_n)$. The subscript n identifies the current period and m indicates the period when the security was purchased. Since the amount of capital gain or loss on a security class sold will depend on the difference between the purchase price and sales price, the portfolio manager must keep track of the amount of each security class held by its date of purchase. Further, the variables that represent decisions at the start of period n are conditional on the sequence of uncertain events e_n preceding the start of period n, since the model computes the optimal policy for every scenario or uncertain event sequence. More precisely, the decision variables are defined as follows:

$b_n^k(e_n)$ = amount of security class k *purchased* at the beginning of period n conditional on event sequence e_n; in dollars of initial purchase price.

$s_{m,n}^k(e_n)$ = amount of security class k, which had been purchased at the beginning of period m, *sold* at the beginning of period n conditional on event sequence e_n; in dollars of initial purchase price.

$h_{m,n}^k(e_n)$ = amount of security class k, which had been purchased at the beginning of period m, *held* (as opposed to sold) at the beginning of period n conditional on event sequence e_n; in dollars of initial purchase price.

The model in this formulation maximizes the expected value of the portfolio at the horizon subject to five types of constraints: cash flow, inventory balance, initial holdings, net capital loss, and category limits, as well as nonnegativity of the variables. The nonnegativity of the variables merely implies that short sales are not permitted. The mathematical formulation is given in Table B.1, where E_n is the set of all uncertain event sequences prior to period n.

Table B.1 Formulation of the BONDS Model

Objective Function

$$\text{Maximize} \quad \sum_{e_N \in E_N} p(e_N) \sum_{k=1}^{K} \left\{ \sum_{m=0}^{n-1} \left[y_m^k(e_m) + v_{m,N}^k(e_N) \right] h_{m,N}^k(e_N) \right.$$

$$\left. + \left[y_N^k(e_N) + v_{N,N}^k(e_N) \right] b_N^k(e_N) \right\}$$

Cash Flow

$$\sum_{k=1}^{K} b_n^k(e_n) - \sum_{k=1}^{K} \left[\sum_{m=0}^{n-2} y_m^k(e_m) h_{m,n-1}^k(e_{n-1}) + y_{n-1}^k(e_{n-1}) b_{n-1}^k(e_{n-1}) \right]$$

$$- \sum_{k=1}^{K} \sum_{m=0}^{n-1} \left[1 + g_{m,n}^k(e_n) \right] s_{m,n}^k(e_n) = f_n(e_n) \qquad (\forall e_n \in E_n, n = 1, 2, \ldots, N)$$

Inventory Balance

$$-h_{m,n-1}^k(e_{n-1}) + s_{m,n}^k(e_n) + h_{m,n}^k(e_n) = 0 \qquad (m = 0, 1, \ldots, n - 2)$$

$$-b_{n-1}^k(e_{n-1}) + s_{n-1,n}^k(e_n) + h_{n-1,n}^k(e_n) = 0$$

$$(\forall e_n \in E_n; n = 1, 2, \ldots, N; k = 1, 2, \ldots, K)$$

Initial Holdings

$$k_{0,0}^k(e_0) = h_0^k \qquad (k = 1, 2, \ldots, K)$$

Capital Losses

$$- \sum_{k=1}^{K} \sum_{m=n'}^{n} g_{m,n}^k(e_n) s_{m,n}^k(e_n) \leqq L_n(e_n) \qquad (\forall e_n \in E_n, \forall n \in N')$$

Category Limits

$$\sum_{k \in Ki} \left[b_n^k(e_n) + \sum_{m=0}^{n-1} h_{m,n}^k(e_n) \right] \gtreqqless C_n^i(e_n)$$

$$(\forall e_n \in E_n, \quad n = 1, 2, \ldots, N, \quad i = 1, 2, \ldots, I)$$

Nonnegativity

$$b_n^k(e_n) \geqq 0, \quad s_{m,n}^k(e_n) \geqq 0, \quad h_{m,n}^k(e_n) \geqq 0$$

$$(m = 1, 2, \ldots n - 1, \quad \forall e_n \in E_n, \quad n = 1, 2, \ldots, N, \quad k = 1, 2, \ldots, K)$$

Cash Flow

The cash flow equations require that the cash used for purchasing securities be equal to the sum of the cash generated from the coupon income on holdings during the previous period, cash generated from sales of securities, and exogenous cash flow. We can define the income yield from coupon interest, the capital gain or loss from selling a security, and the exogenous cash flow as follows:

$g_{m,n}^{k}(e_n)$ = capital gain or loss on security class k, which had been purchased at the beginning of period m and was sold at the beginning of period n conditional on event sequence e_n; per dollar of initial purchase price.

$y_n^{k}(e_n)$ = income yield from interest coupons on security class k, which was purchased at the beginning of period n, conditional on event sequence e_n; per dollar of initial purchase price.

$f_n(e_n)$ = incremental amount of funds either made available to or withdrawn from the portfolio at the beginning of period n conditional on event sequence e_n; in dollars.

The yield and gain coefficients are defined as aftertax, and transaction costs are taken into account by adjusting the gain coefficient by the appropriate bid-asked spread. The index $m = 0$ refers to holdings of the security classes in the initial portfolio. The exogenous cash flow $f_n(e_n)$ may be either positive or negative depending on whether cash is being made available to or withdrawn from the portfolio, respectively. Finally, the cash flow constraints hold with equality, implying that the portfolio is at all times fully invested.

Inventory Balance

The "commodities" that need to be accounted for are the holdings of each security class purchased in a particular period. Hence the inventory balance equations state that the amount of a commodity sold plus the amount of that commodity held at the beginning of a period must equal the amount of that commodity on hand at the end of the previous period. The amount on hand at the end of the previous period is either the amount purchased or the amount held at the beginning of the previous period.

Current Holdings

The inventory balance constraints allow us easily to take into account the securities held in the initial portfolio. If the amounts of these holdings are:

h_0^k = amount of security class k held in the initial portfolio; in dollars of initial purchase price

we merely set the values of the variables $h_{0,0}^k(e_0)$, which refer to the holdings of securities in the initial portfolio, to these amounts.

Capital Loss

The portfolio manager's risk aversion is reflected by a set of constraints limiting the net realized capital losses within any year and the potential for unrealized losses over the planning horizon. If we let

$L_n(e_n)$ = upper bound on the realized net capital loss (after taxes) from sales during the year ending with period n, conditional on event sequence e_n; in dollars

the loss constraints sum up over the periods contained in a particular year the gains or losses from sales of securities in that year and limit this value. N' is the set of indices of periods corresponding to the end of fiscal years, and n' is the index of the first period in a year defined by an element of N'. Since the model essentially forces the sale of all securities at the horizon without transaction costs, the unrealized loss constraints have the same form as the realized loss constraints.

Category Limits

The constraints on broad categories of assets merely state that the holdings of a particular asset category at some point in time must be above or below a level specified conditional on each scenario. An example would be placing a lower limit on the amount of Governments held for pledging purposes. Letting K^i be the index set of the ith asset category and defining

$C_n^i(e_n)$ = lower (upper) bound on the level of holdings of asset category i at the beginning of period n, conditional on event sequence e_n; in dollars of initial purchase price

these constraints are straightforward.

Objective Function

The objective function of this model is the maximization of the expected value of the portfolio at the end of the final period. Since the holdings at the end of the last period are determined by the decisions at the beginning of the last period, we have written the objective function in terms of the interest income and the expected value of the holdings over the last period. More precisely we can define:

$v_{m,N}(e_N)$ = expected (over period N) cash value per dollar of initial purchase price of security class k that had been purchased at the beginning of period m and held at the beginning of the last period in the model

$p(e_N)$ = probability that event sequence, or scenario, e_N obtains

For simplicity we have in fact assumed that the value of the securities at the horizon is after taxes but before transaction costs.

PROBLEM SIZE AND STRUCTURE

In order to have an understanding of the potential size of the model we have formulated, we will compute the number of constraints implied under various model assumptions. Assume for the moment that the number of events in each time period is the same and equal to D. Further, let there be a total of n time periods with n_i periods in year i. Then, if K is the total number of different security classes in all categories and I is the number of broad categories, the number of equations can be calculated as follows:

$$\text{Cash flow:} \qquad 1 + D + D^2 + \cdots + D^{n-1}$$

$$\text{Net capital loss:} \qquad D^{n_1} + D^{n_1+n_2} + \cdots$$

$$\text{Class composition:} \qquad (I-1)[1 + D + D^2 \cdots D^{n-1}]$$

$$\text{Inventory balance:} \qquad K[D + 2D^2 + \cdots + nD^{n-1}]$$

Consider Table B.2, which indicates the number of each type of constraint under a variety of assumptions. It is clear that even for a relatively small number of events and time periods the problem size rapidly becomes completely unmanageable. However, it is also clear that the main difficulty lies with the number of inventory balance constraints. Hence an efficient solution procedure should treat these constraints implicitly instead of explicitly.

Table B.2 Number of Constraints in Various Models

$$I = 2, K = 8$$

Period/year	D = 3			D = 5		
	$n_1 = 1, n_2 = 1$ $n_3 = 1$	$n_1 = 2, n_2 = 1$ $n_3 = 1$	$n_1 = 3, n_2 = 1$ $n_3 = 1$	$n_1 = 1, n_2 = 1$ $n_3 = 1$	$n_1 = 2, n_2 = 1$ $n_3 = 1$	$n_1 = 3, n_2 = 1$ $n_3 = 1$
Cash flow	13	40	121	31	160	781
Net capital loss	39	117	350	155	775	3,875
Class composition	13	40	121	31	160	781
Inventory balance	168	816	3408	440	3440	23,440
Total constraints	233	1613	4000	657	4535	28,877

In Figure B.1 we indicate the matrix structure for a model involving three time periods and only three securities. Note that the inventory balance constraints exhibit what is referred to as a block diagonal structure. Given this matrix structure, the inventory balance constraints can be treated implicitly rather than explicitly by applying the decomposition approach of mathematical programming. Rather than solving the original problem, the decomposition procedure consists of cycling between (1) solving a linear program whose size is equal to the sum of the cash flow, net capital loss, and class composition constraints and (2) solving a collection of subproblems, one for each diagonal block in the inventory balance equations. The procedure can be used when the original problem is too large to solve directly and an efficient solution procedure exists for solving the subproblems.

THE DECOMPOSITION APPROACH

In the general decomposition approach a subset of the constraints are treated implicitly as subproblems, thus reducing the number of constraints that need to be treated explicitly. Solutions to these subproblems generate information in the form of columns for a linear programming approximation of the original problem, called the *restricted master program*. By iterating between the subproblems and the restricted master, it is possible to eventually generate enough columns to find an optimal solution to the original problem. This procedure solves a number of smaller problems several times instead of solving a large complex problem directly. The effectiveness of the method depends crucially upon the ease with which the subproblems can be solved.

In the BONDS model we are able to define subproblems having a recursive solution procedure that is very efficient. We have defined the commodities that need to be accounted for as the holdings of each security class purchased at the start of a given period. For example, security class k purchased at the start of period 1 would be one commodity, and the same security class purchased at the start of period 2 would be another. The constraints of a particular subproblem are then the inventory balance constraints associated with a particular commodity.

To illustrate the subproblems, consider first the period-1 commodities. Security class k is available for purchase at the start of period 1. If a decision to purchase is made, this security class is then available for sale at the start of period 2, or it may be held during the second period. The amount that was held is then available for sale or holding at the start of the third pe-

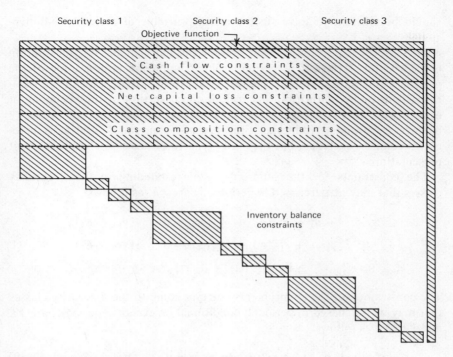

Figure B.1.   Matrix structure for three security classes.

riod. This multistage problem involving a sequence of buy, sell, and hold decisions can be solved with a recursive procedure described in the next section. The problem has a dynamic programming structure wherein the state of the system at time n is defined by the amount of the commodity held. This amount is constrained by the inventory balance equations, which limit the amount sold in any period to be less than or equal to the amount on hand.

Note that if security class k is purchased at the start of period 2, its purchase price and income yield are conditional upon the uncertain event which occurred during period 1. Thus a subproblem is defined for each commodity and each sequence of uncertain events that precede the purchase date of that commodity. As would be expected, the subproblems have no decision variables in common with one another since each set of inventory balance constraints simply keeps track of the holdings of a particular commodity. The commodity definition adopted leads to a relatively large number of subproblems. The rationale, however, is that the subproblems should be efficient to solve since the state variable of each is one-dimensional.

For ease of exposition we will present the mathematics of the solution procedure for a three-time period problem only and ignore some of the possible constraints. We limit the discussion to one broad category of securities, with many maturities, and include the cash flow at the beginning of each period, realized losses over the first two periods, and all inventory balance constraints. Additional time periods, constraints, and asset categories could be included, but they only tend to obscure an already difficult presentation.

The constraints for the subproblems corresponding to the k security classes that may be purchased in period one are $\forall k$, as follows:

$$- b_1^k + s_{1,2}^k(e_1) + h_{1,2}^k(e_1) = 0 \qquad (\forall e_1 \in E_1)$$

$$- h_{1,2}^k(e_1) + s_{1,3}^k(e_2) + h_{1,3}^k(e_2) = 0 \qquad (\forall e_2 \in E_2) \qquad (1)$$

$$b_1^k \geqq 0, \quad s_{1,2}^k(e_1) \geqq 0, \quad h_{1,2}^k(e_1) \geqq 0, \quad s_{1,3}^k(e_2) \geqq 0, \quad h_{1,3}^k(e_2) \geqq 0$$

The constraints for the subproblems corresponding to the k security classes that may be purchased in period 2, conditional on events in period 1, are $\forall k$ and $\forall e_1 \epsilon E_1$, as follows:

$$- b_2^k(e_1) + s_{2,3}^k(e_2 \mid e_1) + h_{2,3}^k(e_2 \mid e_1) = 0 \qquad [\forall e_2 \in E_2(e_1)] \qquad (2)$$

$$b_2^k(e_1) \geqq 0, \quad s_{2,3}^k(e_2 \mid e_1) \geqq 0, \quad h_{2,3}^k(e_2 \mid e_1) \geqq 0$$

The notation $e_2 \mid e_1$ denotes the uncertain events in period 2 conditional on events in period 1. $E_2(e_1)$ is the set of all events in period 2 that follow a particular event in period 1.

For eight security classes, three time periods, and three uncertain events in each period there are thirty-two subproblems. There are eight subproblems of the form (1) corresponding to the eight commodities available for purchase at the start of period 1 and twenty-four of the form (2). The basic structure of the subproblems for an arbitrary number of time periods and uncertain events should be evident, since the subproblem constraints merely reflect the holdings of each commodity for each possible sequence of uncertain events. Note that each commodity is purchased only once and then sold or held during subsequent periods.

The interesting point to note about the subproblem constraints is that they are homogeneous systems of equations (i.e., zero right-hand sides). In decomposition the fundamental theorem employed is that a convex polyhedral set may be represented by a convex combination of its extreme points plus a nonnegative combination of its extreme rays (see Dantzig [1963]). The solutions of (1) and (2) have only one extreme point, all decision variables equal to zero. For any nonzero point satisfying the subproblem constraints, a scalar times that point also satisfies the constraints, and hence, with a linear objective function, there exists an associated unbounded solution. As a result we need only consider the extreme rays of the subproblems. It is critical, for an effective procedure, to be able to construct these extreme rays in an efficient manner. In the next section we show how to do this.

The restricted master for this decomposition scheme, wherein subproblems are defined for each commodity and event sequence, is given in Table B.3. Note that the usual convex combination constraints (e.g., $\Sigma\lambda_i = 1$) are not present since we need only include nonnegative combinations of extreme rays. Further, there are no subproblem constraints associated with buying a security in period 3 since there are no subsequent sell or hold decisions. Hence these decision variables are not represented in terms of extreme points and extreme rays of a subproblem. Notationally, the λ_n's refer to the weighting in the restricted master of the nth solution of the appropriate subproblem, and the bars over the decision variables indicate subproblem solutions that have been generated. The notation is not precise here, the subscript n being different for each subproblem.

For our problem we can initiate the decomposition procedure by constructing a feasible solution to our original problem. This solution is translated into the coefficients for an initial restricted master, which is then solved. The optimal dual solution associated with the constraints of the restricted master, denoted by $\pi_n(\cdot)$, is indicated in Table B.3. These dual variables are used to modify the objective functions of the subproblems at each iteration, and these subproblems are then solved as indicated in the next section. The resulting extreme rays are then added as columns to the restricted master and the procedure is repeated. The algorithm terminates when no new extreme rays are generated at some iteration. A proof of the convergence of the method is given in Dantzig [1963].

SOLVING THE SUBPROBLEMS

The key to successfully using the decomposition procedure is an efficient solution procedure for the subproblems. In this section we present an extremely efficient procedure that may be easily implemented on a computer. The subproblems for each security class that may be purchased in period 1 are $\forall k$.

Table B.3 Restricted Master

Maximize

$$\sum_k \{ \sum_n [\sum_{e_2} p(e_2) \{ y_1^k + v_{1,3}^k(e_2) \} \bar{h}_{1,3,n}^k(e_2)] \lambda_{1,n}^k$$

$$+ \sum_{e_1} \sum_n [\sum_{e_2} p(e_2 \mid e_1) \{ y_2^k(e_1) + v_{2,3}^k(e_2 \mid e_1) \} \bar{h}_{2,3,n}^k(e_2 \mid e_1)] \lambda_{2,n}^k(e_1)$$

$$+ \sum_{e_2} p(e_2) [y_3^k(e_2) + v_{3,3}^k(e_2)] b_3^k(e_2) \}$$

subject to:

Cash Flow, Period 1

$$\pi_1: \quad \sum_k \{ \sum_n [\bar{b}_{1,n}^k] \lambda_{1,n}^k \} = f_1$$

Cash Flow, Period 2

$$\pi_2(e_1): \quad \sum_k \{ \sum_n [-y_1^k \bar{b}_{1,n}^k - \{ 1 + g_{1,2}^k(e_1) \} \bar{s}_{1,2,n}^k(e_1)] \lambda_{1,n}^k$$

$$+ \sum_{e_1} \sum_n [\bar{b}_{2,n}^k(e_1)] \lambda_{2,n}^k(e_1) \} = f_2(e_1) \qquad (\forall e_1 \in E_1)$$

Cash Flow, Period 3

$$\pi_3(e_2): \quad \sum_k \{ \sum_n [-y_1^k \bar{h}_{1,2,n}^k(e_1) - (1 + g_{1,3}^k(e_2)) \bar{s}_{1,3,n}^k(e_2)] \lambda_{1,n}^k$$

$$+ \sum_{e_1} \sum_n [-y_2^k(e_1) \bar{b}_{2,n}^k(e_1) - \{ 1 + g_{2,3}^k(e_2) \} \bar{s}_{2,3,n}^k(e_2)] \lambda_{2,n}^k(e_1)$$

$$+ b_3^k(e_2) \} = f_3(e_2) \qquad (\forall e_2 \in E_2)$$

Realized Losses, Periods 2 and 3

$$\pi_4(e_2): \quad \sum_k \{ \sum_n [-g_{1,2}^k(e_1) \bar{s}_{1,2,n}^k(e_1) - g_{1,3}^k(e_2) \bar{s}_{1,3,n}^k(e_2)] \lambda_{1,n}^k$$

$$+ \sum_{e_1} \sum_n [-g_{2,3}^k(e_2) \bar{s}_{2,3,n}^k(e_2) \lambda_{2,n}^k(e_1) \} \leqq L_3(e_2) \qquad (\forall e_2 \in E_2)$$

$$\lambda_{1,n}^k \geqq 0, \quad \lambda_{2,n}^k(e_1) \geqq 0, \quad b_3^k(e_2) \geqq 0$$

Maximize

$$- [\pi_1 - y_1^k \sum_{e_1} \pi_2(e_1)] b_1^k$$

$$+ \sum_{e_1} [\{1 + g_{1,2}^k(e_1)\} \pi_2(e_1) + g_{1,2}^k(e_1) \sum_{e_2} \pi_4(e_2 \mid e_1)] s_{1,2}^k(e_1)$$

$$+ \sum_{e_1} [y_1^k \sum_{e_2} \pi_3(e_2 \mid e_1)] h_{1,2}^k(e_1)$$

$$+ \sum_{e_2} [\{1 + g_{1,3}^k(e_2)\} \pi_3(e_2) + g_{1,3}^k(e_2) \pi_4(e_2)] s_{1,3}^k(e_2)$$

$$+ \sum_{e_2} [p(e_2) \{y_1^k + v_{1,3}^k(e_2)\}] h_{1,3}^k(e_2)$$

subject to (3)

$$- b_1^k + s_{1,2}^k(e_1) + h_{1,2}^k(e_1) = 0 \qquad (\forall e_1 \in E_1)$$

$$- h_{1,2}^k(e_1) + s_{1,3}^k(e_2) + h_{1,3}^k(e_2) = 0 \qquad (\forall e_2 \in E_2)$$

$$b_1^k \geqq 0, \quad s_{1,2}^k(e_1) \geqq 0, \quad h_{1,2}^k(e_1) \geqq 0, \quad s_{1,3}^k(e_2) \geqq 0, \quad h_{1,3}^k(e_2) \geqq 0$$

where the objective function has been appropriately modified by the dual variables of the restricted master. The subproblems for each security class that may be purchased in period 2 conditional on the events of period 1 are $\forall k$ and $\forall e_1 \in E_1$.

Maximize

$$- [\pi_2(e_1) - y_2^k(e_1) \sum_{e_2} \pi_3(e_2 \mid e_1)] b_2^k(e_1)$$

$$+ \sum_{e_2} [\{1 + g_{2,3}^k(e_2 \mid e_1)\} \pi_3(e_2 \mid e_1) + g_{2,3}^k(e_2 \mid e_1) \pi_4(e_2 \mid e_1)] s_{2,3}^k(e_2 \mid e_1)$$

$$+ \sum_{e_2} [p(e_2 \mid e_1) \{y_2^k(e_2 \mid e_1) + v_{2,3}^k(e_2 \mid e_1)\}] h_{2,3}^k(e_2 \mid e_1)$$

subject to (4)

$$- b_2^k(e_1) + s_{2,3}^k(e_2 \mid e_1) + h_{2,3}^k(e_2 \mid e_1) = 0 \qquad (\forall e_2 \in E_2(e_1))$$

$$b_2^k(e_1) \geqq 0, \quad s_{2,3}^k(e_2 \mid e_1) \geqq 0, \quad h_{2,3}^k(e_2 \mid e_1) \geqq 0$$

The basic structure of the subproblems in each case is identical. When we consider more than three time periods, we have the same structure only with necessary additional variables and constraints. The underlying structure is simply that the hold variables determine the amount of the commodity on hand at the start of the subsequent period. This amount on hand is then either sold or held and the process repeated.

These subproblems turn out to be very easy to solve because of their simple structure and homogeneity. First, every unbounded solution of subproblems of the form (3) has $b_1^k > 0$. If not, the subproblem constraints imply the null solution. Similarly, every unbounded solution of subproblems of the form (4) has $b_2^k (e_1) > 0$. Further, if in solving a subproblem it is found profitable to buy one unit of a commodity, it is profitable to buy as much as possible since the objective function is linear and the constraints are homogenous. Let us look at the problem of buying one unit of a particular commodity. It it is profitable to do so, we have constructed a ray yielding arbitrarily large profit for an arbitrarily large multiple of that solution. Hence we have the following *ray-finding problem* that determines the selling and holding strategy that maximizes the return from buying one unit of a security purchased in period 1.

Maximize

$$\sum_{e_1} [\{1 + g_{1,2}^k(e_1)\}\pi_2(e_1) + g_{1,2}^k(e_1) \sum_{e_2} \pi_4(e_2 \mid e_1)]s_{1,2}^k(e_1)$$

$$+ \sum_{e_1} [y_1^k \sum_{e_2} \pi_3(e_2 \mid e_1)]h_{1,2}^k(e_1)$$

$$+ \sum_{e_2} [\{1 + g_{1,3}^k(e_2)\}\pi_3(e_2) + g_{1,3}^k(e_2)\pi_4(e_2)]s_{1,3}^k(e_2)$$

$$+ \sum_{e_2} [p(e_2)\{y_1^k + v_{1,3}^k(e_2)\}]h_{1,3}^k(e_2)$$

subject to   (5)

$$s_{1,2}^k(e_1) + h_{1,2}^k(e_1) = 1 \qquad (\forall e_1 \in E_1)$$

$$- h_{1,2}^k(e_1) + s_{1,3}^k(e_2) + h_{1,3}^k(e_2) = 0 \qquad (\forall e_2 \in E_2)$$

$$s_{1,2}^k(e_1) \geqq 0, \quad h_{1,2}^k(e_1) \geqq 0, \quad s_{1,3}^k(e_2) \geqq 0, \quad h_{1,3}^k(e_2) \geqq 0$$

This ray-finding problem has an extremely simple solution, which can be easily seen by looking at its dual, namely:

Minimize

$$\sum_{e_1} w_1(e_1) \qquad\qquad\qquad\qquad (6)$$

subject to

$$w_1(e_1) \geqq (1 + g_{1,2}^k(e_1))\pi_2(e_1)$$
$$+ g_{1,2}^k(e_1) \sum_{e_2} \pi_4(e_2 \mid e_1)$$
$$\left. \begin{array}{l} \\ \\ \end{array} \right\} (\forall e_1 \in E_1)$$
$$w_1(e_1) - \sum_{e_2} w_2(e_2 \mid e_1) \geqq y_1^k \sum_{e_2} \pi_3(e_2 \mid e_1)$$

$$w_2(e_2) \geqq (1 + g_{1,3}^k(e_2))\pi_3(e_2)$$
$$+ g_{1,3}^k(e_2)\pi_4(e_2)$$
$$\left. \begin{array}{l} \\ \\ \end{array} \right\} (\forall e_2 \in E_2)$$
$$w_2(e_2) \geqq p(e_2)(y_1^k + v_{1,3}^k(e_2))$$

Since we wish to minimize $\sum_{e_1} w_1(e_1)$, and $w_1(e_1)$ and $w_2(e_2)$ are linked only by the constraints

$$w_1(e_1) \geqq \sum_{e_2} w_2(e_2 \mid e_1) + y_1^k \sum_{e_2} \pi_3(e_2 \mid e_1) \tag{7}$$

we need only choose $w_2(e_2)$ as small as possible and then choose $w_1(e_1)$ as small as possible. Hence:

$$w_2(e_2) = \text{Max}[\{1 + g_{1,3}^k(e_2)\}\pi_3(e_2) + g_{1,3}^k(e_2)\pi_4(e_2);$$
$$p(e_2)\{y_1^k + v_{1,3}^k(e_2)\}] \qquad (\forall e_2 \in E_2)$$
$$\tag{8}$$
$$w_1(e_1) = \text{Max}[\{1 + g_{1,2}^k(e_1)\}\pi_2(e_1) + g_{1,2}^k(e_1) \sum_{e_2} \pi_4(e_2 \mid e_1);$$
$$\sum_{e_2} w_2(e_2 \mid e_1) + y_1^k \sum_{e_2} \pi_3(e_2 \mid e_1)] \qquad (\forall e_1 \in E_1)$$

constitutes a recursive algorithm for finding the optimal solution to the dual of the ray-finding problem. If the optimal value of the objective function of the dual exceeds the purchase cost of the commodity, which is:

$$\pi_1 - y_1^k \sum_{e_1} \pi_2(e_1) \tag{9}$$

then we have found a *profitable* ray of the subproblem. The actual ray is given by $b_1^k = 1$ and a sequence of zeros and ones for the sell and hold variables, a one corresponding to a tight constraint in the dual of the ray finding problem. If the set of tight constraints in this dual problem is not unique, this merely implies an indifference between selling and holding at some stage, and the choice may be made arbitrarily. This solution procedure is a general one and holds for an arbitrary number of events and time periods.

At each iteration all profitable rays found are added as columns to the restricted master. The restricted master is then solved, again yielding new dual variables that modify the objective functions of the subproblems, and the process is repeated. If no profitable ray is found for any subproblem, the process terminates and we have the optimal solution. The value of the optimal solution is merely given by the nonnegative combination of the subproblem solutions, as indicated by the final restricted master. In general we need *not* add any unprofitable ray to the restricted master. However, a ray that is unprofitable at one iteration may become profitable at a future iteration as the objective functions of the subproblems are modified by the dual variables. Hence, if one profitable ray is generated at an iteration, all new rays generated, profitable or not, are in fact added to the restricted master as columns. As the restricted master is augmented by more and more columns, those columns not in the current basis are retained provided storage limitations permit. As storage limitations become binding, those columns that price out most negatively are dropped.

INFORMATION REQUIREMENTS
AND SAMPLE RESULTS OF
THE BONDS MODEL

To indicate how the BONDS model can be applied and the options available to a user, Appendix C describes the information that must be supplied to the model and some of the results provided by the model. This discussion is illustrated by a sample run of the BONDS model, including a printout from the computer run. The sample shown is taken from the historical simulation experiment discussed in Chapter 10. We used the BONDS model to "manage" a hypothetical portfolio of municipal securities over the 10-year period from 1964 to 1973. In the simulation the model was run as of January of each year to obtain a set of portfolio decisions. These decisions took into account the portfolio remaining from the previous January's results, the municipal yield curve as of the decision date, and some expectations about future yield curves. This and other information must be supplied to the model as described in the section below. The second section discusses the decisions of the model resulting from these inputs.

INPUT DATA

The sample to be discussed is the run of the BONDS model for the January 1973 decisions. Thus the input information must describe the initial portfolio that existed at that time, the January 1973 yield curve, and a specification of future interest rate scenarios including their probability. Specification of the large number of possible scenarios can be difficult, but we have structured the input requirements to take advantage of the statistical techniques and simplifications discussed in Chapter 3.

In the discussion below, each of the input items is described in the order it appears in the computer printout. Each item is also identified by the four letter code used to indicate its type of information for the computer program.

Number of Bonds (NBND)

In the January 1973 run, seven maturity categories of bonds were included in the initial portfolio and eight maturities were available for purchase, so that there was a total of 15 "bonds." There was only one yield class of bonds, "good grade" municipals as defined by Salomon Brothers, and it was assumed that all future purchases would be made at par. It would have been possible to designate one or more of the bonds as bonds that would be purchased at a discount or premium. In addition, there could have been more than one yield class of bonds. Other classes might have included U.S. Treasuries and/or other quality groups of municipals. Thus bonds available for purchase are identified by their maturity, their yield class, and their coupon rate relative to the market yield for their maturity. The maximum number of bonds is forty, but this limit does not include a one-period bond automatically made available for purchase by the model.

A model parameter that must be supplied with the information on number of bonds is the maximum number of columns the master program can retain in the decomposition solution procedure. This procedure is most efficient if a large number of columns are allowed to be retained, but the user is able to reduce the number if needed to fit the portfolio problem within the computer capacity available.

Number of Asset Classes (CLAS)

Up to three classes of bonds are allowed in the model, and it is possible to specify upper and lower bounds on the dollar amount in each class. For example, if the portfolio model contained both Treasuries and municipals, the bank might want to specify a minimum amount of Treasuries that must be held. The number of classes and the type of each constraint, that is, upper or lower limits, are identified in this input item.

Initial Portfolio (IPRT)

Input information is needed for each bond in the initial portfolio. This information includes an identifying number assigned by the user, the maturity of the bond in years or fractions thereof, the coupon rate, the total par value, the original purchase price, and the class of the bond. In an actual application of the model the individual bonds held by a bank would be grouped into maturity categories. Then the average coupon rate and the book and par values would be computed for each category.

Number of Periods (NPER)

The maximum number of periods allowed in the model is five, although the problem size can get very large if more than four periods are specified. Three periods were specified for the sample run.

Number of Events in Each Period (NEVT)

In the sample run there were three possible random events in each period. During each period of the model, interest rates could rise, stay the same, or fall, with some probability. In general, it is necessary to specify the number of such random events in each period. However, when the number of events is the same for all time periods, it is possible to use a "999" code, as in the sample run, rather than list a parameter for each period separately.

Periods with Loss Constraints (APLC)

Loss constraints are specified in the sample run for the initial portfolio (period 0) and for the end of each period of the model. The constraint on the initial portfolio limits the amount of losses that can be realized in the model's first decision. Constraints for periods 1 and 2 limit realized losses at the end of those periods, and the final constaint limits unrealized losses at the horizon. For some purposes it may not be desirable to have loss constraints at the end of each period. If the first two periods are 6 months long, for example, a bank would probably want to limit the sum of the losses over the first two periods rather than have individual limits. This can be accomplished in the model by omitting period 1 from the loss constraint parameters.

Capital Gains Tax (CGTX)

The capital gains tax in the sample run is set at 0.50 to approximate the corporate income tax rate. In an actual application it would reflect a bank's state and local taxes, if any, as well as the federal tax rate.

Bid-Asked Spread (BKPT)

Spreads between bid and asked prices are specified for each class of bond. These spreads are specified as a "step function," in which each spread applies to a range of maturities. In the municipal bond run we have assumed a spread of 0.125% for maturities up to 2 years, 0.25% for maturities from 2 up to 3 years, 0.375% up to 7 years, 0.625% up to 11 years, and a spread of 0.75% for maturities of 11 years or longer. These can be seen in the BKPT lines of the input section. Each line of input specifies the class of the bond, the shortest maturity that has the spread specified, and the spread. Up to five steps can be specified for each bond class.

Yield Curve Input Option (YSET)

Future yield curves can be specified in one of two ways for the model. First, they can be generated as changes from the starting yield curve, which is the procedure described in Chapter 3 and used in the sample run. This is accomplished by setting the YSET variable equal to zero. The alternative procedure is to specify directly each yield curve that might occur in the future periods of the model. This adds to the input requirements, but it is a better procedure if the starting yield curve had an unusual shape that should not be reflected in future yield curves. To use this option, a code of 1 is indicated on the YSET line, and it is also necessary to specify which of the yield curves provided later is the starting yield curve.

Specification of Yield Curves (YDPT)

Each yield curve in the model is specified by three points on the curve. The remainder of the curve is then filled in by the model using the function described in Chapter 3. For example, the starting yield curve in the January 1973 run is specified by the three YDPT lines. Each line includes a "1" to indicate that the yield is for class 1 bonds, a maturity, and the yield for that maturity. In this case the maturities specified were 1, 20, and 30 years, and the yields were 3.1%, 4.923% and 5.2%, respectively. Each line also includes a "1" in the fourth column of numbers to indicate that these points are for yield curve number 1. Since future yield curves will be based on changes from this one and there is only one class of bonds, it is the only curve that needs to be specified. If the alternative procedure were used, each of the possible future yield curves would also have to be specified and a number would be assigned to each. Similarly, a yield curve would have to be specified for each class of bonds if more than one class were included.

Bond Maturities (MATR)

A bond number must be assigned for each maturity and yield class that is either in the initial portfolio or available for purchase. In the sample run, bond numbers 1 through 8 represent bonds available for purchase. They have maturities of 2, 3, 4, 5, 10, 15, 20, and 30 years, respectively. Maturity categories 9 through 15 indicate the maturity groupings included in the initial portfolio. Each of these fifteen categories is also identified as a class 1 bond.

Length of Periods (LPER)

The length of each time period in the model must be specified in years. In the sample run, each period is 1 year long, but any length greater than zero is allowed.

Probabilities (PROB)

The probability of each ramdom event in the model is specified in the PROB input lines. The procedure used can be explained most easily by reference to the PROB lines of the sample run. The first three lines refer to the probability of each event in period 1, indicated by the 1's in the first column of numbers. There are three possible events, indicated by the numbers 1, 2, and 3 in the second column. The probabilities of each of these events are given in the third column as .33333, .33334, and .33333, respectively. These were set so the probabilities of rates rising, staying the same, and falling would be equal, but the middle number was increased to .33334 so that the probabilities would add exactly to 1.

The probabilities of events that can occur in period 2 are, in general, conditional upon which event occurs in period 1. This is allowed in the model, but it is not needed in the sample run, since the probabilities of rate changes in period 2 are independent of the previous period. The period 2 probabilities are indicated by a 2 in the first column of numbers. In one second column, 999s are used to specify that the period 2 probabilities are the same for all events of period 1. Each event of the second period is numbered in column 3, and equal probabilities are specified in column 4.

For period 3, we believed that some of the events should be conditional upon what happened in previous periods. In particular, the municipal yield curve was low enough in January 1973 that we believed it would not fall three years in a row. If interest rates fell in 1973 and 1974, periods 1 and 2, we felt it would have essentially no chance of going lower, and it would be very likely to rebound from the low level. To express these conditional probabilities it was necessary to specify the probability of each period 3 event, conditional upon each of the events possible in periods 1 and 2.

The PROB table allows this information to be specified. Period 3 probabilities are identified by a 3 in the first column of numbers. The next two columns identify the number of an event in periods 1 and 2, respectively. Column 4 specifies an event in period 3, and the probability of this event is given in the last column. This can be illustrated by the last PROB line. It indicates there is a .10 probability of event 3 occurring in period 3, if event 3 has also occurred in both periods 1 and 2. In other words, if interest rates have fallen in both the previous periods, there is only a 10% chance that rates will remain at the low level. There is a 90% chance that rates will rise to the next higher level under these conditions. This is specified by the probability of event 2 given in the next to last PROB line. In the second from last PROB line we specified the probability of event 1 under these assumptions to be .00001. We wanted only two rate levels to be possible if rates fell twice, so we specified event 1 as a null event, with essentially a zero probability.

Option for One-Period Liability (SLIB)

Although the maturity categories of the BONDS model all refer to assets of various types, the model does allow for the sale of a liability whose maturity is equal to the length of the current period. This option allows the user to explore the implications of using liabilities to either fund an outflow or purchase additional securities. If the option is desired, a SLIB line is included in the input. The information it contains is the spread between the cost of this liability and the yield on an asset of the same maturity. If the model has 1-year time periods, for example, and the spread is set at 0.005, then the cost of a 1-year liability in each period is 50 basis points above the yield on the one-period security. There is no SLIB line in the sample run because we did not want to allow the model to sell liabilities.

Income Tax Rate (CPTX)

This line is used to specify the tax on coupon income from each class of bonds. In the sample run the tax rate is set at zero because the class of bonds is tax-exempt.

Base Year in Yield-Curve Change Model (BSYR)

If future yield curves are based on changes from the starting curve, the amounts of these changes are specified for a particular maturity. Changes in two other maturities are then computed from this change. The base maturity in the sample is the 1-year maturity. If more than one yield class were included in the model, a base year would be needed for these additional classes.

Changes in the Yield on the Base Maturity (CYBY)

These input lines specify the amount of change in the interest rate on the base maturity that occurs for each random event. The first three CYBY lines indicate the changes that can occur for events 1, 2, and 3 in period 1. These changes in the 1-year rate are an increase of 0.01105 (i.e., 110.5 basis points), no change, and down 0.01105, respectively. Whichever change occurs in period 1, the same changes are possible in period 2, as indicated by the next three CYBY cards.

As with the PROB cards, changes in interest rates can be made conditional upon previous random events. The basic format is the same for these input lines as it is for the PROB lines. The last CYBY line, for example, indicates that for period 3, if event 3 occurs in both periods 1 and 2, then event 3 in this period is no change in rates. The previous line specifies that event 2 under these same assumptions is an increase of 110.5 basis points. This information combined with the PROB table indicates what is expected to happen if rates fall 2 years in succession. There is a 10% chance that they will stay at that level and a 90% chance that they will rise one level, represented by a 110.5 basis point increase in the 1-year rate.

The sample CYBY table is typical of those used when future yield curves are based on changes from the starting curve. The other alternative is to specify each of the future yield curves that might occur. For example, in a two-period model there might be a starting yield curve assigned the number 1. Before the second period it might rise one level to curve number 2, it might stay at the same level but return to a more normal shape (indicated by a curve number 3), or it might fall to a curve assigned the number 4. This pattern of possibilities is specified with the CYBY inputs, but the changes specified would refer to yield curve numbers rather than changes in the base rate. In this example, events 1, 2, and 3 would be specified by +1 (i.e., an increase from curve 1 to yield curve 2), +2, and +3, respectively. Whichever approach is used to specify future yield curves, a separate set of CYBY input is required for each curve class.

Key Years in Specification of Yield Curve Changes (KYR1 and KYR2)

When future yield curves are based on changes from the initial curve, as they are in this example, each future curve needs to be defined by three maturities. One of them is the base maturity identified above as the 1-year bond. These two input lines specify the other two maturities and some parameters used in calculating their future yields. The two lines in the sample run identify the maturities as 20 and 30 years, and specify that changes in the 20-year should equal 67% of changes in the 1-year rate.

Changes in the 30-year rate are set at 61% of the 1-year rate changes. To illustrate how these parameters are used, if event 1 occurs in the first period, the 1-year rate will rise 110.5 basis points, as specified above. The 20- and 30-year rates will rise 67 and 61% of this amount, respectively. This defines three yields on the new yield curve, and the remainder can be filled in using the function described in Chapter 3.

More complicated change parameters are allowed in the model. In each key year line, three parameters are specified to define an equation such as:

$$R_{20,t} = a + b(R_{1,t} - R_{1,t-1}) + cR_{20,t-1}$$

In the KYR1 line of the sample run, $a = 0$, $b = 0.6702$, $c = 1$. The effect of these parameters is to set the change of the 20-year rate equal to 0.6702 of the change in the 1-year rate. These parameters are consistent with an empirical study of past relationships, but others could easily have been used. Note that a set of key year lines are required for each yield class.

Parameters for Bond Discounts and Premiums (DSPD)

The first input line, NBND, specified the number of bonds that would be purchased at a discount or premium. The DSPD lines, not needed in the sample run, are used to identify the specific bonds and the amount of discount or premium for each. Each line contains a bond number and a "spread" for the bond. For example, a spread of 0.005 on bond 3 would indicate that the coupon rate on bond 3 would be 50 basis points below the market yield on bonds of ths maturity and class at the time of its purchase. Thus, bond 3 would always be purchased at a discount if bought by the model. If desired, the spread between the coupon and market yield can be made conditional on the previous events. To accomplish this, each DSPD line contains information in addition to bond number and spread. It also identifies the period in which the spread applies and the numbers of events on which the spread is conditional. The format is similar to that of the PROB and CYBY lines.

Exogenous Cash Flows (EFLO)

In each period of the model there may be inflows or outflows of cash exogenous to the model. There may be an outflow of funds to finance an expected deposit runoff, for example, if interest rates rise. These inflows and outflows can be specified for each period and for each sequence of events, using the same format as in the PROB and CYBY input lines.

For the sample run we assumed that there would be no exogenous cash flows after the start of the model but that there would be an initial inflow resulting from the interest income on the portfolio held during the previous year, 1972. This interest income was $5635, as shown in the first EFLO line. The zero in the first column of numbers refers to the start of the model. The next line contains a 1., 999., and 0.0. This indicates that for all events in period 1 the exogenous cash flow is zero. Since no further EFLO lines have been included, the model makes the same assumption for events of all future periods.

Loss Constraints (LCNS)

These input lines specify the amount of loss allowed at the end of each period for each event sequence. In the sample run, realized losses of $676.33 were allowed in the model's first decisions, that is, at period zero. Similar realized losses were allowed at the end of periods 1 and 2. It would have been possible to vary the limit on realized losses, depending on the events which occurred, but we allowed the same amount for each sequence of interest rates. This is accomplished with the 999 code as before. The last LCNS line specifies an upper limit on unrealized losses at the horizon of $3381.66, independent of which events occurred. This amount is 2.5% of the starting book value of the portfolio.

Printout Option (POUT)

The POUT line specifies the amount of output desired from the run. The sample run contains the minimum amount of output. It would also have been possible to have the computer print out data on bond prices and complete yield curves for each sequence of events, horizon values of the portfolio for each event sequence, and a variety of information about the results of the run, including shadow prices, the final matrix, reduced prices, and the weighting vector.

Run Parameters (MXIT & SUBJ)

The final two input lines in the sample run specify a maximum number of iterations for the model and indicate the end of the input for this run.

RESULTS OF THE MODEL

The optimization model provides a set of recommended decisions for each period and each sequence of random events that can occur. For the actions to be taken in January 1973, it recommended that bonds in three maturity categories be purchased. The suggested purchases were $54,555 of bond 2, $13,871 of bond 4, and $10,786 of bond 8. These bond numbers correspond to maturities of 3, 5, and 30 years, respectively. To finance these purchases, the model sold bonds in the initial portfolio corresponding to bond numbers 10 (2 years), 11 (2 years), 12 (22 years) and 15 (29 years). Two categories of 2-year bonds were used in the initial portfolio because they had different coupon rates. This difference is reflected in the cash received from the sale of each category, which show a slight loss on sale of bond 10 but a small gain from sale of bond 11. Bonds that were in the January 1973 portfolio and were not sold by the model are shown in the HOLD line. The SURE ASSET line refers to the one-period bond that is automatically made available for purchase, but the model did not acquire any in the first period.

The first set of period 2 decisions refer to the actions that would be taken if interest rates rise, event 1. The interest income from bonds held during the first period is shown in the table. This income plus receipts from maturities and some sales would be used to buy $51,254 of a 1-year bond and $36,489 of a 3-year bond. Since interest rates have risen once, these relatively short-term purchases have to be made to keep the unrealized losses at the horizon from becoming too large. In this table, cash is provided by the maturity of bond 9 and the sale of bond 11, both of which were in the initial January 1973 portfolio. In addition, bonds purchased last period are also sold. These are the number 2 bonds that had a 3-year maturity at the time of purchase.

Different actions would be taken if rates did not change (event 2) or fell (event 3). These are shown in the succeeding period 2 tables. If event 2 occurred, the model would purchase some 5- and 30-year bonds out of interest income and maturities. No bonds would be sold. If rates fell, the model would lengthen the portfolio further by purchasing more of the 30-year bond and none of the 5-year maturity. Some 2-year bonds would also be sold out of the initial portfolio to help finance the 30-year purchases.

Similar decision tables are provided for the period 3 decisions, one for each of the nine possible sequences of interest rates. The first period 3 table indicates actions that would be taken if rates rose and then increased again, event sequence 1,1. The second table refers to a sequence in which rates rise and then do not change, event sequence 1, 2, and so on, through each of the nine tables for period 3 decisions.

The period 1 decisions recommended by the model are the ones that would be actively considered by a portfolio manager. Decisions shown for periods 2 and 3 represent approximate contigency actions to be taken depending on what happens. When making current decisions, it is important to consider what future actions might be taken, as the model does. However, actual decisions for periods 2 and 3 will be based on interest rates and other information available at the time. The model will be updated and run again to help make these future decisions.

MUNICIPAL ROLLOVER - JAN '73 DATA

INPUT DATA

NUMBER OF BONDS = 15   NO. TRADED AT PREMIUM OR DISCOUNT =

BONDS IN INITIAL PORTFOLIO

BOND NO.	MATURITY	COUPON	VAL. AT $100/BOND
9	1.000	0.060890	12387.47
10	2.000	0.030775	27123.43
11	2.000	0.037406	47015.78
12	22.000	0.034000	3036.81
13	26.000	0.052000	2739.95
14	28.000	0.056500	25070.47
15	29.000	0.051000	12257.65

NO. BONDS IN INITIAL PORTFOLIO =   7

NUMBER OF PERIODS =   3

NO. EVENTS IN PERIOD 999 =   3.

LOSS CONSTRAINTS SPECIFIED FOR PERIODS   0   1   2   3

ARRAY(DIM) MUST BE DIMENSIONED AT LEAST   32120
DIMENSION GIVEN IS   32120

REMAINING INPUT CARDS

CGTX	0.50000	0.00000	0.00000
BKPT	1.00000	0.50000	0.12500
BKPT	1.00000	2.00000	0.25000
BKPT	1.00000	3.00000	0.37500
BKPT	1.00000	7.00000	0.62500
BKPT	1.00000	11.00000	0.75000
YSET	0.00000	0.00000	0.00000
YDPT	1.00000	1.00000	0.03100
YDPT	1.00000	20.00000	0.04923
YDPT	1.00000	30.00000	0.05200
MATR	1.00000	2.00000	1.00000
MATR	2.00000	3.00000	1.00000
MATR	3.00000	4.00000	1.00000
MATR	4.00000	5.00000	1.00000
MATR	5.00000	10.00000	1.00000

0   NO. OF COLUMNS =   6.00 TIMES NO. OF ROWS

ORIGINAL PRICE	YIELD CLASS
12387.47	1.
27123.43	1.
47015.78	1.
3036.81	1.
2739.95	1.
25070.47	1.
12257.65	1.

0.00000	0.00000	0.00000	0.00000
0.00000	0.00000	0.00000	0.00000
0.00000	0.00000	0.00000	0.00000
0.00000	0.00000	0.00000	0.00000
0.00000	0.00000	0.00000	0.00000
0.00000	0.00000	0.00000	0.00000
0.00000	0.00000	0.00000	0.00000
1.00000	0.00000	0.00000	0.00000
1.00000	0.00000	0.00000	0.00000
1.00000	0.00000	0.00000	0.00000
0.00000	0.00000	0.00000	0.00000
0.00000	0.00000	0.00000	0.00000
0.00000	0.00000	0.00000	0.00000
0.00000	0.00000	0.00000	0.00000
0.00000	0.00000	0.00000	0.00000

MATR	6.00000	15.00000	1.00000
MATR	7.00000	20.00000	1.00000
MATR	8.00000	30.00000	1.00000
MATR	9.00000	1.00000	1.00000
MATR	10.00000	2.00000	1.00000
MATR	11.00000	2.00000	1.00000
MATR	12.00000	22.00000	1.00000
MATR	13.00000	26.00000	1.00000
MATR	14.00000	28.00000	1.00000
MATR	15.00000	29.00000	1.00000
LPER	1.00000	1.00000	0.00000
LPER	2.00000	1.00000	0.00000
LPER	3.00000	1.00000	0.00000
PROB	1.00000	1.00000	0.33333
PROB	1.00000	2.00000	0.33334
PROB	1.00000	3.00000	0.33333
PROB	2.00000	999.00000	1.00000
PROB	2.00000	999.00000	2.00000
PROB	2.00000	999.00000	3.00000
PROB	3.00000	1.00000	1.00000
PROB	3.00000	1.00000	1.00000
PROB	3.00000	1.00000	1.00000
PROB	3.00000	1.00000	2.00000
PROB	3.00000	1.00000	2.00000
PROB	3.00000	1.00000	2.00000
PROB	3.00000	1.00000	3.00000
PROB	3.00000	1.00000	3.00000
PROB	3.00000	1.00000	3.00000
PROB	3.00000	2.00000	999.00000
PROB	3.00000	2.00000	999.00000
PROB	3.00000	2.00000	999.00000
PROB	3.00000	3.00000	1.00000
PROB	3.00000	3.00000	1.00000
PROB	3.00000	3.00000	1.00000
PROB	3.00000	3.00000	2.00000
PROB	3.00000	3.00000	2.00000
PROB	3.00000	3.00000	2.00000
PROB	3.00000	3.00000	3.00000
PROB	3.00000	3.00000	3.00000
PROB	3.00000	3.00000	3.00000
CPTX	0.00000	1.00000	0.00000
BSYR	1.00000	0.00000	0.00000
CYBY	1.00000	1.00000	0.01105
CYBY	1.00000	2.00000	0.00000
CYBY	1.00000	3.00000	-0.01105
CYBY	2.00000	999.00000	1.00000
CYBY	2.00000	999.00000	2.00000
CYBY	2.00000	999.00000	3.00000
CYBY	3.00000	1.00000	1.00000
CYBY	3.00000	1.00000	1.00000
CYBY	3.00000	1.00000	1.00000
CYBY	3.00000	1.00000	2.00000
CYBY	3.00000	1.00000	2.00000
CYBY	3.00000	1.00000	2.00000
CYBY	3.00000	1.00000	3.00000
CYBY	3.00000	1.00000	3.00000
CYBY	3.00000	1.00000	3.00000
CYBY	3.00000	2.00000	999.00000
CYBY	3.00000	2.00000	999.00000
CYBY	3.00000	2.00000	999.00000

0.00000	0.00000	0.00000	0.00000
0.00000	0.00000	0.00000	0.00000
0.00000	0.00000	0.00000	0.00000
0.00000	0.00000	0.00000	0.00000
0.00000	0.00000	0.00000	0.00000
0.00000	0.00000	0.00000	0.00000
0.00000	0.00000	0.00000	0.00000
0.00000	0.00000	0.00000	0.00000
0.00000	0.00000	0.00000	0.00000
0.00000	0.00000	0.00000	0.00000
0.00000	0.00000	0.00000	0.00000
0.00000	0.00000	0.00000	0.00000
0.00000	0.00000	0.00000	0.00000
0.00000	0.00000	0.00000	0.00000
0.00000	0.00000	0.00000	0.00000
0.00000	0.00000	0.00000	0.00000
0.33333	0.00000	0.00000	0.00000
0.33334	0.00000	0.00000	0.00000
0.33333	0.00000	0.00000	0.00000
1.00000	0.33333	0.00000	0.00000
2.00000	0.33334	0.00000	0.00000
3.00000	0.33333	0.00000	0.00000
1.00000	0.33333	0.00000	0.00000
2.00000	0.33334	0.00000	0.00000
3.00000	0.33333	0.00000	0.00000
1.00000	0.33333	0.00000	0.00000
2.00000	0.33334	0.00000	0.00000
3.00000	0.33333	0.00000	0.00000
1.00000	0.33333	0.00000	0.00000
2.00000	0.33334	0.00000	0.00000
3.00000	0.33333	0.00000	0.00000
1.00000	0.33333	0.00000	0.00000
2.00000	0.33334	0.00000	0.00000
3.00000	0.33333	0.00000	0.00000
1.00000	0.33333	0.00000	0.00000
2.00000	0.33334	0.00000	0.00000
3.00000	0.33333	0.00000	0.00000
1.00000	0.00001	0.00000	0.00000
2.00000	0.89999	0.00000	0.00000
3.00000	0.10000	0.00000	0.00000
0.00000	0.00000	0.00000	0.00000
0.00000	0.00000	0.00000	0.00000
0.00000	0.00000	0.00000	0.00000
0.00000	0.00000	0.00000	0.00000
0.00000	0.00000	0.00000	0.00000
0.01105	0.00000	0.00000	0.00000
0.00000	0.00000	0.00000	0.00000
−0.01105	0.00000	0.00000	0.00000
1.00000	0.01105	0.00000	0.00000
2.00000	0.00000	0.00000	0.00000
3.00000	−0.01105	0.00000	0.00000
1.00000	0.01105	0.00000	0.00000
2.00000	0.00000	0.00000	0.00000
3.00000	−0.01105	0.00000	0.00000
1.00000	0.01105	0.00000	0.00000
2.00000	0.00000	0.00000	0.00000
3.00000	−0.01105	0.00000	0.00000
1.00000	0.01105	0.00000	0.00000
2.00000	0.00000	0.00000	0.00000
3.00000	−0.01105	0.00000	0.00000

```
                    CYBY          3.00000          3.00000          1.00000
                    CYBY          3.00000          3.00000          1.00000
                    CYBY          3.00000          3.00000          1.00000
                    CYBY          3.00000          3.00000          2.00000
                    CYBY          3.00000          3.00000          2.00000
                    CYBY          3.00000          3.00000          2.00000
                    CYBY          3.00000          3.00000          3.00000
                    CYBY          3.00000          3.00000          3.00000
                    CYBY          3.00000          3.00000          3.00000
                    KYR1         20.00000          0.00000          0.67020
                    KYR2         30.00000          0.00000          0.61190
                    EFLO          0.00000       5635.00000          0.00000
                    EFLO          1.00000        999.00000          0.00000
                    LCNS          0.00000        676.33000          0.00000
                    LCNS          1.00000        999.00000        676.33000
                    LCNS          2.00000        999.00000        999.00000
                    LCNS          3.00000        999.00000        999.00000
                    POUT          1.00000          0.00000          0.00000
                    MXIT         25.00000          0.00000          0.00000
                    SUBJ          0.00000          0.00000          0.00000


        INPUT COMPLETE FOR JOB NUMBER     1


        CODE FOR AMOUNT OF PRINTING =  1
        CAPITAL GAINS TAX = 0.50
        COUPON INCOME TAX = 0.00
        MAXIMUM NO. OF ITERATIONS = 25
        MAXIMUM CPU TIME NOT SPECIFIED. DEFAULT VALUE OF     10.00


        YIELD CLASS    1     INPUT DATA
            TIME             1.00      20.00       30.00
            YIELD        0.031000  0.049232   0.052000

            BASE YEAR -      1.00
            KEY YEAR 1 -    20.00           ALPHA = 0.0000000
            KEY YEAR 2 -    30.00           ALPHA = 0.0000000
```

1.00000	0.01105	0.00000	0.00000
2.00000	0.00000	0.00000	0.00000
3.00000	-0.01105	0.00000	0.00000
1.00000	0.01105	0.00000	0.00000
2.00000	0.00000	0.00000	0.00000
3.00000	-0.01105	0.00000	0.00000
1.00000	0.02000	0.00000	0.00000
2.00000	0.01105	0.00000	0.00000
3.00000	0.00000	0.00000	0.00000
1.00000	0.00000	0.00000	0.00000
1.00000	0.00000	0.00000	0.00000
0.00000	0.00000	0.00000	0.00000
0.00000	0.00000	0.00000	0.00000
0.00000	0.00000	0.00000	0.00000
0.00000	0.00000	0.00000	0.00000
676.33000	0.00000	0.00000	0.00000
999.00000	3381.66000	0.00000	0.00000
0.00000	0.00000	0.00000	0.00000
0.00000	0.00000	0.00000	0.00000
0.00000	0.00000	0.00000	0.00000

MINUTES ASSUMED.

BETA = 0.6702000   GAMMA = 1.0000000
BETA = 0.6119000   GAMMA = 1.0000000

```
BOND MATURITIES     BOND      MATURITY
                    NUMBER    (YEARS)    CLASS
                    ------    --------   -----

                      1        2.00       1
                      2        3.00       1
                      3        4.00       1
                      4        5.00       1
                      5       10.00       1
                      6       15.00       1
                      7       20.00       1
                      8       30.00       1
                      9        1.00       1
                     10        2.00       1
                     11        2.00       1
                     12       22.00       1
                     13       26.00       1
                     14       28.00       1
                     15       29.00       1


BID - ASKED SPREAD INPUT DATA - CLASS  1

    POINT NO. 1     STARTING TIME =      0.50
    POINT NO. 2     STARTING TIME =      2.00
    POINT NO. 3     STARTING TIME =      3.00
    POINT NO. 4     STARTING TIME =      7.00
    POINT NO. 5     STARTING TIME =     11.00
```

INITIAL PORTFOLIO

PAR VALUE	BOOK VALUE	YIELD
12387.	12387.	0.06089
27123.	27123.	0.03078
47016.	47016.	0.03741
3037.	3037.	0.03400
2740.	2740.	0.05200
25070.	25070.	0.05650
12258.	12258.	0.05100

NEW SPREAD =   0.1250
NEW SPREAD =   0.2500
NEW SPREAD =   0.3750
NEW SPREAD =   0.6250
NEW SPREAD =   0.7500

MUNICIPAL ROLLOVER - JAN '73 DATA

PERIOD	NO. OF EVENTS	LENGTH (YEARS)	VALUES OF E1 E2 E3 E4 E5				
0							
1	3	1.00	1				
			2				
			3				
2	3	1.00	1	1			
			1	2			
			1	3			
			2	1			
			2	2			
			2	3			
			3	1			
			3	2			
			3	3			
3	3	1.00	1	1	1		
			1	1	2		
			1	1	3		
			1	2	1		
			1	2	2		
			1	2	3		

CONDITIONAL PROBABILITY	EXOGENOUS FLOW	LOSS CONSTRAINT
	5635.	676.
.3333300	0.	676.
.3333400	0.	676.
.3333300	0.	676.
.3333300	0.	676.
.3333400	0.	676.
.3333300	0.	676.
.3333300	0.	676.
.3333400	0.	676.
.3333300	0.	676.
.3333300	0.	676.
.3333400	0.	676.
.3333300	0.	676.
.3333300	0.	3382.
.3333400	0.	3382.
.3333300	0.	3382.
.3333300	0.	3382.
.3333400	0.	3382.
.3333300	0.	3382.

```
1   3   1
1   3   2
1   3   3

2   1   1
2   1   2
2   1   3

2   2   1
2   2   2
2   2   3

2   3   1
2   3   2
2   3   3

3   1   1
3   1   2
3   1   3

3   2   1
3   2   2
3   2   3

3   3   1
3   3   2
3   3   3
```

```
.3333300          0.          3382.
.3333400          0.          3382.
.3333300          0.          3382.


.3333300          0.          3382.
.3333400          0.          3382.
.3333300          0.          3382.


.3333300          0.          3382.
.3333400          0.          3382.
.3333300          0.          3382.


.3333300          0.          3382.
.3333400          0.          3382.
.3333300          0.          3382.


.3333300          0.          3382.
.3333400          0.          3382.
.3333300          0.          3382.


.3333300          0.          3382.
.3333400          0.          3382.
.3333300          0.          3382.


.0000100          0.          3382.
.8999900          0.          3382.
.1000000          0.          3382.
```

MUNICIPAL ROLLOVER - JAN '73 DATA

        PERIOD   1 EXOGENOUS FLOW =   5635.00
            IE1 =   0   IE2 =   0   IE3 =   0   IE4 =   0

BOND NUMBER   1   2   3
                        9   10   11
PURCHASE
                     0.00   54555.17   0.00
                     0.00   0.00   0.00

SURE ASSET TRANSACTIONS   INTEREST   0.00

BONDS PURCHASED IN PERIOD   0
  SELL
    BOOK VALUE
                     0.00   0.00   0.00
                     0.00   27123.43   31696.86
    CASH VALUE
                     0.00   0.00   0.00
                     0.00   26989.42   31741.64

  HOLD (BOOK VALUE)
                     0.00   0.00   0.00
                 12387.47   0.00   15318.92

FINAL RESULTS

IE5 =   0

4	5	6	7	8
12	13	14	15	
13871.45	0.00	0.00	0.00	10785.93
0.00	0.00	0.00	0.00	
MATURED	0.00	PURCHASED	0.00	
0.00	0.00	0.00	0.00	0.00
3036.81	0.00	0.00	12257.65	
0.00	0.00	0.00	0.00	0.00
2705.40	0.00	0.00	12141.07	
0.00	0.00	0.00	0.00	0.00
0.00	2739.95	25070.47	0.00	

```
PERIOD   2  EXOGENOUS FLOW =              0.00
       IE1 =   1   IE2 =   0   IE3 =   0   IE4 =    0


BOND NUMBER              1                2                3
                         9               10               11
INTEREST
                      0.00          2014.49             0.00
                    754.27             0.00           573.02
PURCHASE
                      0.00         36489.26             0.00
                      0.00             0.00             0.00

SURE ASSET TRANSACTIONS         INTEREST             0.00

BONDS PURCHASED IN PERIOD    0
  SELL
    BOOK VALUE
                      0.00             0.00             0.00
                  12387.47             0.00         15318.92
    CASH VALUE
                      0.00             0.00             0.00
                  12387.47             0.00         15274.87

  HOLD (BOOK VALUE)
                      0.00             0.00             0.00
                      0.00             0.00             0.00

BONDS PURCHASED IN PERIOD    1
  SELL
    BOOK VALUE
                      0.00         54555.17             0.00
                      0.00             0.00             0.00
    CASH VALUE
                      0.00         54063.96             0.00
                      0.00             0.00             0.00

  HOLD (BOOK VALUE)
                      0.00             0.00             0.00
                      0.00             0.00             0.00
```

IE5 =   0

4	5	6	7	8
12	13	14	15	
554.98	0.00	0.00	0.00	560.87
0.00	142.48	1416.48	0.00	
0.00	0.00	0.00	0.00	0.00
0.00	0.00	0.00	0.00	

MATURED   0.00   PURCHASED   51253.63

0.00	0.00	0.00	0.00	0.00
0.00	0.00	0.00	0.00	
0.00	0.00	0.00	0.00	0.00
0.00	0.00	0.00	0.00	
0.00	0.00	0.00	0.00	0.00
0.00	2739.95	25070.47	0.00	

0.00	0.00	0.00	0.00	0.00
0.00	0.00	0.00	0.00	
0.00	0.00	0.00	0.00	0.00
0.00	0.00	0.00	0.00	
13871.45	0.00	0.00	0.00	10785.93
0.00	0.00	0.00	0.00	

```
        PERIOD   2  EXOGENOUS FLOW =            0.00
             IE1 =   2   IE2 =   0   IE3 =   0   IE4 =   0


BOND NUMBER                    1                2                3
                               9               10               11
INTEREST
                            0.00          2014.49             0.00
                          754.27             0.00           573.02



PURCHASE
                            0.00             0.00             0.00
                            0.00             0.00             0.00

SURE ASSET TRANSACTIONS              INTEREST             0.00

BONDS PURCHASED IN PERIOD    0
  SELL
    BOOK VALUE
                            0.00             0.00             0.00
                        12387.47             0.00             0.00
    CASH VALUE
                            0.00             0.00             0.00
                        12387.47             0.00             0.00

  HOLD (BOOK VALUE)
                            0.00             0.00             0.00
                            0.00             0.00         15318.92

BONDS PURCHASED IN PERIOD    1
  SELL
    BOOK VALUE
                            0.00             0.00             0.00
                            0.00             0.00             0.00
    CASH VALUE
                            0.00             0.00             0.00
                            0.00             0.00             0.00

  HOLD (BOOK VALUE)
                            0.00         54555.17             0.00
                            0.00             0.00             0.00
```

IE5 =   0

4	5	6	7	8
12	13	14	15	
554.98	0.00	0.00	0.00	560.87
0.00	142.48	1416.48	0.00	
4288.55	0.00	0.00	0.00	14115.51
0.00	0.00	0.00	0.00	
MATURED	0.00	PURCHASED	0.00	
0.00	0.00	0.00	0.00	0.00
0.00	0.00	0.00	0.00	
0.00	0.00	0.00	0.00	0.00
0.00	0.00	0.00	0.00	
0.00	0.00	0.00	0.00	0.00
0.00	2739.95	25070.47	0.00	
0.00	0.00	0.00	0.00	0.00
0.00	0.00	0.00	0.00	
0.00	0.00	0.00	0.00	0.00
0.00	0.00	0.00	0.00	
13871.45	0.00	0.00	0.00	10785.93
0.00	0.00	0.00	0.00	

```
        PERIOD   2   EXOGENOUS FLOW =           0.00
           IE1 =   3   IE2 =   0   IE3 =   0   IE4 =   0


BOND NUMBER                    1              2              3
                               9             10             11
INTEREST
                            0.00         2014.49           0.00
                          754.27            0.00         573.02
PURCHASE
                            0.00            0.00           0.00
                            0.00            0.00           0.00

SURE ASSET TRANSACTIONS          INTEREST           0.00

BONDS PURCHASED IN PERIOD    0
  SELL
    BOOK VALUE
                            0.00            0.00           0.00
                        12387.47            0.00       15318.92
    CASH VALUE
                            0.00            0.00           0.00
                        12387.47            0.00       15441.07


  HOLD (BOOK VALUE)
                            0.00            0.00           0.00
                            0.00            0.00           0.00

BONDS PURCHASED IN PERIOD    1
  SELL
    BOOK VALUE
                            0.00            0.00           0.00
                            0.00            0.00           0.00
    CASH VALUE
                            0.00            0.00           0.00
                            0.00            0.00           0.00

  HOLD (BOOK VALUE)
                            0.00        54555.17           0.00
                            0.00            0.00           0.00
```

```
IE5 =    0


       4              5              6              7              8
      12             13             14             15

  554.98          0.00           0.00           0.00         560.87
    0.00        142.48        1416.48           0.00

    0.00          0.00           0.00           0.00       33845.14
    0.00          0.00           0.00           0.00

MATURED           0.00        PURCHASED         0.00



    0.00          0.00           0.00           0.00           0.00
    0.00          0.00           0.00           0.00

    0.00          0.00           0.00           0.00           0.00
    0.00          0.00           0.00           0.00



    0.00          0.00           0.00           0.00           0.00
    0.00       2739.95       25070.47           0.00



    0.00          0.00           0.00           0.00           0.00
    0.00          0.00           0.00           0.00

    0.00          0.00           0.00           0.00           0.00
    0.00          0.00           0.00           0.00

13871.45          0.00           0.00           0.00       10785.93
    0.00          0.00           0.00           0.00
```

```
       PERIOD   3  EXOGENOUS FLOW =        0.00
           IE1 =   1   IE2 =   1   IE3 =   0   IE4 =   0


BOND NUMBER                1              2              3
                           9             10             11
INTEREST
                        0.00        1715.46           0.00
                        0.00           0.00           0.00
PURCHASE
                        0.00           0.00           0.00
                        0.00           0.00           0.00

SURE ASSET TRANSACTIONS         INTEREST     2155.21

BONDS PURCHASED IN PERIOD    0
  SELL
    BOOK VALUE
                        0.00           0.00           0.00
                        0.00           0.00           0.00
    CASH VALUE
                        0.00           0.00           0.00
                        0.00           0.00           0.00

  HOLD (BOOK VALUE)
                        0.00           0.00           0.00
                        0.00           0.00           0.00

BONDS PURCHASED IN PERIOD    1
  SELL
    BOOK VALUE
                        0.00           0.00           0.00
                        0.00           0.00           0.00
    CASH VALUE
                        0.00           0.00           0.00
                        0.00           0.00           0.00

  HOLD (BOOK VALUE)
                        0.00           0.00           0.00
                        0.00           0.00           0.00

BONDS PURCHASED IN PERIOD    2
  SELL
    BOOK VALUE
                        0.00           0.00           0.00
                        0.00           0.00           0.00
    CASH VALUE
                        0.00           0.00           0.00
                        0.00           0.00           0.00

  HOLD (BOOK VALUE)
                        0.00       36489.26           0.00
                        0.00           0.00           0.00
```

```
IE5 =    0


       4              5              6              7              8
      12             13             14             15

 554.98           0.00           0.00           0.00         560.87
   0.00         142.48        1416.48           0.00

   0.00           0.00           0.00           0.00           0.00
   0.00           0.00           0.00           0.00

 MATURED       51253.63     PURCHASED       69033.44



   0.00           0.00           0.00           0.00           0.00
   0.00           0.00       11910.66           0.00

   0.00           0.00           0.00           0.00           0.00
   0.00           0.00       11234.33           0.00


   0.00           0.00           0.00           0.00           0.00
   0.00        2739.95       13159.81           0.00



   0.00           0.00           0.00           0.00           0.00
   0.00           0.00           0.00           0.00

   0.00           0.00           0.00           0.00           0.00
   0.00           0.00           0.00           0.00

13871.45           0.00           0.00           0.00       10785.93
   0.00           0.00           0.00           0.00



   0.00           0.00           0.00           0.00           0.00
   0.00           0.00           0.00           0.00

   0.00           0.00           0.00           0.00           0.00
   0.00           0.00           0.00           0.00


   0.00           0.00           0.00           0.00           0.00
   0.00           0.00           0.00           0.00
```

```
        PERIOD   3   EXOGENOUS FLOW =           0.00
             IE1 =   1   IE2 =   2   IE3 =   0   IE4 =   0


BOND NUMBER              1               2               3
                        9              10              11
INTEREST
                     0.00         1715.46            0.00
                     0.00            0.00            0.00
PURCHASE
                     0.00            0.00        57473.68
                     0.00            0.00            0.00

SURE ASSET TRANSACTIONS         INTEREST         2155.21

BONDS PURCHASED IN PERIOD   0
  SELL
    BOOK VALUE
                     0.00            0.00            0.00
                     0.00            0.00            0.00
    CASH VALUE
                     0.00            0.00            0.00
                     0.00            0.00            0.00

  HOLD (BOOK VALUE)
                     0.00            0.00            0.00
                     0.00            0.00            0.00

BONDS PURCHASED IN PERIOD   1
  SELL
    BOOK VALUE
                     0.00            0.00            0.00
                     0.00            0.00            0.00
    CASH VALUE
                     0.00            0.00            0.00
                     0.00            0.00            0.00

  HOLD (BOOK VALUE)
                     0.00            0.00            0.00
                     0.00            0.00            0.00

BONDS PURCHASED IN PERIOD   2
  SELL
    BOOK VALUE
                     0.00            0.00            0.00
                     0.00            0.00            0.00
    CASH VALUE
                     0.00            0.00            0.00
                     0.00            0.00            0.00

  HOLD (BOOK VALUE)
                     0.00        36489.26            0.00
                     0.00            0.00            0.00
```

IE5 =   0

4	5	6	7	8
12	13	14	15	
554.98	0.00	0.00	0.00	560.87
0.00	142.48	1416.48	0.00	
0.00	0.00	0.00	0.00	325.43
0.00	0.00	0.00	0.00	

MATURED   51253.63   PURCHASED   0.00

0.00	0.00	0.00	0.00	0.00
0.00	0.00	0.00	0.00	
0.00	0.00	0.00	0.00	0.00
0.00	0.00	0.00	0.00	
0.00	0.00	0.00	0.00	0.00
0.00	2739.95	25070.47	0.00	

0.00	0.00	0.00	0.00	0.00
0.00	0.00	0.00	0.00	
0.00	0.00	0.00	0.00	0.00
0.00	0.00	0.00	0.00	
13871.45	0.00	0.00	0.00	10785.93
0.00	0.00	0.00	0.00	

0.00	0.00	0.00	0.00	0.00
0.00	0.00	0.00	0.00	
0.00	0.00	0.00	0.00	0.00
0.00	0.00	0.00	0.00	
0.00	0.00	0.00	0.00	0.00
0.00	0.00	0.00	0.00	

```
PERIOD   3   EXOGENOUS FLOW =        0.00
        IE1 =   1   IE2 =   3   IE3 =   0   IE4 =   0


BOND NUMBER              1              2              3
                        9              10             11
INTEREST
                     0.00        1715.46           0.00
                     0.00           0.00           0.00
PURCHASE
                     0.00           0.00           0.00
                     0.00           0.00           0.00

SURE ASSET TRANSACTIONS         INTEREST      2155.21

BONDS PURCHASED IN PERIOD   0
  SELL
    BOOK VALUE
                     0.00           0.00           0.00
                     0.00           0.00           0.00
    CASH VALUE
                     0.00           0.00           0.00
                     0.00           0.00           0.00

  HOLD (BOOK VALUE)
                     0.00           0.00           0.00
                     0.00           0.00           0.00

BONDS PURCHASED IN PERIOD   1
  SELL
    BOOK VALUE
                     0.00           0.00           0.00
                     0.00           0.00           0.00
    CASH VALUE
                     0.00           0.00           0.00
                     0.00           0.00           0.00

  HOLD (BOOK VALUE)
                     0.00           0.00           0.00
                     0.00           0.00           0.00

BONDS PURCHASED IN PERIOD   2
  SELL
    BOOK VALUE
                     0.00           0.00           0.00
                     0.00           0.00           0.00
    CASH VALUE
                     0.00           0.00           0.00
                     0.00           0.00           0.00

  HOLD (BOOK VALUE)
                     0.00       36489.26           0.00
                     0.00           0.00           0.00
```

```
IE5 =    0


        4              5              6              7
       12             13             14             15              8

    554.98          0.00           0.00           0.00          560.87
       0.00        142.48        1416.48           0.00

       0.00          0.00           0.00           0.00        57799.11
       0.00          0.00           0.00           0.00

MATURED        51253.63       PURCHASED           0.00



       0.00          0.00           0.00           0.00           0.00
       0.00          0.00           0.00           0.00

       0.00          0.00           0.00           0.00           0.00
       0.00          0.00           0.00           0.00


       0.00          0.00           0.00           0.00           0.00
       0.00       2739.95       25070.47           0.00



       0.00          0.00           0.00           0.00           0.00
       0.00          0.00           0.00           0.00

       0.00          0.00           0.00           0.00           0.00
       0.00          0.00           0.00           0.00

  13871.45          0.00           0.00           0.00        10785.93
       0.00          0.00           0.00           0.00



       0.00          0.00           0.00           0.00           0.00
       0.00          0.00           0.00           0.00

       0.00          0.00           0.00           0.00           0.00
       0.00          0.00           0.00           0.00


       0.00          0.00           0.00           0.00           0.00
       0.00          0.00           0.00           0.00
```

279

```
        PERIOD   3  EXOGENOUS FLOW =            0.00
             IE1 =   2   IE2 =   1   IE3 =   0   IE4 =   0


BOND NUMBER                    1               2               3
                               9              10              11
INTEREST
                            0.00         2014.49            0.00
                            0.00            0.00          573.02
PURCHASE
                        88436.03            0.00            0.00
                            0.00            0.00            0.00

SURE ASSET TRANSACTIONS         INTEREST        0.00

BONDS PURCHASED IN PERIOD    0
  SELL
    BOOK VALUE
                            0.00            0.00            0.00
                            0.00            0.00        15318.92
    CASH VALUE
                            0.00            0.00            0.00
                            0.00            0.00        15318.92

  HOLD (BOOK VALUE)
                            0.00            0.00            0.00
                            0.00            0.00            0.00

BONDS PURCHASED IN PERIOD    1
  SELL
    BOOK VALUE
                            0.00        54555.17            0.00
                            0.00            0.00            0.00
    CASH VALUE
                            0.00        54385.58            0.00
                            0.00            0.00            0.00

  HOLD (BOOK VALUE)
                            0.00            0.00            0.00
                            0.00            0.00            0.00

BONDS PURCHASED IN PERIOD    2
  SELL
    BOOK VALUE
                            0.00            0.00            0.00
                            0.00            0.00            0.00
    CASH VALUE
                            0.00            0.00            0.00
                            0.00            0.00            0.00

  HOLD (BOOK VALUE)
                            0.00            0.00            0.00
                            0.00            0.00            0.00
```

```
IE5 =    0


        4              5              6              7              8
       12             13             14             15

   726.56          0.00           0.00           0.00        1294.87
     0.00        142.48        1416.48           0.00

     0.00          0.00           0.00           0.00           0.00
     0.00          0.00           0.00           0.00

MATURED            0.00       PURCHASED          0.00



     0.00          0.00           0.00           0.00           0.00
     0.00          0.00           0.00           0.00

     0.00          0.00           0.00           0.00           0.00
     0.00          0.00           0.00           0.00


     0.00          0.00           0.00           0.00           0.00
     0.00       2739.95       25070.47           0.00



     0.00          0.00           0.00           0.00           0.00
     0.00          0.00           0.00           0.00

     0.00          0.00           0.00           0.00           0.00
     0.00          0.00           0.00           0.00

 13871.45          0.00           0.00           0.00       10785.93
     0.00          0.00           0.00           0.00



  4288.55          0.00           0.00           0.00        8781.81
     0.00          0.00           0.00           0.00

  4215.82          0.00           0.00           0.00        8347.80
     0.00          0.00           0.00           0.00


     0.00          0.00           0.00           0.00        5333.70
     0.00          0.00           0.00           0.00
```

```
        PERIOD   3   EXOGENOUS FLOW =          0.00
              IE1 =   2   IE2 =   2   IE3 =   0   IE4 =   0


BOND NUMBER                    1              2              3
                               9             10             11
INTEREST
                            0.00        2014.49           0.00
                            0.00           0.00         573.02
PURCHASE
                            0.00           0.00           0.00
                            0.00           0.00           0.00

SURE ASSET TRANSACTIONS             INTEREST           0.00

BONDS PURCHASED IN PERIOD    0
  SELL
    BOOK VALUE
                            0.00           0.00           0.00
                            0.00           0.00       15318.92
    CASH VALUE
                            0.00           0.00           0.00
                            0.00           0.00       15318.92

  HOLD (BOOK VALUE)
                            0.00           0.00           0.00
                            0.00           0.00           0.00

BONDS PURCHASED IN PERIOD    1
  SELL
    BOOK VALUE
                            0.00       54555.17           0.00
                            0.00           0.00           0.00
    CASH VALUE
                            0.00       54679.03           0.00
                            0.00           0.00           0.00

  HOLD (BOOK VALUE)
                            0.00           0.00           0.00
                            0.00           0.00           0.00

BONDS PURCHASED IN PERIOD    2
  SELL
    BOOK VALUE
                            0.00           0.00           0.00
                            0.00           0.00           0.00
    CASH VALUE
                            0.00           0.00           0.00
                            0.00           0.00           0.00

  HOLD (BOOK VALUE)
                            0.00           0.00           0.00
                            0.00           0.00           0.00
```

```
IE5 =    0


         4              5              6              7            8
        12             13             14             15
    726.56          0.00           0.00           0.00        1294.87
      0.00        142.48        1416.48           0.00

 51902.48          0.00           0.00           0.00       24263.38
      0.00          0.00           0.00           0.00

 MATURED           0.00        PURCHASED          0.00



      0.00          0.00           0.00           0.00           0.00
      0.00          0.00           0.00           0.00

      0.00          0.00           0.00           0.00           0.00
      0.00          0.00           0.00           0.00


      0.00          0.00           0.00           0.00           0.00
      0.00       2739.95       25070.47           0.00



      0.00          0.00           0.00           0.00           0.00
      0.00          0.00           0.00           0.00

      0.00          0.00           0.00           0.00           0.00
      0.00          0.00           0.00           0.00

 13871.45          0.00           0.00           0.00       10785.93
      0.00          0.00           0.00           0.00



      0.00          0.00           0.00           0.00           0.00
      0.00          0.00           0.00           0.00

      0.00          0.00           0.00           0.00           0.00
      0.00          0.00           0.00           0.00

  4288.55          0.00           0.00           0.00       14115.51
      0.00          0.00           0.00           0.00
```

283

```
        PERIOD   3   EXOGENOUS FLOW =           0.00
            IE1 =   2   IE2 =   3   IE3 =   0   IE4 =   0


BOND NUMBER               1                 2                 3
                          9                10                11
INTEREST
                        0.00           2014.49              0.00
                        0.00              0.00            573.02
PURCHASE
                        0.00              0.00              0.00
                        0.00              0.00              0.00

SURE ASSET TRANSACTIONS         INTEREST              0.00

BONDS PURCHASED IN PERIOD    0
  SELL
    BOOK VALUE
                        0.00              0.00              0.00
                        0.00              0.00          15318.92
    CASH VALUE
                        0.00              0.00              0.00
                        0.00              0.00          15318.92

  HOLD (BOOK VALUE)
                        0.00              0.00              0.00
                        0.00              0.00              0.00

BONDS PURCHASED IN PERIOD    1
  SELL
    BOOK VALUE
                        0.00          54555.17              0.00
                        0.00              0.00              0.00
    CASH VALUE
                        0.00          54977.29              0.00
                        0.00              0.00              0.00

  HOLD (BOOK VALUE)
                        0.00              0.00              0.00
                        0.00              0.00              0.00

BONDS PURCHASED IN PERIOD    2
  SELL
    BOOK VALUE
                        0.00              0.00              0.00
                        0.00              0.0C              0.00
    CASH VALUE
                        0.00              0.00              0.00
                        0.00              0.00              0.00

  HOLD (BOOK VALUE)
                        0.00              0.00              0.00
                        0.00              0.00              0.00
```

IE5 =   0

| 4 | 5 | 6 | 7 | 8 |
12	13	14	15	
726.56	0.00	0.00	0.00	1294.87
0.00	142.48	1416.48	0.00	
0.00	0.00	0.00	0.00	80836.62
0.00	0.00	0.00	0.00	
MATURED	0.00	PURCHASED	0.00	
0.00	0.00	0.00	0.00	0.00
0.00	0.00	0.00	0.00	
0.00	0.00	0.00	0.00	0.00
0.00	0.00	0.00	0.00	
0.00	0.00	0.00	0.00	0.00
0.00	2739.95	25070.47	0.00	
0.00	0.00	0.00	0.00	0.00
0.00	0.00	0.00	0.00	
0.00	0.00	0.00	0.00	0.00
0.00	0.00	0.00	0.00	
13871.45	0.00	0.00	0.00	10785.93
0.00	0.00	0.00	0.00	
4288.55	0.00	0.00	0.00	0.00
0.00	0.00	0.00	0.00	
4372.50	0.00	0.00	0.00	0.00
0.00	0.00	0.00	0.00	
0.00	0.00	0.00	0.00	14115.51
0.00	0.00	0.00	0.00	

```
        PERIOD   3   EXOGENOUS FLOW =           0.00
             IE1 =   3   IE2 =   1   IE3 =   0   IE4 =   0


BOND NUMBER                    1              2                 3
                               9             10                11

INTEREST
                             0.00       2014.49            0.00
                             0.00          0.00            0.00
PURCHASE
                             0.00          0.00        75336.29
                             0.00          0.00            0.00

SURE ASSET TRANSACTIONS            INTEREST             0.00

BONDS PURCHASED IN PERIOD    0
  SELL
    BOOK VALUE
                             0.00          0.00            0.00
                             0.00          0.00            0.00
    CASH VALUE
                             0.00          0.00            0.00
                             0.00          0.00            0.00

  HOLD (BOOK VALUE)
                             0.00          0.00            0.00
                             0.00          0.00            0.00

BONDS PURCHASED IN PERIOD    1
  SELL
    BOOK VALUE
                             0.00      54555.17            0.00
                             0.00          0.00            0.00
    CASH VALUE
                             0.00      54679.03            0.00
                             0.00          0.00            0.00

  HOLD (BOOK VALUE)
                             0.00          0.00            0.00
                             0.00          0.00            0.00

BONDS PURCHASED IN PERIOD    2
  SELL
    BOOK VALUE
                             0.00          0.00            0.00
                             0.00          0.00            0.00
    CASH VALUE
                             0.00          0.00            0.00
                             0.00          0.00            0.00

  HOLD (BOOK VALUE)
                             0.00          0.00            0.00
                             0.00          0.00            0.00
```

```
IE5 =    0


        4                5                6                7                8
        12               13               14               15


   554.98            0.00             0.00             0.00          2091.97
        0.00           142.48          1416.48            0.00

     0.00             0.00             0.00             0.00             0.00
        0.00             0.00             0.00             0.00

MATURED              0.00       PURCHASED              0.00



     0.00             0.00             0.00             0.00             0.00
        0.00             0.00             0.00             0.00

     0.00             0.00             0.00             0.00             0.00
        0.00             0.00             0.00             0.00


     0.00             0.00             0.00             0.00             0.00
        0.00          2739.95         25070.47            0.00



     0.00             0.00             0.00             0.00             0.00
        0.00             0.00             0.00             0.00

     0.00             0.00             0.00             0.00             0.00
        0.00             0.00             0.00             0.00


 13871.45            0.00             0.00             0.00         10785.93
        0.00             0.00             0.00             0.00



     0.00             0.00             0.00             0.00         15237.05
        0.00             0.00             0.00             0.00

     0.00             0.00             0.00             0.00         14436.86
        0.00             0.00             0.00             0.00


     0.00             0.00             0.00             0.00         18608.09
        0.00             0.00             0.00             0.00
```

```
PERIOD    3   EXOGENOUS FLOW =           0.00
        IE1 =    3    IE2 =    2    IE3 =    0    IE4 =    0


BOND NUMBER                    1                    2                    3
                               9                   10                   11
INTEREST
                            0.00              2014.49                 0.00


                            0.00                 0.00                 0.00
PURCHASE
                            0.00                 0.00                 0.00
                            0.00                 0.00                 0.00

SURE ASSET TRANSACTIONS            INTEREST                 0.00

BONDS PURCHASED IN PERIOD     0
  SELL
    BOOK VALUE
                            0.00                 0.00                 0.00
                            0.00                 0.00                 0.00
    CASH VALUE
                            0.00                 0.00                 0.00
                            0.00                 0.00                 0.00

  HOLD (BOOK VALUE)
                            0.00                 0.00                 0.00
                            0.00                 0.00                 0.00

BONDS PURCHASED IN PERIOD     1
  SELL
    BOOK VALUE
                            0.00             54555.17                 0.00
                            0.00                 0.00                 0.00
    CASH VALUE
                            0.00             54977.29                 0.00
                            0.00                 0.00                 0.00

  HOLD (BOOK VALUE)
                            0.00                 0.00                 0.00
                            0.00                 0.00                 0.00

BONDS PURCHASED IN PERIOD     2
  SELL
    BOOK VALUE
                            0.00                 0.00                 0.00
                            0.00                 0.00                 0.00
    CASH VALUE
                            0.00                 0.00                 0.00
                            0.00                 0.00                 0.00

  HOLD (BOOK VALUE)
                            0.00                 0.00                 0.00
                            0.00                 0.00                 0.00
```

```
IE5 =    0


        4               5               6               7               8
       12              13              14              15
   554.98            0.00            0.00            0.00         2091.97


        0.00          142.48         1416.48            0.00

        0.00            0.00            0.00            0.00        61197.70
        0.00            0.00            0.00            0.00

MATURED                 0.00        PURCHASED           0.00



        0.00            0.00            0.00            0.00            0.00
        0.00            0.00            0.00            0.00

        0.00            0.00            0.00            0.00            0.00
        0.00            0.00            0.00            0.00


        0.00            0.00            0.00            0.00            0.00
        0.00         2739.95        25070.47            0.00



        0.00            0.00            0.00            0.00            0.00
        0.00            0.00            0.00            0.00

        0.00            0.00            0.00            0.00            0.00
        0.00            0.00            0.00            0.00

    13871.45            0.00            0.00            0.00        10785.93
        0.00            0.00            0.00            0.00



        0.00            0.00            0.00            0.00            0.00
        0.00            0.00            0.00            0.00

        0.00            0.00            0.00            0.00            0.00
        0.00            0.00            0.00            0.00


        0.00            0.00            0.00            0.00        33845.14
        0.00            0.00            0.00            0.00
```

```
        PERIOD   3  EXOGENOUS FLOW =        0.00
            IE1 =   3   IE2 =   3   IE3 =   0   IE4 =   0


    BOND NUMBER              1              2              3
                            9             10             11
    INTEREST
                          0.00        2014.49           0.00
                          0.00           0.00           0.00
    PURCHASE



                     55797.46           0.00           0.00
                          0.00           0.00           0.00
    SURE ASSET TRANSACTIONS         INTEREST           0.00

    BONDS PURCHASED IN PERIOD    0
      SELL
        BOOK VALUE
                          0.00           0.00           0.00
                          0.00           0.00           0.00
      CASH VALUE
                          0.00           0.00           0.00
                          0.00           0.00           0.00

      HOLD (BOOK VALUE)
                          0.00           0.00           0.00
                          0.00           0.00           0.00

    BONDS PURCHASED IN PERIOD    1
      SELL
        BOOK VALUE
                          0.00           0.00           0.00
                          0.00           0.00           0.00
      CASH VALUE
                          0.00           0.00           0.00
                          0.00           0.00           0.00

      HOLD (BOOK VALUE)
                          0.00       54555.17           0.00
                          0.00           0.00           0.00

    BONDS PURCHASED IN PERIOD    2
      SELL
        BOOK VALUE
                          0.00           0.00           0.00
                          0.00           0.00           0.00
      CASH VALUE
                          0.00           0.00           0.00
                          0.00           0.00           0.00

      HOLD (BOOK VALUE)
                          0.00           0.00           0.00
                          0.00           0.00           0.00
```

```
IE5 =    0


        4              5              6              7              8
       12             13             14             15
554.98           0.00           0.00           0.00        2091.97
       0.00         142.48        1416.48           0.00


        0.00           0.00           0.00           0.00           0.00
        0.00           0.00           0.00           0.00
MATURED              0.00      PURCHASED           0.00


        0.00           0.00           0.00           0.00           0.00
        0.00           0.00       11910.66           0.00
        0.00           0.00           0.00           0.00           0.00
        0.00           0.00       13775.24           0.00


        0.00           0.00           0.00           0.00           0.00
        0.00        2739.95       13159.81           0.00


        0.00           0.00           0.00           0.00           0.00
        0.00           0.00           0.00           0.00
        0.00           0.00           0.00           0.00           0.00
        0.00           0.00           0.00           0.00
13871.45           0.00           0.00           0.00       10785.93
        0.00           0.00           0.00           0.00


        0.00           0.00           0.00           0.00       33845.14
        0.00           0.00           0.00           0.00
        0.00           0.00           0.00           0.00       35801.82
        0.00           0.00           0.00           0.00


        0.00           0.00           0.00           0.00           0.00
        0.00           0.00           0.00           0.00
```

REFERENCES

Almon, Shirley, "The Distributed Lag between Capital Appropriations and Expenditures," *Econometrica,* Vol. 33, No. 1 (January 1965), pp. 178–196.

Baumol, William J. and Richard E. Quandt, "Investment and Discount Rates under Capital Rationing—A Programming Approach," *The Economic Journal,* Vol. 75, No. 298 (June 1965), pp. 317–329.

Booth, G. Geoffrey, "Programming Bank Portfolios under Uncertainty: An Extension," *Journal of Bank Research,* Vol. 2, No. 4 (Winter 1972), pp. 28–40.

Bower, Richard S. and H. Clay Simpson, Jr., "Realizing the Promise of Computer Time Sharing in Banks," *The Bankers Magazine,* Vol. 153, No. 1 (Winter 1970), pp. 57–68.

Bradley, Stephen P. and Dwight B. Crane, "A Dynamic Model for Bond Portfolio Management," *Management Science,* Vol. 19, No. 2 (October 1972), pp. 139–191.

Bradley, Stephen P. and Dwight B. Crane, "Managing a Bank Bond Portfolio over Time," in M. A. H. Dempster, Ed., *Stochastic Programming* (London: Academic Press), 1975 (forthcoming).

Bradley, Stephen P. and Dwight B. Crane, "Management of Commercial Bank Government Security Portfolios: An Optimization Approach under Uncertainty," *Journal of Bank Research,* Vol. 4, No. 1 (Spring 1973), pp. 18–30.

Bradley, Stephen P., Ronald S. Frank, and Sherwood C. Frey, Jr., "Determining the Appropriate Discount Rates in Pure Capital Rationing," Graduate School of Business Administration, Harvard University, Working Paper No. 75-4 (January 1975).

Brimmer, Andrew F., "Commercial Bank Lending and Monetary Management," a speech presented to the 57th Annual Fall Conference of the Robert Morris Association, Los Angeles, California, October 1971.

Budzeika, George, "A Model of Business Loan Behavior at Large New York City Banks," *Journal of Bank Research,* Vol. 1, No. 4 (Winter 1971), pp. 58–72.

Chambers, D. and A. Charnes, "Intertemporal Analysis and Optimization of Bank Portfolios," *Management Science,* Vol. 7, No. 4 (July 1961), pp. 393–410.

Charnes, A. and S. C. Littlechild, "Intertemporal Bank Asset Choice with Stochastic Dependence," Systems Research Memorandum No. 188, The Technological Institute, Northwestern University (April 1968).

Charnes, A. and Sten Thore, "Planning for Liquidity in Financial Institutions: The Chance-Constrained Method," *The Journal of Finance*, Vol. 21, No. 4 (December 1966), pp. 649-674.

Cheng, Pao Lun, "Optimum Bond Portfolio Selection," *Management Science*, Vol. 8, No. 4 (July 1962), pp. 490-499.

Chervany, Norman L., John S. Strom, and Ralph Boehlke, "An Operations Planning Model for the Northwestern National Bank of Minneapolis," in Albert N. Schrieber, Ed., *Corporate Simulation Models* (Providence, R. I.: College of Simulation and Gaming of the Institute of Management Science, and Seattle, Washington: Graduate School of Business Administration), 1970.

Cohen, Kalman J. and Frederick S. Hammer, "Linear Programming and Optimal Bank Asset Management Decisions: Some Preliminary Note Equations and Exhibits," unpublished manuscript, November 1966.

Cohen, Kalman J. and Frederick S. Hammer, "Linear Programming and Optimal Bank Asset Management Decisions," *The Journal of Finance*, Vol. 22, No. 2 (May 1967), pp. 147-165.

Cohen, Kalman J. and Sten Thore, "Programming Bank Portfolios Under Uncertainty," *Journal of Bank Research*, Vol. 1, No. 1 (Spring 1970), pp. 42-61.

Cramer, Harold, *Mathematical Methods of Statistics* (Princeton: Princeton University Press), 1946.

Crane, Dwight B., "Assessment of Yields on U.S. Government Securities," Graduate School of Business Administration, Harvard University, Working Paper No. 71-26 (December 1971).

Crane, Dwight B., "A Stochastic Programming Model for Commercial Bank Bond Portfolio Management," *Journal of Financial and Quantitative Analysis*, Vol. 6, No. 3 (June 1971), pp. 955-976.

Crane, Dwight B. and James R. Crotty, "A Two-State Forecasting Model: Exponential Smoothing and Multiple Regression," *Management Science*, Vol. 13, No. 8 (April 1967), pp. 501-507.

Daellenback, Hans G. and Stephen H. Archer, "The Optimal Bank Liquidity: A Multi-Period Stochastic Model," *Journal of Financial and Quantitative Analysis*, Vol. 4, No. 3 (September 1969), pp. 329-343.

Dantzig, George B., *Linear Programming and Extensions* (Princeton: Princeton University Press), 1963.

de Leeuw, Frank, "A Model of Financial Behavior," in James S. Duesenberry et al., Eds., *Brookings Econometric Model of the United States Economy* (Rand McNally and North Holland), 1965.

Eppen, Gary D. and Eugene F. Fama, "Solutions for Cash Balance and Simple Dynamic Portfolio Problems with Proportional Costs," *Journal of Business*, Vol. 41 (January 1968), pp. 94-112.

Eppen, Gary D. and Eugene F. Fama, "Three Asset Cash Balance and Dynamic Portfolio Problems," *Management Science*, Vol. 17, No. 5 (January 1971), pp. 311-319.

Fisher, Lawrence and Roman L. Weil, "Coping with the Risk of Interest-Rate Fluctuations: Returns to Bondholders from Naive and Optimal Strategies," *Journal of Business*, Vol. 44, No. 4 (October 1971), pp. 408-431.

Fried, Joel, "Bank Portfolio Selection," *Journal of Financial and Quantitative Analysis*, Vol. 5, No. 2 (June 1970), pp. 203-227.

Hamburger, Michael J. and Cynthia M. Latta, "The Term Structure of Interest Rates: Some Additional Evidence," *Journal of Money, Credit and Banking*, Vol. 1, No. 1 (February 1969), pp. 71-83.

Hempel, George H., "Basic Ingredients of Commercial Banks' Investment Policies," *The Bankers Magazine*, Vol. 155, No. 4 (Autumn 1972), pp. 50–59.

Hempel, George H. and Stephen R. Kretschman, "Comparative Performance of Portfolio Maturity Policies of Commercial Banks," *Mississippi Valley Journal of Business and Economics*, Vol. 9, No. 1 (Fall 1973), pp. 55–75.

Hempel, George H. and Jess B. Yawitz, "Maximizing Bond Returns," *The Bankers Magazine*, Vol. 157, No. 3 (Summer 1974), pp. 103–114.

Johnston, J., *Econometric Methods* (New York: McGraw-Hill), 1963.

Kane, Edward J., "Is There a Predilected Lock-In Effect?," *National Tax Journal*, Vol. XXI, No. 4 (December 1968), pp. 365–385.

Komar, Robert I., "Developing a Liquidity Management Model," *Journal of Bank Research*, Vol. 2, No. 1 (Spring 1971), pp. 38–52.

Lifson, K. A. and Brian R. Blackmarr, "Simulation and Optimization Models for Asset Deployment and Funds Sources Balancing Profit, Liquidity and Growth," *Journal of Bank Research*, Vol. 4, No. 3 (Autumn 1973), pp. 239–255.

Lyon, Roger A., *Investment Portfolio Management in the Commercial Bank* (New Brunswick, N.J.: Rutgers University Press), 1960.

Malkiel, Burton G., "Expectations, Bond Prices, and the Term Structure of Interest Rates," *Quarterly Journal of Economics*, Vol. LXXVI, No. 2 (May 1962), pp. 197–218.

Markowitz, Harry M., *Portfolio Selection: Efficient Diversification of Investments* (New Haven: Yale University Press), Monograph 16, Cowles Foundation for Research in Economics at Yale University, 1970. Originally published by John Wiley & Sons, Inc., New York, 1959.

Meiselman, David, *The Term Structure of Interest Rates* (Englewood Cliffs, N.J.: Prentice-Hall), 1962.

Modigliani, Franco and Richard Sutch, "Debt Management and the Term Structure of Interest Rates: An Empirical Analysis of Recent Experience," *Journal of Political Economy*, Vol. 75 (August 1967), pp. 569–589.

Modigliani, Franco and Richard Sutch, "Innovations in Interest Rate Policy," *American Economic Review*, Vol. 56, No. 2 (May 1966), pp. 178–197.

Modigliani, Franco and Richard Sutch, "The Term Structure of Interest Rates: A Re-examination of the Evidence," *Journal of Money, Credit and Banking*, Vol. 1, No. 1 (February 1969), pp. 112–120.

Pierson, Gail, "Effect of Economic Policy of the Term Structure of Interest Rates," *The Review of Economics and Statistics*, Vol. 52, No. 1 (February 1970), pp. 1–11.

Pye, Gordon, "A Markov Model of the Term Structure," *Quarterly Journal of Economics*, Vol. LXXX, No. 1 (February 1966), pp. 60–72.

Robertson, James M., "A Mixed Integer Programming Bank Asset Management Model," unpublished paper presented at the 17th TIMS International Conference, London, July 1970.

Robinson, Randall S., "BANKMOD: An Interactive Simulation Aid for Bank Financial Planning," *Journal of Bank Research*, Vol. 4, No. 3 (Autumn 1973), pp. 212–224.

Robinson, Roland I., *The Management of Bank Funds* (New York: McGraw-Hill), 2nd ed., 1962.

Roll, Richard, *The Behavior of Interest Rates: An Application of the Efficient Market Model to U.S. Treasury Bills* (New York: Basic Books), 1970.

Roll, Richard, "Investment Diversification and Bond Maturity," *Journal of Finance*, Vol. 26, No. 1 (March 1971), pp. 51–66.

Salomon Brothers, *An Analytical Record of Yields and Yield Spreads,* 1974.

Telser, Lester, "Safety First and Hedging," *Review of Economic Studies,* Vol. 23, 1955–1956.

Thomson, Michael R., "Forecasting for Financial Planning," *Journal of Bank Research,* Vol. 4, No. 3 (Autumn 1973), pp. 225–231.

Watson, Ronald D., "Tests of Maturity Structures of Commercial Bank Government Securities Portfolios: A Simulation Approach," *Journal of Bank Research,* Vol. 3, No. 1 (Spring 1972), pp. 34–46.

Wolf, Charles R., "A Model for Selecting Commercial Bank Government Security Portfolios," *The Review of Economics and Statistics,* Vol. 51, No. 1 (February 1969), pp. 40–52.

Woodworth, G. Walter, *The Management of Cyclical Liquidity of Commercial Banks* (Boston: The Bankers Publishing Company), 1967, pp. 116–119.

INDEX

DATE DUE